1930

The Story of a Baseball Season When Hitters Reigned Supreme

Lew Freedman

SPORTS PUBLISHING

Sports Publishing books may be purchased in bulk at special discounts for sales promotion, corporate gifts, fund-raising, or educational purposes. Special editions can also be created to specifications. For details, contact the Special Sales Department, Sports Publishing, 307 West 36th Street, 11th Floor, New York, NY 10018 or sportspubbooks@skyhorsepublishing.com.

Sports Publishing® is a registered trademark of Skyhorse Publishing, Inc.®, a Delaware corporation.

Visit our website at www.sportspubbooks.com.

10 9 8 7 6 5 4 3 2 1

Library of Congress Cataloging-in-Publication Data is available on file.

Jacket design by Kai Texel
Front jacket photo credit: Getty Images
Back jacket photo courtesy of the Boston Public Library, Leslie Jones Collection

Print ISBN: 978-1-68358-420-9
Ebook ISBN: 978-1-68358-421-6

Printed in the United States of America

CONTENTS

PREFACE

THE 1930 MAJOR League Baseball season was unique. It was a hitter's paradise, a fantasy world for the batter. It was a fluke, an aberration in the history of the game. The National League was founded in 1876, a quarter of a century ahead of the American League, and the sport was still going strong into the twenty-first century . . . but 1930 was an outlier. Never before or since have batters had their way with pitchers so readily, so easily, as they did during the summer of 1930.

The sixteen big-league teams put up pinball numbers in the scoring column and, at the same time, pitchers were in a nearly universal funk. It was as if almost every single major-league pitcher forgot how to throw; as if nearly everyone needed Tommy John surgery to fix what ailed them.

Of course, Tommy John the pitcher was not born until 1943, and the medical procedure that would repair so many injured elbows was not invented until decades later. Surely, most of the pitchers who suffered bombardment and humiliation in 1930 would have gladly sought out a seemingly magic antidote to the agonies of the moment.

More than ninety years have passed since the baseball campaign of 1930, so eyewitnesses are exceptionally scarce; all of the active participants deceased. Only baseball historians and avid fans recall the craziness of this solitary year. For fans of a particular team, the 1930 season does not stand out on a list, in terms of results.

Perhaps only those with allegiance to the Philadelphia Athletics or St. Louis Cardinals would take notice.

For the other fourteen teams—especially those that moved on to other locations over time—the season of 1930 would appear on no lists of accomplishments for fans to savor when discussing the good ol' days. But what a season it would have been to watch unfold, more so for breathtaking individual achievements that stood out like flashing neon lights.

Above all, this was the year of Hack Wilson, who ruled the NL—and all of baseball—with two remarkable batting statistics. Lewis Robert "Hack" Wilson owned 1930, his club of a bat producing long-revered and admired statistics, at least one of which has never been duplicated. He was the Babe Ruth of the National League for one, brief, shining moment. Even as the actual Babe Ruth was still slugging away in the American League.

The 1930 season is to be remembered for Bill Terry as well, with the New York Giants first baseman's .400 average a forerunner of awareness that such batsmen were about to become endangered species.

Chuck Klein of the Philadelphia Phillies, also on his way to the Hall of Fame, might well have won a Triple Crown in any other season (40 HRs, 170 RBIs, .386 BA). Instead, his power totals in home runs, runs batted in, and average led the National League in nothing.

Wally Berger's 38 home runs for the Boston Braves set a record for rookies that stood until 1987, when Mark McGwire blasted 49 homers for the Oakland A's.

It was the year of George "Showboat" Fisher, too; budding superstar, it might be thought. But rather it turned into the year of "Showboat" Fisher; a supernova, flashing briefly across the night sky and then becoming lost in some distant galaxy.

1930

Some of the best pitchers in history—Hall of Famers, in fact—were bruised and battered by the time the 1930 season ended. These men recorded terrific accomplishments over long careers, but in 1930 they seemed more like journeymen.

Two starting pitchers, rarities among their brethren, were able to retire hitters in the same fashion they always had and would. Predominant among the breed was Lefty Grove and Dazzy Vance. While nearly all others faltered, they continued to excel somehow when it came to denying runs. They were in leagues of their own.

Grove and Vance were just about the only ones who didn't have to take cover from the barrage of line drives clouted up the middle and over the heads of the others who were bold enough to take a turn on the mound. "Duck!" had to be the best advice shouted by teammates that season.

For the first time in baseball history, a team scored more than 1,000 runs in a season (and this was during a 154-game season), when the New York Yankees compiled 1,062. Also, for the second time in history, too, since the Cardinals were right behind New York with 1,004 runs scored.

The National League as a whole batted .303, and that was with pitchers in the lineup full-time. The Giants' team average was .319. The Phillies hit .315, and St. Louis .314. The two worst-hitting team totals were .281, the statistics of the Cincinnati Reds and Boston Braves.

Not only did all eight regular position players for the Cardinals bat at least .303, but four more backups, appearing in at least 45 games, also hit at least .321. Overall, sixty-two players hit .300 during the 1930 season, forty-two of them batting at least .320, and seventeen hitting at least .350. And twenty players stroked at least 200 hits. For many good players, collecting 200 safeties in a season was a once-in-a-career accomplishment.

As the inverse of the eye-opening hitting statistics, some of the worst earned-run averages imaginable were recorded by pitchers who, in other eras, might have swiftly been demoted to the minors. The Washington Senators' 3.96 was the only team earned-run average under 4.00. The Phillies' was a hold-your-nose 6.71.

The 1930 season was a tipping point for baseball and the country as a whole. For the decade of the 1920s, baseball had embraced the refreshing breeze of the "Lively Ball Era" in conjunction with the Roaring Twenties. Now, at the start of a new decade, the sport was pondering if it had fallen for too much of a good thing just as the Great Depression was beginning to deliver a sobering blow to the good times of the last decade.

Americans were about to be bludgeoned on the baseball field and at the bank.

PRELUDE

BABE RUTH DID not invent the home run, but he might as well have.

Until George Herman "Babe" Ruth Jr. revolutionized baseball with his powerful uppercut swing, big stick, and larger-than-life personality, the sport was played in a different manner. The game was about scoring one run at a time, station-to-station, base-to-base, as opposed to clearing the bases with a single swipe.

Ruth, born February 6, 1895, in Baltimore, Maryland, was right on time, possessor of a blossoming man-child personality and a devil-may-care attitude. That, combined with his prowess on the baseball field transformed him into one of the grandest of mainstream celebrities at a time when the United States was ripe for indulgence.

"The Sultan of Swat," "The Bambino," Ruth elbowed his way into a space in an American pantheon of heroes when no one recognized the need, while simultaneously filling his soul with adulation after being dumped in an orphanage and shortchanged on love.

He was an American original in America's favorite game, making his major-league debut in 1914 and mostly serving as a marvelous pitcher for the world champion Boston Red Sox until he and the team recognized he was an even more marvelous batter.

Through the good fortune of timing and coming of age perfectly, when Major League Baseball crafted renovation of the sport through rules alteration, Ruth was present to showcase the possibilities.

In 1918, the lefty swinging Ruth led the American League in home runs—with 11. A year later, unleashed as a hitter for the first time, with pitching shoved to the side as a secondary responsibility, Ruth clouted 29 homers. That not only led the league, but set a new single-season record for the sport.

Rather than cling tightly to this treasure, the Red Sox foolishly sold Ruth to the New York Yankees for $125,000 in time for the 1920 season. It is likely the largest fleecing in baseball history. This neatly overlapped with rules changes that effectively concluded baseball's "Deadball Era," when baseballs were softer, traveled lesser distances, were beaten to a pulp before being removed from games, and pitchers were allowed to spit, scrape, cut, and otherwise bend the ball to their will.

Game scores were lower; in 1908, teams averaged a mere 3.4 runs per game. There was more weight put on stolen bases than home runs. The all-time exemplar of what was termed "the scientific game" was Ty Cobb, a fierce and superb all-around player who felt this was the true style to play. But those who supervised the game felt that offense was lacking.

New baseballs were manufactured, tighter wound around cork: the so-called livelier ball. Instead of attempting to keep balls in play as long as possible, it was decided that when balls got dirty, they should be replaced. That made it easier for hitters to see the pitch. The rules makers also came down hard on pitchers, outlawing the shine ball, emery ball, and the spitter, except for those who were already reliant on it. Those hurlers were grandfathered in, though it was not until 1934 when Burleigh Grimes retired that the spitball became completely illegal.

Soon enough after 1920, however, as was much later proclaimed in a baseball advertisement, it became apparent that "chicks dig the long ball." As did everyone else. Ruth, the 6-foot-2, 215-pound (before he ate too many hot dogs and drank too much beer) slugger, was the pathfinder.

In 1920, Ruth smashed 54 home runs—another new record—and hit 59 in 1921, breaking his own record for the third straight season. He sent electric voltage through the sport and by 1923, New York's new home park of Yankee Stadium opened. With Ruth hitting a homer on Opening Day of the season, sportswriter Fred Lieb referred to the ballpark as "The House That Ruth Built." Crowds were enormous—on the road as well—with fans desperate to see Ruth bash one deep.

As if Babe Ruths could be purchased right off a shelf in a store, other teams felt they needed to get one of them, too. Hitters broke in who had not been weaned on the old-style game, but were brought up with the mindset of swinging away.

In 1920, when Ruth clouted his 59 homers, none of the other 15 teams in the American League hit that many. The St. Louis Browns' 50 homers came in second to Ruth. In the National League, only the Philadelphia Phillies, with 64 homers, exceeded Ruth's total.

As a bonus, Ruth's bombastic presence and extraordinary performance helped baseball recover from the Black Sox Scandal, as the superior Chicago White Sox fixed the outcome of the 1919 World Series, falling to the Cincinnati Reds. This black mark led to the creation of the position of commissioner as the new supreme authority in baseball. Judge Kenesaw Mountain Landis promptly banned eight members of the White Sox from the game for life.

This was an embarrassing time for baseball and dented public confidence. The concurrent rise of the Babe, though, overshadowed the negative and infused new life in the sport. While the scandal otherwise might well have developed enervating cynical fans, Ruth, the home run, and more scoring provided the antidote.

New York Giants Hall of Fame infielder Freddie Lindstrom was one observer who encapsulated that.

"The Babe was baseball's savior," Lindstrom said. "No doubt about it. Babe Ruth was the greatest morale force in the history of baseball because of his tremendous bat." Lindstrom was from Chicago and just turning fourteen when the Black Sox Scandal occurred, and he said he was quite demoralized by the news. "We couldn't believe it."[1]

In the decade between the emergence of Ruth's resurrection act and 1930, baseball was dramatically reshaped. The Babe had become a king, but there were many other hitters who helped retake control of the sport from those once-overwhelming pitchers. As so, the lid was taken off the offense.

The Yankees became the biggest gate attraction, establishing themselves as a powerhouse. For their dominance in 1927, the team gained the sobriquet of "Murderers' Row." And while Babe Ruths did not grow on trees, it turned out that once unleashed, other power hitters could excite the populace.

Ruth upped his own single-season record to 60 homers in 1927, and no one else threatened 50, but players like teammate Lou Gehrig, Cy Williams, Rogers Hornsby, Chuck Klein, Jim Bottomley, and Hack Wilson became well known for their long-ball talents, too.

Then, in time for 1930, almost as if an earthquake had reconfigured the paths of two rivers to create a confluence, something seemed slightly amiss in the manufacture of baseballs. It seems that when the season began, pitchers discovered the grip was different; the makers had not raised the stitches appropriately high. This spelled doom for many pitchers relying on curves or other breaking stuff. Most were about to embark on a nightmare season.

Oh, yes, it might be bluntly said there was a shortage of good pitching dotting rosters that season as well. Many of the consistently clobbered pitchers probably did not really belong in the big leagues at all. They could tell their grandkids some distant day in the future they once hurled for the Philadelphia Phillies, but they had to hope the younger relatives never looked up their stats in *The Baseball Encyclopedia*.

1

THE GREAT DEPRESSION

PRESIDENT HERBERT HOOVER was present at the Washington Senators' season-opening game of 1930 to continue the tradition of the highest elected official in the United States throwing out the ceremonial first pitch.

Hoover was seated in a special presidential box next to the Senators home dugout. Not known as a great athlete, though he did have a serious passion for fishing, when Hoover rose from his seat to toss the pitch he showed he didn't have his best stuff. If Hoover had been winding up and firing from the mound to the plate, it would not have been called a strike.

If this was a respite from his onerous duties, taking in a ballgame was only temporary amusement. The thriving United States of the 1920s was imploding, entering an economic crisis that was the worst in the nation's history.

The Great Depression, the economic plague would come to be called, would ruin many financially. On April 14, it was early in the collapse, but the storm had arrived, if not yet unleashed its full force.

When the 16 big-league teams gathered for spring training, Babe Ruth was a holdout. The immensely popular Ruth helped bring crowds to Yankee Stadium that bulged to more than 70,000 at times. In 1923, their first season in Yankee Stadium, the club attracted more than one million fans. In 1924, likewise. This was true again in 1926. Attendance was closer to 1.2 million in 1927, the year of the Murderers' Row Yankees.

The Yankees won almost all of the time, fielded the biggest hitters, and were situated in the media capital of the country. And Ruth was the ringmaster of this circus, his every move chronicled by an adoring press, often his moon face leaping from the pages of the New York dailies, beloved by children who dreamed of spending just a moment with the Big Guy as he scrawled his autograph.

It had been a decade since Boston had parted ways with Ruth, the most valuable property in baseball, and the Yankees reaped the bountiful harvest. Once he came under the sway of Christy Walsh, the first genuine player-agent, he was made aware of his true earning potential.

Ruth's annual salary grew, even if negotiations between him and general manager Ed Barrow and Yankees owner Jacob Ruppert were sometimes more like a tug of war than push and pull over dollars and sense.

The Depression really began on September 4, 1929, before the end of the previous baseball season. This was swiftly followed by the Black Tuesday stock market crash of October 29, 1929, which spurred the steady decline of the world's gross domestic product. The World Series had been over for just ten days and it had been a rosy season for baseball. The American League's Philadelphia Athletics bested the National League's Chicago Cubs in five games.

The severity of the Depression was not immediately recognized and there was optimism in some quarters of a quick reversal. That did not occur.

Babe felt he was worth big bucks and by all objective measures was absolutely correct. Ruth had just completed a $70,000-a-year contract. Two-thirds of American families lived on $2,500 a year. As Ruth advanced into his thirties (he turned thirty-five before the 1930 season was due to start), he wanted more. Maybe he sensed his heyday was winding down.

Ruth approached the front office with a demand for a three-year, $85,000-a-year deal. Barrow and Ruppert resisted. As Opening Day drew nearer, Ruth finally capitulated. He settled for a two-year contract at $80,000 a season, still a remarkable sum for the era. This was especially true for a time of uncertainty, though the depths of those Depression woes were not yet 100 percent clear.

This was the signing occasion when Ruth uttered one of his most memorable bon mots. Upon learning the munificence of Ruth's new salary, newspapermen declared he was making more money than the president. Ruth wittily responded, "I had a better year than he did." Strangely, for such an oft-quoted sentence, with some variations, the words have been attributed to Ruth with no apparent original source.

It definitely seems like something Ruth would have said. In any case, once his new arrangement was sealed with the Yankees, Ruth was out-earning Hoover, whose salary was $75,000 a year.

Given the serious problems facing the United States, it was quite the legitimate argument that Ruth also did have a better year than Hoover.

Hoover has not been treated very kindly by history. In fact, early on in his presidency he was aggressive in seeking to combat the mushrooming Depression, from proposing a $160 tax cut to securing big business executives' support for $1.8 billion in investment. Henry Ford, as big a magnate as there was, announced he would raise daily wages from six dollars to seven dollars at his Ford plants. In response, unions backed off demands for more money.

But the Depression steamrolled everything. At its worst, within a couple of years, one in four Americans was unemployed. Millions could not pay their rent and were evicted. Major cities relied on soup kitchens to feed the hungry. The homeless set up shanty towns that were called "Hoovervilles" to deride the president.

Baseball was by far the most popular sport in the United States in the 1920s and 1930s, but it was about to suffer its own decline due to the Depression as well. After Ruth's high-end, two-year contract expired, his next salary called for $52,000.

By then, attendance was plummeting as fans were more worried about where their next meals were coming from than spending money on baseball tickets.

Things were fairly robust in 1930. The Chicago Cubs had the best attendance in the sport, with 1,463,624 fans cramming into Wrigley Field. The Yankees drew 1,169,230. Brooklyn also attracted more than a million fans with the turnstiles humming for 1,097,329 visitors. But by 1933, it was a whole different world. No team drew a million fans, and no team averaged 10,000 fans a game. The Yankees were tops with 728,014 fans for the season. The lowly St. Louis Browns couldn't give tickets away, as the expression goes. The Browns' season total was a stunning 88,113. For the entire year.

The sport's average crowd sank to lower than 5,000 fans per game in '33, the bottom. Not only Babe Ruth, but all other players ceased receiving raises. It took a full decade for the Depression to wane, and it took amped up production as the United States turned to World War II for the economy to completely revive.

2

HACK WILSON—MAN OF THE HOUR

HIS FIRST NAME was Lewis, but Hack is what he did with his mighty lumber. The Chicago Cubs outfielder, who lived a life of some fabulous highs, and whose life is often viewed as a tragedy, is best remembered for his performance in 1930.

While some other ballplayers truly were akin to Halley's Comet, Wilson was the real deal, piling up worthy statistics in the second half of the 1920s while building a genuine resume of respect.

Lewis Robert Wilson was born in Ellwood City, Pennsylvania, in 1900, growing up in the heart of steel country. Wilson's physical stature was always something underestimated. Unlike the preferred athlete, he was not lanky. Wilson was stocky and short by major-league standards, even during his era, listed as standing 5-foot-6. But he was an extraordinarily powerful man. His shoulders were broad, and while his legs may have been short, they were heavily muscled. His arms appeared to be as thick as his bat.

Visually, Wilson did not make a good first impression when baseball scouts came around. He thrived on stickball when young and was gregarious with friends. He wanted to be liked and considered one of the gang. Life was not particularly easy in a mill town an hour from Pittsburgh. Wilson's father, Robert, worked in the mills and was a drinking man. Then he got a teenager pregnant, who sought legitimacy for the boy. Robert did not wish to marry. This disappointed Wilson's mother, who was also a heavy drinker.

The boy had little parental guidance and, at age sixteen, quit school to work. He got a job at a print works and also caddied, but devoted free time to baseball. "Even in those days, I pictured myself a big-leaguer," Wilson said.[1]

It was work in harsh environments, lifting and carrying, lifting and carrying, which built Wilson's strength. "I worked at the print shop for two years," Wilson said, "during which time I carried a million pounds of lead and was getting to be a big, husky kid."[2]

Eventually, Wilson and his father moved to the town of Eddystone. In the mid-teen years of the twentieth century, Wilson was enamored by the periodic appearance of a big leaguer named Bris Lord, who played for the Philadelphia Athletics. Lord passed through town and his shiny car caught Wilson's fancy.

He later recalled talking to himself, inspired by Lord's vehicle. "Keep on trying, Lewis," he said, "and you too will be a big-league ballplayer and own your own automobile."[3]

How many American boys with even a smidgeon of baseball ability thought that way? And how few of them ever made it to the big time? Wilson was one dreamer that became an exception.

At twenty-one, Wilson made his debut in the minors with the Martinsburg Mountaineers in the Class D Blue Ridge League. He appeared in just 30 games, yet batted .356. That limited exposure was partially due to injury, but he was showing those teams who doubted him. Back for more seasoning the following year, he hit .366 with 30 home runs.

Wilson spent most of the 1923 season with Class B Portsmouth of the Virginia League, and his batting eye was even sharper, based on a .388 average. But Wilson could play and the team owner offered him around $25,000, hoping to score a nice payday. Hall of Fame manager John J. McGraw came to watch Wilson play, and although Wilson bashed the ball around, McGraw was hesitant. This was another case of prejudice because of Wilson's build. Sometimes weightlifters and muscle-bound wrestlers are said to have "no neck." That was exactly what McGraw said of Wilson. "That guy don't look like a ballplayer," McGraw said. "He's too short and he has no neck."[4]

This was not the only time McGraw misjudged Wilson. McGraw, an old-time practitioner of the scientific approach to the game, which had been so good to him as a player and a manager, was not yet sold on the long ball.

Yet McGraw's owner friend in Virginia hounded him to take Wilson because he strongly believed in the youngster's talent. After considerable lobbying, McGraw purchased Wilson for $11,000. The New York Giants brought Wilson to the National League, but only worked him into three games at the end of the 1923 season.

The Giants were a powerhouse in this era. In 1921 and 1922, the club won the NL pennant and the World Series. The next two seasons, the Giants also won the flag, making it four in a row. But they fell to the Yankees in 1923 and to the Washington Senators in 1924. Wilson did not appear in one game of the championship round in 1923 . . . but things changed in 1924.

Although Wilson was not an instant superstar the next season, he did everything at a high rate of speed. His body screamed that he could not run, but he could—especially in the field. He became a starter in 1924, and was in the majors to stay. He played in 107 games for the Giants, hitting .295 and clouting 10 home runs. At times he looked tough in the batter's box and then suddenly seemed vulnerable to a good curveball. George Kelly shared a lineup spot with Wilson because when Hack slumped, McGraw was quick to replace him. Even though he was a consistent starter, his skipper was yet to truly trust him.

Still, in 1924, Wilson played in all seven Series games, although he batted just .233, going 7-for-30. Yet, for a guy who had been snubbed and whom even his manager had not felt was terribly impressive, Wilson had come far quickly.

Unlike some, Wilson did not come to New York with a ready-made nickname. Although "Hack" fit, and his acceptance of the nickname is still part of his image of taking his hacks at the plate, it is also said that once he became a solid player in '24, a newspaper took a fan vote to bestow some kind of moniker on him to replace the formal and more pedestrian Lewis. That activity produced "Hack." While there may have been trepidation from the Giants front office, the fans liked the guy.

Wilson became entangled in a controversial fielding play in a big game against the Dodgers that, in the retelling, seems astonishing. There were so many fans present that day that they were not all confined to the grandstands; the overflow was bunched together in the outfield.

Brooklyn's Johnny Mitchell blasted a shot to center. Wilson, who took pride in his hustle and fielding, sprinted for the ball. He essentially barged into the crowd, thrust his hand in the air . . . and disappeared from view. Time elapsed with no sign of Wilson. Then a fan tossed the player's cap back onto the grass. That was followed by his glove sailing through the air. Then Wilson burst from the mob, his bare right hand clutching the ball. He waved and claimed he caught it clean.

Umpire Bill Klem did not believe Wilson's catch was kosher, however. He was no eyewitness, his view blocked by the fans, but he ruled the hit a ground-rule double. Wilson was furious. It was the greatest catch of his life and he felt cheated.

In a much later newspaper interview, Wilson was asked if he really did catch the ball. "Even the Giants asked me that after the game," he said of his teammates. And when I insisted I did, I felt some of them didn't believe me. But I swear to heaven I caught the ball."[5]

Wilson said he tracked the ball through the crowd and timed his leap to make the grab, thrusting his glove in the air, and then tumbling to the ground. He was aware there was a child seated on the ground and he tried to land carefully with his legs splayed so he did not injure the youngster with his spikes.

As he tilted off-balance, one fan seized his glove and another grabbed his hat, but he protected the ball in his right, bare hand.

Wilson's prime days in New York did not last very long. He was suckered into swinging at too many curveballs he missed, had ankle problems that inhibited some of his movement, and never really got on the right side of McGraw. By 1925, McGraw was losing interest and patience in Wilson. Hack was deployed in only 62 games and batted just .239. In August of that season, Wilson was exiled to Toledo of the American Association in a trade for Earl Webb, who would have better days with the Boston Red Sox. Toledo also got a player to be named later in Pip Koehler. Wilson was disheartened by the deal, but ended up benefiting greatly.

This was a McGraw mistake. In 55 games with Toledo, Wilson batted .343 and was drafted by the Chicago Cubs. It was a wise move.

"We stole him from the Giants," said Cubs manager Joe McCarthy. "They had sent him to the minors and forgotten to recall him. A critical mistake. So he was unprotected when the draft came around. McGraw hit the ceiling when he heard about it. I don't think he ever got over it. Wilson led the league [in home runs] four of the next five years."[6]

In 1925, Wilson could barely distinguish himself as one of the Giants' top five outfielders. In 1926, he was fifth in the National League MVP voting. He played in 142 games, scored 97 runs, led the league with 21 homers, knocked in 109 runs, batted .321, and registered an on-base percentage of .406.

Following his early struggles, this is when Hack Wilson *became* Hack Wilson. Over the following three seasons—1927, 1928, and 1929—Wilson smacked 30, 31, and 39 home runs, also leading the NL in the first of those two seasons. His average was also above par, hitting .318 (1927), .313 (1928), and .345 (1929). In 1929, Hack led the league in runs batted in with 159.

So it would be inaccurate to suggest Wilson came out of nowhere when he recorded his phenomenal slugging season of 1930. He had been trending in that direction.

This was also true about his off-field behavior. Wilson enjoyed going to speakeasies and nightclubs (remember that this was during Prohibition and imbibing was illegal) and drank heavily. He was viewed as a life-of-the-party guy, but in a good way. It was not a common occurrence for other ballplayers to take a teammate aside and whisper that they might need assistance with their "habits." Baseball players drank when they were on the road, based in cities for several games in a row, particularly in this era before night ball. The games were played in the afternoon and the players had every night free unless they were hopping a train to the next city.

Many Cubs kept company with Hack in those late-hours joints. They drank often, too, and Wilson was known as a star who picked up the tab for the whole gang. Applying more modern standards, Wilson would have been identified as an alcoholic and judged that way.

It is challenging enough to hit a baseball thrown by a professional pitcher, so not being sober in the batter's box can be dangerous. Wilson recognized his own foibles to a degree and insisted he was never drunk on the field.

"I've never played a game drunk," he said. "Hungover, yes. But drunk, no."[7]

Maybe alcohol fueled Wilson's fearsome temper—he never wished to back away from a fight, and his strength gave him the same advantage in combat that he brought to his at-bats. "That's the way it was with Hack," McCarthy said. "Good-natured as he could be, but things seemed to happen to him."[8]

McCarthy said those who might seek a fight with Wilson never did so twice. Once, Wilson carried over a battle that began the night before at the ballpark to the train station where the Cubs and Cincinnati Reds were boarding. He planned revenge, and when a peacemaker with Cincinnati tried to hold him back, Wilson leveled them both. A *Chicago Tribune* story reported, "Hack Wilson . . . yesterday hit three baseballs for singles and two Cincinnati pitchers on the nose."[9]

Wilson probably hit the baseballs on the nose, too.

3

BILL TERRY OUTHITTING THEM ALL

BILL TERRY WAS never as flamboyant as Babe Ruth, never the slugger the likes of Jimmie Foxx, and sometimes took a back seat to Rogers Hornsby. Yet while the man was somewhat overshadowed in the 1920s because he was not a power hitter at a time when the home run was ascendant, he was as solid a hitter as anyone of his era.

William Howard Terry was born October 30, 1898, in Atlanta, Georgia. He was a Southern man who starred for a Northern team, playing his entire 14-year career for the New York Giants. He did not get his first big-league at-bat until the 1923 season, when he was already twenty-four. He hit just .143 in nine plate appearances, so there was no telling this was a guy who would become an 11-time .300-plus hitter.

By 1922, John J. McGraw was well into his 30-year tenure with the Giants. McGraw was the kingpin manager of the National League and often scouted his own players to keep the Giants winners, taking ten pennants and three World Series championships.

Evidence of how hard-nosed McGraw could be in running his club—and make no mistake, it was *his* club—was in the nickname "Little Napoleon." Yes, McGraw was a dictator. He was also called "Muggsy" by some, but not too loudly since he was not keen on the moniker.

As part of their preseason spring training annual ritual, the Giants worked their way north before settling into the big-league opener at the Polo Grounds or elsewhere in the NL. Typically, the team made a stop in Memphis, Tennessee. Talent whisperers had McGraw's ear, touting a young pitcher who briefly shined in the Southern Association, then left the game to go into the oil business. These baseball wisemen friendly to McGraw said this fella was a can't-miss guy.

Terry, who stood 6-foot-1 and weighed a sturdy 200 pounds, met McGraw in his room at the Peabody Hotel, then as now, the most famous hotel in the city. McGraw was interested, especially since Terry made a good presentation: he was well-dressed, of pleasant demeanor, and had a good build. When he asked Terry how much money he wanted to join the Giants, Terry responded he had a secure job that was helping take care of his growing family and would need at least as much as he was making at Standard Oil of Louisiana.

Yes, he knew this was the Giants, the multiple-time champion Giants, no minor-league club. Terry responded he wanted a three-year contract starting at $800 a month. McGraw recoiled at the amount. Terry basically then said it seemed the two men had nothing to talk about. No deal was hatched that day.

Terry had a passion for baseball from his youth, though initially it was all about pitching. It was quite some time before hitting took precedence and he became a stylish first baseman.

"I was interested in baseball," Terry said. "I was interested in playing it, from the time I was a little kid. I never will forget, my father decided I couldn't throw hard, so he got a mitt someplace, said, 'I want to see how hard you throw.' Well, we went out in the backyard and he marked out the distance—and he couldn't catch me. I'd get warmed up and I'd turn the ball loose —Jiminy Christmas—I'd hit him all over."[1]

A lefty batter, Terry was also a southpaw thrower. He did not come from a close-knit family. His parents were often at war and eventually split up for good when he was a teen. He left school at thirteen and took various jobs. It was no wonder he sought a reliable income when he latched onto Standard Oil; he wanted his own family to have the security he missed out on.

Terry experienced some good moments hurling for semi-pro teams and in the low minors, topping out with Class B Shreveport. He finished 14–11 with a 3.00 earned-run average in that last season. That was in 1917. Then Terry got married—his wife's family had moved to Memphis—and he did not play another professional inning until 1922. It was hardly a recommended career path.

While some teams wanted to rent Terry's skills, he turned them down for a lower-level steady job, making batteries. The oil company had its own baseball team and while working full-time for the outfit, Terry played weekends for the Standard Oil Polearines.

Terry actually helped found that team, managed it, and when not pitching, took the field at first base. That was how he trained himself around the bag. There is no indication Terry was discontented with his lot. He was happy with wife Elvena, his regular job, his baby son, and enjoyed playing competitive ball part-time.

If things had ended there, the world would not had heard of Bill Terry. He began receiving some regional baseball notoriety in the Memphis newspapers and sometimes when traveling, playing in such cities as Little Rock, Arkansas.

Only a month passed between the meeting between Terry and McGraw before the Giants called back. McGraw did not direct-dial—he had someone else do it—but Terry was promised a job on the terms he outlined during his face-to-face meeting with McGraw. Terry met the Giants on the road and McGraw had him practice to examine the goods with his own eyes, though it makes one wonder what would have happened if McGraw was disappointed after the recommendations.

After only a few days with the Giants, McGraw said the organization needed help in Toledo with the Class AA club. He couched Terry's shift to Ohio in terms of doing the team a favor. Terry ascertained his wages would remain the same, so he departed for an 88-game stay in Toledo. Even though he was supposed to be a pitcher, going 9–9 with a 4.25 earned-run average, he impressed more with the bat, averaging .336. The transformation to position player was nearly complete.

Terry spent most of 1923 with the Toledo Mud Hens, showing up in just three games for the Giants with one hit in seven at-bats. The time spent in Toledo was worth the investment, in terms of experience for Terry and in terms of the Giants really seeing what he could do. He played in 109 games for Toledo and hit .377 with 14 home runs that summer, but mostly became known as a swinger who swatted the ball to the outfield gaps, collecting hard singles and doubles. Terry was not a renowned slugger, although he did hit as many as 28 homers in a season in the majors (1932).

Given how young he was, Terry must have made a different type of impression with the Giants because he was named the Mud Hens manager on August 1. That almost seemed like a retirement job, not for a player so young, though it was really just a stopgap move for Terry and the team. He didn't even finish the season. When his grandmother died, Terry left for the funeral and never returned to Toledo.

Although he was with the Giants for good starting in 1924, it almost seemed as if he brought the wrong bats with him. He got into 77 games and hit just .239, certainly not what was expected after his season in Toledo. The main problem was a broken ankle incurred while sliding on the basepaths.

In 1925, Terry batted .319 with 11 home runs and 70 runs batted in through 133 games for the Giants, but even that was not the true beginning of his emergence as a Hall Famer. In 1926, Terry appeared in 98 games and batted just .289. He was a holdout as the team prepared for the season—as was the team's other first baseman, George Kelly. Something had to give and it was Kelly, who signed first.

Terry tried to stay in touch with McGraw, but with Kelly in the fold and Terry not yet showing the type of steady production he expected, McGraw told reporters he was sitting on it, not responding because "a submission to Terry's financial demands would probably be too great a strain on the bond market."[2]

Terry sounded somewhat imperial in his rejection of the Giants' offer, saying, "I'll go back home and go to work before I'll play at those figures."[3]

Terry had become a home developer and landlord, so he could fall back on another job to make a respectable living. Kelly was on fire in spring training, yet Terry could make good on his threat to leave the sport and take another direction in life. That was not truly in his heart, but he felt his chief responsibility was to provide for his family.

From their first meeting, McGraw and Terry dickered over price. As the Giants broke camp and followed the usual path north, they once again parked at the Peabody Hotel. Terry made overtures, calling McGraw in his room, but he ducked him. He didn't want to talk. So Terry issued a public statement, saying, "I have called McGraw's room several times and knocked at his door several times," Terry said, "and as long as I get no answer, I assume he doesn't want to see me. . . . if they are not willing to do business, I suppose that it means I will stay in Memphis and forget the idea of playing baseball."[4]

It was these types of passive-aggressive confrontations that drove a bit of a wedge between McGraw and Terry. Terry was never really one of the spirited manager's favorites. He wanted players who bled baseball, like Frankie Frisch and others, who would listen to him and not defy him, whether it was about money or not. McGraw seemed to hold a grudge, handing first base to Kelly for the most part and relying on Terry more as a pinch-hitter. (In 46 of those 98 games, Terry had just one plate appearance.)

Golf aside, and thinking in general, McGraw may well have been focused on Terry in a comment: "The first-class baseball player must think, talk and eat baseball, in addition to playing it, and I don't want any of my players sitting around and talking nothing but golf in the heat of the pennant race."[5]

The chill remained past Opening Day. Terry finally reported on April 26. That was Terry's last holdout for some time. Finally, in 1927, Terry became a star, a player McGraw could at least love on the field. That year he batted .326 with 20 home runs, accompanied by 121 RBIs. Showing some speed afoot, Terry slashed 13 triples.

Intriguingly, the Giants had an all Hall of Fame infield of Terry at first, Rogers Hornsby at second, Travis Jackson at shortstop, and Freddie Lindstrom at third . . . yet could only finish 92–62, two games out of first.

The next season, 1928, Terry again batted .326, with 17 home runs and 101 RBIs. Given his time away from the sport, Terry was already twenty-nine years old. Yet his performances would be marked by an upward trajectory.

By then, McGraw was starting to make enemies on his own team and, three decades into his role, was starting to become grumpy and physically unwell. He still had the power to shake things up, however. The Giants parted with Hornsby, sending him to the Chicago Cubs. But in '29, outfielder Mel Ott hit in the .320s for the second year in a row, and Carl Hubbell blossomed into an 18-game winner.

In 1929, Terry was a .372 hitter with 14 home runs, 117 RBIs, 10 stolen bases, a .418 on-base percentage, and 226 hits. He was one of the best batsmen in baseball and was primed for what would become his greatest and most memorable season.

4

BABE RUTH STILL IN THERE SLUGGING

BY 1930, BABE Ruth was already the greatest slugger of all time. He was the dominant power hitter before the decade changed, and was still batting those balls to the moon for several years into the '30s.

For Ruth, 1930 was merely a train stop; merely one of his many phenomenal statistical years. The man who essentially invented the home run was a run-of-the-mill great, meaning he set no records that season. Of course, by then he had plastered his name next to several highests, biggests, and most astonishing numbers.

Although some players had better all-around years than Ruth here and there, there was no argument put forth, no case to be made, that he was not still king of the castle. This was a man who had struck 54, 59, and 60 home runs in different seasons. People may have made fun of his conditioning as his stomach began to balloon, but no one ever suggested Ruth lacked the eyesight to destroy pitchers' confidence.

The baseball world may have been catching up in some ways, but Ruth still put together a typical statistical year in 1930—one of several he had equaled—that would make other batters envious and that would be worthy of Most Valuable Player consideration many years over the ensuing decades.

Since a handful of others registered some of the most amazing stats of their careers in that season—or in a few cases, that were ever seen—given his year-by-year standards, Ruth was merely "great" in the season of the hitter.

At thirty-five years of age, Ruth played 145 games for the Yankees, made 676 plate appearances, led the American League in home runs with 49 (the eleventh of the twelve times he would top the circuit), knocked in 153 runs, stole 10 bases, batted .359, led the league in walks (136), on-base percentage (.493), and slugging (.732).

For almost anyone else in history—Hall of Famers included—that might be a career year. For Ruth, that was the kind of season he had routinely been recording for the past decade. Best remembered for his 714 home runs, he also drove in 2,214 runs—leading the league in that category five times. He walked more than anyone else, and his lifetime on-base percentage was a ridiculous .474, partnered with an astounding record career slugging of .690. While Ruth captured just one batting title, his lifetime average was .342.

Ruth made a million friends for the sport, charmed children everywhere he traveled, and his larger-than-life personality pretty much made him the best-known man—not merely athlete—in the country. Almost totally overlooked just about as soon as Ruth began banging home runs beyond the tall and deep walls of ballparks was how excellent a pitcher he was. The southpaw won 94 games, set a World Series record for consecutive scoreless innings, and posted a career earned-run average of 2.28. Taken together, the hitting and pitching achievements buttress the case that Ruth was the greatest ballplayer of all.

By 1919, as Ruth was making the transition from full-time pitcher to full-time outfielder and hitter, he was still a bit of a hybrid. He won nine games on the mound, but led the AL with 11 homers and hit .300. He wanted to be paid as a star and this holdout/negotiation with the infamous Red Sox owner Harry Frazee, led to the end of Ruth's ride in Boston. While Frazee was a theatre impresario, the tale that he sold Ruth to the Yankees for $125,000 so he could finance the Broadway show *No, No Nanette* was not accurate. While Frazee did put on that musical, it was not until several years later. When he sold Ruth to New York, Frazee became one of the most hated men (if not public enemy No. 1) in Boston baseball history.

Ruth wanted $10,000 to play another year for Boston and Frazee either did not have the cash, or simply refused to pay the freight.

This is how Ruth remembers the money confrontation: "I put my price at $10,000 and felt I had it coming. But Frazee yelled as if I were trying to rob the cash drawer at the old Frazee Theatre in New York. For $10,000, he said he'd expect at least John Barrymore. I asked him what good Barrymore's profile would be with the bases filled in a tight ballgame."[1]

Frazee was not smart enough to realize he already had the John Barrymore of baseball in his employ and Ruth could sell many more tickets than the thespian. Ruth was as much the showman as Barrymore.

So history was written, or rewritten. Ed Barrow led the Red Sox to a World Series crown in 1918 from the dugout. In 1919 Barrow asked Ruth if he wanted to stay on the mound or move to the outfield permanently. Ruth replied, "Well, I certainly like to hit." Barrow said, "If you love to hit that much, I'll just have to keep you in the game every day."[2]

Ruth set a new home run record in 1919, the first season after World War I had ended. He smacked 29 and some fans threw him a special day of recognition in appreciation. Ruth received some gifts and when a sportswriter asked the Bambino what Frazee gave him, Ruth said, "A cigar."[3] Frazee did not admire the Babe's candor. If the intention was to make Frazee look cheap, Ruth was successful. Perhaps that lit the fuse that ticked Frazee off enough to succumb to Yankee wooing.

Frazee was tired of Ruth. Barrow moved to New York as business manager-general manager and engineered the trade bringing Ruth to the Bronx. Big, haunting mistake by Frazee. A superstar was born in New York and it wasn't Lady Gaga.

Babe Ruth defined the home run and the home run defined him for posterity. But a review of his best batting averages in the 1920s leads one to wonder how many times he may have hit .400 if he had concentrated on base hits more than the long ball. In different seasons, Ruth batted .376, .378, .393, .378, .372, and .373. Likewise, one can only wonder what kind of lifetime batting totals he might have compiled if he hadn't focused on pitching at the front end of his career and if he had focused on conditioning in his thirties. There would have been stupefying numbers next to his name in the record books, à la Cy Young in pitching, records never to be broken. Of course, when Ruth retired in 1935, those career statistics were believed untouchable.

Also, what fun would a Babe Ruth who was serious, sober, and single-minded have been instead of the freewheeling fellow who became so beloved? Take away the trappings and the booming shots into the stratosphere and Ruth was Lou Gehrig, a great who projected low-key sincerity, or Rogers Hornsby, another great, but a cold customer.

Ruth was not a highly educated man. He spent much of his youth in an orphanage in Baltimore, St. Mary's Industrial School for Boys, and he was no Phi Beta Kappa. But he did have an innate sense of his own worth and a manner which combined with his baseball exploits made him extraordinarily popular. It didn't take long after joining the Yankees for him to recognize the home run was his financial ticket.

It was Hall of Fame Yankees manager Miller Huggins who said, "New York is a home run town."[4] That made the immature Ruth and the glitzy city a match.

Ruth laughed his way around the bases as his tape-measure jobs landed on nearby planets. Originally, when he set the homer mark of 29, he realized some scribes and baseball people believed he had taken the seasonal record as far as it could go. When he amassed a new record of 54 homers, he increased the record by nearly 50 percent, skipping the 30s and 40s altogether. He was fully cognizant no one believed the record would increase.

"They thought my 54 of 1920 was such an unheard-of accomplishment that no one again could ever push it up that high," Ruth said.[5]

Wrong again. Ruth bashed 59 home runs in 1921. Then came 1927, the Murderers' Row Yankees who obliterated the American League pennant race with a 110-44 record when Ruth broke his own standard with 60 home runs. That was the single-season mark for 34 years until Roger Maris collected his 61 homers. What is usually overlooked is that Ruth came back with 54 home runs again in 1928. That meant during the 1920s, he clubbed 50 or more home runs four times.

As the decade turned to 1930, no other player had ever hit 50 in a season. In the National League, Hornsby, then with the St. Louis Cardinals, hit 42 in 1922, and Chuck Klein of the Philadelphia Phillies hit 43 in 1929.

It was all a blast to Ruth. He was making more money than he imagined. He was the biggest star on the winningest team. Women threw themselves at him. He drove fine automobiles, replacing them on a whim, dressed in high fashion, sometimes in suits, wearing spats. He played golf in a better wardrobe than Bobby Jones, mingled in high society and among the biggest star athletes from other sports.

Except for Prohibition, which Ruth pretty successfully eluded, there were barely any restraints on his behavior. He was unleashed from the hard-knocks upbringing of the orphanage and felt no authority figure, Huggins, Barrow, or Yankees owner Jake Ruppert, could govern his domain. In one of the most enduring of baseball comments, when New York outfielder Ping Bodie was asked what it was like to room on the road with Ruth, he said, "I don't know. I don't room with Babe Ruth. I room with his suitcase."[6]

Everyone wanted to meet Babe Ruth, to hang out with Babe Ruth and Ruth loved the limelight. To him, everyone was a friend. Perhaps one of the funnier aspects of the idea of Ruth's hobnobbing was that he couldn't remember names. That did not merely apply to the man in the street, or rookies on his team, but to other famous Americans. Ruth didn't really grasp who other celebrities were, or why they were famous. He was just out to have a good time.

Once, a teammate asked Ruth what he had done the night before. "I was at a party with those movie people," Ruth said. The other player probed for names. "Oh, you know, what the hell are their names?" Ruth said.[7] Their names were Douglas Fairbanks and Mary Pickford. In the 1920s, you could hardly get more famous than that duo.

Ruth was in full-fledged rebellion against authority figures. He had had enough of being told what to do and now that he had money he felt he could be his own boss. What he wasn't quite good enough at was representing himself in outside deals.

Christy Walsh wiggled his way into Ruth's inner circle and became baseball's first agent, helping him acquire endorsements and become a supplier of columns for newspapers around the country. Walsh enhanced Ruth's financial situation and his reputation. He also did his best to guard it when Ruth's behavior sometimes swerved off the rails in various escapades. Walsh acted as a guidance counselor of sorts, helping to steer Ruth into publicized activities that boosted his reputation.

When Ruth was made to understand he was harming himself and disappointing kids with sometimes scandalous behavior, he backed off, swore off drinking for a time, and retreated to his Sudbury, Massachusetts, farm where he chopped wood and toned up his muscles.

Ruth was proud to be part of the 1927 Yankees, referring to it as the greatest team in history, a label that has only intermittently been challenged. He also remained gratified by the impregnability of his single-season homer record of 60.

"They were made before many of the parks had been artificially changed as so to favor the home-run hitter," Ruth said. "I hit them into the same parks where only a decade before 10 or 12 homers were good enough to win the title."[8]

Not only were the balls being manufactured with tighter knit centers to fly farther on contact, but ballpark fences were drawn in. More players emulated Ruth's looser, uppercut swing. Yet

Ruth was right. He was ahead of the curve, the first guy to weaponize the home run. He single-handedly revolutionized baseball. The 1930 season culminated that revolution begun a decade earlier.

5

THE NEW YORK YANKEES

WHEN THE NEW York American League franchise began in 1903, taking over a spot from the Baltimore Orioles, it was called the Highlanders. In 1913, they would be renamed the Yankees. There were only a few seasons in the first two decades of the twentieth century that the team was any good, claiming a few second-place finishes during that time.

However, as soon as the franchise acquired Babe Ruth, the team's status changed. The Babe showed up in the Bronx in 1920 and became the cornerstone of the franchise; the man the front office built around.

New York won its first pennant in 1921, although the Yankees lost the World Series to the New York Giants. The Yankees topped the American League again in 1922, but again dropped the Series to the Giants. In 1923, the year Yankee Stadium opened with its 58,000 capacity, the Yankees won their third straight pennant and finally triumphed in the Series against their crosstown foes, the Giants. They would also set a new single-game record for Opening Day capacity that season, with 74,000 fans in attendance.

Following two down years, the Yankees resumed prominence, taking three pennants in a row: 1926, 1927, and 1928. Although the rise of the Philadelphia Athletics coincided with the final days of the decade, when the 1930 season began no one but the foolish dismissed the Yankees' chances.

Not that anyone could tell given his production, but Ruth was edging toward old baseball age. He was no single stalwart on the club, though, the starting lineup employing a handful of future Hall of Famers. Besides Ruth, the Yankees had Lou Gehrig at first—the greatest ever to play the position and whose own slugging often brought home more runs than Ruth did in a given season.

Bill Dickey, only twenty-three, owned the catcher's role. Tony Lazzeri anchored second. Earle Combs held one of the outfield positions, along with Ruth. Five Hall of Famers were regulars. Third baseman Ben Chapman joined that quintet as an above-.300 hitter. Although they were not all of prime vintage, there were four members of the pitching staff that would also become enshrined in Cooperstown: Red Ruffing, Herb Pennock, Waite Hoyt, and Lefty Gomez.

Gomez was a rookie in 1930, and only went 2–5. At twenty-one years of age, he was not yet ready for prime time, though he would soon be. A West Coast guy from a family with seven children, Gomez was toiling with the San Francisco Seals when informed the Yankees had bought his contract. "I am so lucky!" was Gomez's reaction.[1]

Gomez was a hilarious man, a brilliant after-dinner speaker at sports banquets, and just the guy to keep a team loose in the clubhouse. The Yankees needed that type of influence in 1930. The popular Miller Huggins had died during the 1929 season, and that development generated turbulence. Ruth wanted the manager's job, but the higher-ups didn't see him as being cut out for the role. Coach Art Fletcher was promoted for the season's final 11 games, going 6–5.

The brass selected Bob Shawkey as his permanent successor. Shawkey was a 195-game winner over his 15-year big-league career, but as recently as 1927 had been a teammate of many of the same players. As such, Shawkey may have been too close to some players and wasn't respected as a commander. Still, the Yankees roster was loaded with big-name players who were expected to be pennant contenders.

In some ways, the center fielder Combs slipped into the shadows, though his lifetime average was .325 and he led the AL in triples three times. Combs excelled in the field and spent about twenty years as a coach after retiring as a player. In 1930, he batted .344 as a leadoff man, carried a .424 on-base percentage, struck 22 triples, scored 129 runs, and drove in 82.

Combs was from Richmond, Kentucky, and grew up with the ambition of becoming a school teacher. He completed a two-year college teaching program and returned home to teach in a one-room schoolhouse before he was tempted into a new calling at age twenty-three. After joining the Yankees organization, Combs gave an interview declaring, "The bat is mightier than the pen."[2]

No doubt playing ball paid more since he was making $37 a month at the school and walking four miles each way to and from work. Playing for a coal company team, Combs's talents were discovered by the Louisville Colonels. Soon enough, he was sold to the Yankees for $50,000.

Combs was larger than the average leadoff hitter of the time—at 6 feet tall and 185 pounds—but his skills differed from the power hitters. "Nature, of course, aided me in assuming the lead-off position," he said. "The lead-off man should be fast and have a keen eye. I happened to be born with both."[3] Combs broke in with the Yankees in 1924, and by 1927 had developed a new crouching style in the batter's box.

At the time, leadoff men were the classic table setters assigned the primary task of getting on base. Miller Huggins spelled that out very specifically for Combs. Combs was a line-driver hitter, anyway. Huggins informed him he was going to be "The Waiter," not as in a server bringing the appetizer to the table but in being patient at the plate, since Ruth and Gehrig were hitting behind him and they blasted missiles. "Whenever you get on base, you just get there for Babe Ruth or Lou Gehrig, or one of the other big fellows, to send you the rest of the way around."[4]

Combs lived long enough to receive a telephone call from Cooperstown, New York, informing him he had been selected to the National Baseball Hall of Fame. He was residing in Paint Lick, Kentucky, in 1970, had been retired as a player since 1935 and as a coach since 1954, so he was a bit astonished, to say the least.

"Nearly knocked me off my feet," said Combs, who died six years later at age seventy-seven. "Biggest surprise I've had in my life. That's the last thing in the world I ever expected to happen to me."[5]

Tony Lazzeri was from San Francisco, but came onto the Yankees radar after smacking 60 home runs for Salt Lake City of the Pacific Coast League. Even if it was an abnormally lengthened season, that was still an attention-getter—especially since Lazzeri was primarily a second baseman. He never approached such a figure in the majors, but his lifetime average was .292 and he once drove in 11 runs in a game. He was one of the pillars of the Yankees in the 1920s, and in 1930 batted .303 with 120 RBIs.

Besides the admirable statistics, Lazzeri brought leadership. Ruth's star shined brighter than anyone else's. Gehrig was not a vocal leader. Lazzeri was the rah-rah guy. "Here's the man who really made the 1926 team," Huggins said of Lazzeri. "He was the tower of strength to Gehrig and [shortstop Mark] Koeing when they were unsure of themselves. Ball players like Lazzeri come along once in a generation."[6]

It took Lazzeri five days on a train from San Francisco to reach the Yankees' 1930 spring-training camp in St. Petersburg, Florida. Lazzeri and Ruth were pals in the locker room, often playing pranks on one another, which generally meant wrecking the other guy's baseball gear when he wasn't looking. Each took turns attacking underwear and other garments with scissors.

Once in the clubhouse, Lazzeri fooled Ruth by emptying a bottle of eyedrops and replacing the contents with water. When he was sure Ruth was watching, Lazzeri guzzled the bottle. Ruth proclaimed him crazy. "Look at the dumb guy," Ruth said. "He drinks the eye wash."[7] Lazzeri went out and stroked three hits that day. In response, Ruth asked the trainer for the eye wash the next day, drank it down, and went out and had a fine game. He started a hitting streak and each day imbibed his eyedrops. "Sure tastes terrible, Tony, doesn't it?"[8] Ruth said even as he continued the habit until his hitting streak was snapped.

Lazzeri was a Yankee from 1926 to 1937. Throughout his major-league days, Lazzeri sought to keep his affliction of epilepsy quiet, however, though it is believed the disease cost him his life at forty-two in 1946. He tumbled down a flight of stairs in his home, and while many were certain the fall was due to a seizure, his death certificate listed the cause as a heart attack.

Babe and Gehrig came to the plate in consecutive places in the batting order. They had an excellent supporting cast—including several Hall of Famers, as mentioned—but although he didn't have it in his personality to be so gargantuan, welcoming, and open to the world, Gehrig, not Ruth, would have been viewed as the best player in the game. He was wholesome, friendly, but not so outgoing to play the role of a dandy. He was the good college boy and very much a mama's boy, pleasing her ahead of the public—or anyone else—until he married.

Gehrig, a left-handed hitter only twenty when he left Columbia University for the Yankees, made his first appearance in the majors in 1923. He was a powerfully built man who seemed stronger than 6 feet tall and 200 pounds might have provided for, with broad shoulders and immensely muscled legs.

Through nagging injuries and illnesses, Gehrig's home address was first base. He was a regular by 1925, a star by 1926, and a superstar by 1927. In that spectacular Yankees year etched in lore, Gehrig registered some nearly unbelievable statistics. He slammed 52 home runs (breaching territory where Ruth had led), drove in 173 runs, and batted .373. His on-base percentage was .474, and it was Gehrig who was honored with the American League Most Valuable Player Award that memorable season.

"Larrupin' Lou" was an RBI machine. He led the league in the category five times, and his 1931 total of 185 runs knocked in is so extraordinary that players in the modern era cannot even fathom it. In 1930, the year of the hitter, Gehrig was right near the top of statistical categories with the best of the gang of sluggers. He batted .373, drove in 173 runs, swatted 41 homers, cracked 42 doubles, and accumulated 220 hits.

There were things Gehrig was known for that Ruth was not. His day in, day out dependability is one of the things most famously remembered about Gehrig. He stepped into the Yankees lineup on June 1, 1925, as a fill-in for Wally Pipp at first base, and essentially never left. His nickname became "The Iron Horse," and his playing streak stretched to 2,130 games.

Playing through injuries and illnesses, Gehrig's streak ended on May 2, 1939, just about fourteen years later. Gehrig possessed ten times the humility of Ruth, and Ruth possessed ten times the ego of Gehrig. There is good cause to wonder what both men would have been like if they had each been more in the middle.

The streak ended only because Gehrig was dying—though he did not know that yet. He only knew he had been drained of his strength and power and could no longer perform tasks that had once come easily. He benched himself, and his manager and teammates all knew it was the right thing because he clearly wasn't himself.

No one loses their top-rated talent overnight as Gehrig did without serious physical injury. He checked himself into the Mayo Clinic in Minnesota to get answers. Doctors told him he had an incurable wasting disease called amyotrophic lateral sclerosis, or ALS. Gehrig had never heard of it, nor had his teammates or most of the public. Gehrig battled with dignity, but the illness remains incurable today. He was only thirty-seven when he passed away, an age so young he should have still been out on the diamond.

While the Yankees of 1930 finished the year with six regulars hitting over .300, they did not have six solid arms, which was their one flaw. Of course, no other team could dress up its pitching staff in tuxedos that season, either.

It is often overlooked that, after Red Sox owner Harry Frazee parted with Ruth, he was still under financial duress. Ed Barrow, having grown up with the Sox organization, knew the ins and outs of players' talents. He hoodwinked Frazee.

One pitcher the Yankees scammed out of the Red Sox was Red Ruffing. Ruffing got into his first major-league game with Boston as a nineteen year old in 1924. For six-plus seasons, the young hurler threw for the worst team in the AL, receiving little to no run support. From 1925 through 1929, he posted seasons of 9–18, 6–15, 5–13, 10–25, and 9–22. His psyche had to be destroyed. Yet acquisition by the Yankees provided for one of the most dramatic pitching turnarounds in baseball history. Ruffing ended up with 273 career victories and was a 1967 inductee to the National Baseball Hall of Fame.

Ruffing began the 1930 season with the Red Sox, but after an 0–3 start, Barrow and the Yankees rescued him. Granted, Ruffing's 4.14 earned-run average was not going to win much praise, but over the rest of the season he went 15–5. Ultimately, he won between 18 and 21 games six times for New York, the town and club an obvious tonic for his career.

Of course, this was just a fresh manner of Ruffing proving his toughness. When he was young, working on a coal car, the train shifted and his left foot was crushed, necessitating the need to amputate four toes. Another time, he broke an ankle in a mining accident. Even pitching for the last-place Red Sox was safer than his previous profession.

Surveying his then plight, seemingly doomed to spend eternity in Boston, Ruffing underwent a baseball interview at the tail end of the 1929 season. He was looking ahead optimistically, for some reason. "Perhaps the luck will break better for me in 1930," he said. "Perhaps I'll cut out that one bad inning stuff. Perhaps I'll have better control but, no matter how things go, I'll stick out my chin and keep my head up."[9]

Ruffing played 22 seasons and was forty-two when he retired, following a 9–9 season with the Chicago White Sox. It was time.

Herb Pennock was another future Hall of Famer on the New York pitching staff who was shy of his best in 1930, finishing 11–7 with a 4.32 ERA. At eighteen, Pennock got his first look in the majors in 1912 with the Philadelphia Athletics. The southpaw spent another year observing from the dugout, and then flashed some good stuff with an 11–4 record in 1914. Before long, Pennock was shifted to the Red Sox—when Boston was still good—but missed the 1918 season in military service.

Perhaps the war did him some good, as when he returned to the league in 1919, now twenty-five years of age, he went 16–8 with a 2.71 ERA. He spent three more seasons in Boston, each year winning in double figures, but coping with being a key man for a lousy team.

Barrow felt Pennock could blossom . . . and it worked. Immediately, Pennock raised his stature in the eyes of the AL, winning 19 games for the Yankees in 1923. The lefty posted seasons of 21, 23, 19, and 17 wins for the Yankees, though by 1930 he was thirty-six and dealing with pain in his pitching arm. Pennock at full strength and making medium contributions might have been the difference between a pennant and an also-ran finish, but that was not the case.

Riding a train on a road trip, Pennock knew he was in trouble when his pitching arm was too sore for menial morning tasks. He told roommate Bob Meusel he needed help getting dressed. Pennock told him, "Comb my hair. Button the collar of my shirt. Tie my tie."[10]

Pennock never told Huggins, took his turn on the mound that day against the St. Louis Browns, and by throwing sidearm and stressing his curveball, he survived the outing.

Over 22 seasons, Pennock was usually described as a gentleman. He won 241 games—just shy of 60 percent of his decisions. His nickname was inclusive of his Pennsylvania birthplace and his demeanor: "The Squire of Kennett Square." Pennock was a man of varied interests beyond baseball. He was a gardener, raised foxes, and raised and raced Thoroughbred horses. Later, he became general manager of the Philadelphia Phillies, but would pass away at age fifty-four after having a stroke on his way into the Commodore Hotel in New York City for a baseball executives' meeting.

Of all guys, the pitcher with the highest winning percentage for the Yankees in 1930 was little-remembered Ed Wells. But he, like the other starters, had a high earned-run average—a lefty who had spent a handful of years with the Detroit Tigers and moved to New York in 1929. In 1930, Wells went 12–3, a great winning percentage (.800) accompanied by a rotten earned-run average of 5.20. He never reached double-figure victories again.

Right-hander George Pipgras had a shooting-star career, going 10–3 for the 1927 murderers, 24–13 in 1928, and 18–12 in 1929. Although he was as reliable as anyone on the mound in 1930, his career was on the wane when he finished 15–15.

From a family of baseball pitchers, Pipgras grew up in Iowa. Brothers Fred and Ed hoped to join him on the Yankees, but Fred never got out of the minors and Ed's entire big-league production mounted to five appearances with the Brooklyn Dodgers in 1932, his sole decision a loss.

When he was very raw, George Pipgras saved his floundering career by taking the advice of a friend who put him in touch with a low-level team. Pipgras had 15 cents in his pocket and the train fare from Worthington, Minnesota, to Madison, Wisconsin, was 60 cents. The manager actually wired Pipgras the cash and he thus turned his career around.

Although still unusual enough to be commented on, but not unique, decades ago some players shifted to umpiring after retiring from active duty. Pipgras was one of them.

Pipgras was duck hunting on Boston Red Sox owner Tom Yawkey's South Carolina estate when the magnate said he would be a good arbiter. Pipgras had been pondering becoming a minor-league manager, but changed his goal. American League president Will Harridge followed up with an offer of handling games in the New York-Pennsylvania League.

Pipgras spent the offseason studying baseball rules and when his old team, the Yankees, came to St. Petersburg for spring training, he asked manager Joe McCarthy if he could ump intra-squad games, which is how he gained his initial experience. By 1938, Pipgras was working in the AL as a full-time ump.

Later, he reflected umpiring was actually fun.

"It is pleasant work," Pipgras said. "Perhaps you don't get the same thrill out of umpiring a game in which there have been no kicks as you do over pitching a low-hit shutout, but you're still in baseball, and in quite an important department of the game."[11]

6

THE PHILADELPHIA ATHLETICS

THERE WERE SOME years in the 1920s, and again in the 1930s, when if the New York Yankees sneezed it would send American League pennant pursuers back over the horizon. But 1930 was not one of those years New York could take for granted.

After managing the Pittsburgh Pirates for three seasons in the 1890s, Connie Mack became owner-manager of the Philadelphia A's in 1902. Mack managed more games, won more games, and lost more games than any other manager in history, not surrendering the reins of the Athletics until after the 1950 season.

Mack, who wore a suit and tie in the dugout instead of a uniform to manage, led the A's to great success and three World Series titles in the early days of the American League (1910, 1911, and 1913). However, when the Federal League popped up as a threat and waved big bucks at players, Mack told his stars to go play anywhere they wanted and then deconstructed his team. It took until 1929 for Philadelphia to win another pennant and World Series.

When the 1930 season began, the A's seemed as loaded with power bats as the Yankees. They were certainly not scared of the

New Yorkers. The nature of the 1930 season, with such reliance on offense and so many gift pitches being thrown to the hitters, was tailor-made for A's sluggers.

Philadelphia had four future Hall of Famers on the roster; three position-player starters and one pitcher. All of them were magnificent that year. Catcher Mickey Cochrane batted .357. First baseman Jimmie Foxx smashed 37 home runs with 156 runs batted in to combine with his .335 average. Outfielder Al Simmons mashed 36 homers, outdid Foxx in RBIs with 165 and both of his teammates with a .381 average. They had help, too. Shortstop Jimmy Dykes batted .301 and outfielder Bing Miller came through with a .303 mark with 100 RBIs.

The biggest star of the summer, though, was A's southpaw Lefty Grove. Grove, often irascible, always confident, who owned a wicked fastball and curve, was on his way to 300 wins. But his 1930 was truly astounding. As almost all other pitchers in the league collapsed, Grove's performance stood out by such a huge margin that he was basically the equal of Babe Ruth coming out of nowhere to hit 54 homers in a season.

Grove finished 28–5 with a 2.54 ERA for the 1930 season. He led all of baseball in wins, ERA, strikeouts (209), saves (nine), and winning percentage (.848). Compared to the performance of the rest of the league's hurlers, it may have been the best-ever season by a pitcher, even though, statistically, it wasn't even Grove's finest. Wes Ferrell of the Cleveland Indians had the second-best ERA in the league at 3.31.

Dazzy Vance of Brooklyn was kinda sorta the Grove of the National League, with a 2.61 ERA. No one else in the game was under 3.00—not even future Hall of Famers.

With such stellar numbers, what's most impressive is that Grove wasn't even in perfect health that year. He had been plagued by blisters for years and even at his peak sought to throw around them. "I believe I have tried everything in the land for those two tender spots," Grove said. "It is like a bunch of needles being pushed into my hand, if I bear down on that ball when the blister is ripe. You notice I don't wrap my fingers around the ball as most pitchers do. In fact, I have short fingers, strange as that may seem. My fastball is effective this year, my curve seems to be breaking right, but I can't get rid of the blisters."[1]

Bing Miller's lifetime average over 16 seasons was .311, so his 1930 contribution was far from unexpected. Born Edmund John Miller in Vinton, Iowa, Miller was once asked if he received his "Bing" nickname for smashing the baseball.

"Far from it," Miller said. "I got it from a comic strip before I ever saw a big-league game. The characters were a lot of fellows telling tall stories and the tallest were told by the one who was George Washington Bing."[2] It was his brother Eugene who chose the moniker. This Bing, it turned out, was an avid storyteller himself.

Al Simmons had an awkward batting stance, but resisted efforts to change it. True to himself, Simmons hit .308 as a twenty-two-year-old rookie for the A's in 1924, and only improved from there. He hit .387 the following season, to go along with a startling 253 hits (as well as knocking in 129 runs). In 1930, Simmons's .381 led the American League, and he didn't even do as well as he did the next year, when he hit .391 for a second batting title.

Born in Milwaukee, Aloysius Harry Simmons grew up a long-distance Athletics fan, so he signed with the right team. Actually, Simmons took grief from teammates for hitting with his foot in the "bucket," as it was called, and when skipper Connie Mack saw that habit he grew alarmed. However, after his first impression, Mack watched Simmons slug the ball all over the field.

Still, Simmons approached Mack to talk about his hitting, and it was on this very issue, after Mack was cured of doubts.

"I came to see you about my batting, Mr. Mack," Simmons said. "Your batting, Al? What's wrong with it?" Mack replied. "Well, the older players don't seem to think much of my style. I was wondering what I should to do to change it." Mack, who not so long before had been in the other camp, reassured Simmons. "Nothing," he replied. "Don't worry about what the other players think or say. I'm the one you have to satisfy, and I'm satisfied right now."[3]

Simmons was a holdout in spring training of 1930, announcing that he wanted a salary of $25,000. Mack refused to pay. Time passed, but the negotiators had one last talk, and Mack gave in just prior to the opener against the Yankees.

"Al, it seems we are in need of your services," Mack said. "I suggest you play today." "I'll play if I get my money," Simmons. Mack added, though not happily, "You'll get exactly what you asked for."[4] Simmons was rushed into the lineup and hit a two-run homer in his first at-bat of a 6–2 Philadelphia victory.

Although relief pitching was a much less important element in the game in 1930, Mack saw Grove filling in that way. "If I could only get Grove to finish a ballgame for us between starts," Mack said.[5] Grove made 32 starts in 1930, to go along with 18 relief appearances.

Grove was so far superior to any other pitcher that year he overshadowed even his best supporting teammates by tremendous margins. But, unfortunately for the A's, Grove couldn't pitch in every single game.

To the uninitiated, Rube Walberg could be confused with Rube Waddell because of the similarity of their names and their affiliations with the Philadelphia A's. Although they were a couple of decades apart playing for Mack, Waddell, who was a bit wackier, came along in the early days of the American League. Walberg was a southpaw for the A's in the 1920s and 1930s. Like most pitchers in 1930, Walberg did not have a personal best season. Again, like most pitchers with any success during this era, his best years were sandwiched around that campaign. He won 18 games in 1929 and 20 in 1931—155 in all. He was helpful, but not dominant in 1930, with a 13–12 mark.

George Ervin Walberg was born on a farm in Pine City, Minnesota, in 1896, but as a youngster had no exposure to baseball. He headed for Washington State, began working for a navigation company, and was fascinated by sailors' stories on the ocean. He thought he might go to sea, or even become a lumberjack, but began playing semipro ball. Turned out he had a good arm, and scouts found him.

The New York Giants signed Walberg and brought him to spring training in Texas, but chose not to keep him. The A's took a look, but didn't think Walberg had a full arsenal of stuff. "Don't come back until you have acquired a curveball," Mack said.[6]

He did, and was hired. Walberg suffered from a lack of concentration in 1930, as he had invested heavily in the stock market and had to cope with anxiety over his future as the Depression took hold.

"I own all my stocks outright," Walberg said, "and I know I will see them all come back. I'm young and the United States looks pretty good to me. I also think the new ball, with its raised seams, has helped me."[7]

He was erroneous on both counts. The new ball hurt most pitchers, and the statistical evidence showed Walberg was better off without what the ball had become.

The critical pitcher in the rotation behind Grove, giving the A's what they needed in support, was George Earnshaw. Earnshaw came from a wealthy family and did not need the money the big leagues offered. Initially, he went into the water transportation business as baseball teams sought him. His uncle ran the company, but one day he told Earnshaw that business was not good and neither was his health, so he was quitting. Go find another job, he told George.

Earnshaw was a twenty-eight-year-old rookie with a 7–7 mark in 1928, but shocked the baseball world by going 24–8 the next season (plus a victory in Game Two of the World Series). In 1930, Earnshaw came through with 22 victories, although his earned-run average ballooned to 4.44. He led the AL in games started with 39, but also in bases on balls with 139, which was more his fault than the hitters. At 6-foot-4 and 210 pounds, "Moose" Earnshaw was described otherwise by Babe Ruth for his hardworking nature. Ruth called him "a horse."[8]

Connie Mack once said Gordon "Mickey" Cochrane was the best catcher he ever saw. High praise coming from Mack, who not only saw many during his managerial career, but also manned the position during his playing days. In 1930, Cochrane, twenty-seven, was in his prime, and batted a whopping .357 for the season. He had been the American League Most Valuable Player in 1928 when he didn't hit nearly as well, but was such a tremendous field leader, bringing other attributes to the game, he still gained the recognition.

Catchers were notorious for wearing out and needing rest, yet Cochrane wanted to play every day. Once, Mack took him out of a game because of a mildly strained back. "Don't you worry about me, Mr. Mack," Cochrane said, "it's the game that counts." Mack liked the gumption displayed. "Wasn't that a fine spirt?" is how Mack reacted.[9]

Gordon Stanley Cochrane was born in Bridgewater, Massachusetts, in 1903. His father, an Irish immigrant, and his mother from Scotland, Cochrane, always described as a fiery player, was a tremendous sports star at Boston University, where he played baseball, basketball, football, some hockey, and boxed. Five sports in all, he is regarded as one of the greatest athletes in school history. He also hunted, fished, and performed trap shooting, though he always loved baseball best, sometimes ditching the hoe his father handed him to farm before pulling out a concealed mitt from his shirt.

Cochrane spent parts of 1923 and 1924 in the minors, and Mack purchased him for $50,000 from the Class AA team in Portland, Oregon, where he batted .333 in 99 games. At first he loved Cochrane, then had moments of doubt, and then realized he was something special. Cochrane was eager, but made mistakes on some of the hard plays behind the plate, such as allowing passed balls and catcher's interference.

It was obvious the incumbent, Cy Perkins, was going to lose his starting job to Cochrane soon, and permanently. Instead of taking offense, Perkins became Cochrane's personal coach, educating him on the little things. The men stayed friends for life.

"I taught him all I knew," Perkins said. "At least I didn't hurt him."[10]

Mack preferred calling pitches himself, but Cochrane didn't worry about shaking him off.

"I used to call all the pitches from the bench," Mack said. "But when Mickey came along I met a young fellow who wasn't afraid to tell me I was wrong. Mickey would shake off my sign and do as he pleased. In all the years he caught for me, he wasn't wrong more than a couple of times."[11]

Mack's faith in Cochrane's savvy grew. It wasn't as clear if Mack was as enthusiastic a supporter of Cochrane's musical ability. Cochrane, who played the saxophone, wrote a song in the middle of the 1930 pennant race, though it seemed to have little connection to baseball.

One stanza went,

> I'd like to take you back
> I'd like to help you unpack,
> But you left me before
> And you'd do it some more
> So please keep offa my track.[12]

Also during that season, Cochrane teased Babe Ruth, saying the slugger should take up playing the saxophone, because every man was good for something and Ruth couldn't hit anymore. Nice try; Ruth was hitting with the same amount of power as always.

Cochrane and Mack were good partners, thinking alike, and Cochrane was one of the best-hitting catchers of all time. However, as fond of players as he would get, Mack never let friendship stand in the way of keeping the good ship Athletics alive financially.

In 1933, Cochrane, only thirty, was sold to the Detroit Tigers for $100,000, and would become player-manager for the 1934 season. Always wanting to become a manager, Cochrane was spectacular in his dual role. He hit .320, won the AL MVP award, and was chosen for the new All-Star Game. He also led Detroit to a record of 101–53 and the pennant.

The Tigers had been a middle-of-the-road, somewhat mediocre team for several years. Cochrane made it clear there would be no lollygagging on his watch.

"I played with the Athletics for nine years and in that time we never finished out of the first division and I do not intend to do so now," he said in a community speech.[13] Cochrane reinforced that directly to the ballplayers. "Do you want to be champions, or are you satisfied to hang around the second division and be laughed at?"[14]

A year later, in 1935, the Tigers went all the way, defeating the Chicago Cubs for the World Series crown. In 1937, at thirty-four, Cochrane was still active when an on-field incident changed his life. On May 25, after appearing in 27 games and batting .306, New York's Bump Hadley hit Cochrane in the head with a pitch. Two innings earlier, Cochrane had blasted a game-tying home run. The pitch fractured his skull and sent him to the hospital for seven days.

"His eyes were rolled up," said Yankees catcher Bill Dickey, who stood next to Cochrane as he sprawled on the ground. "I could see nothing, but the whites of them."[15]

This was an era before the speed of pitchers' fastballs were clocked on radar guns. "I lost sight of the ball when it was three feet from me," Cochrane said.[16]

The injury was so severe, Cochrane nearly died. Doctors ordered him to cease playing ball, and Cochrane never played another game. At first he tried to get himself into managing shape.

"Don't know what will happen," Cochrane said. "Sometimes I feel pretty good. Then again I get bad dizzy spells and so tired . . . I feel logy."[17]

Cochrane finished the season as manager and started the next year in that role, but lasted just 98 games with a 47–51 record before being replaced. After surrendering the urge to return to baseball, Cochrane spent time at a friend's Wyoming hunting ranch and then started his own ranch in Montana. A heavy smoker, he was only fifty-nine when he died in 1962 of lymphatic cancer.

The Babe Ruth in the Philadelphia Athletics lineup in 1930 was Jimmie Foxx. Just as he had two "Ms" in his first name and "two Xs" in his last name, Foxx seemed to have double the muscles everywhere. It was a wonder the bat didn't break in his hands on his follow through every swing. The nickname "Double X" implicitly carried the warning, "And don't you forget it." If you did, you could remind yourself of Foxx's hitting attributes through a second nickname, "The Beast."

Yankees pitcher Lefty Gomez, half-comedian, anyway, joked Foxx "had muscles in his hair." Gomez often told stories about how much Foxx scared him at the plate. One laugh-getter was about how the first astronauts to the moon found a baseball Foxx hit off Gomez for a homer decades earlier.

It was also a good thing Foxx was not a mean man, or he might have been too menacing to be around. Off the field, he had almost a puppy's disposition. Foxx took rookies out to dinner on his tab, picked up bills in bars and restaurants for other teammates, and didn't mind when children interrupted his dinner asking for autographs.

But, boy, he carried a big stick on the field. James Emory Foxx was born in Sudlersville, Maryland, in 1907, where he remained a hometown hero. His height was listed at six feet and, somewhat surprisingly, his weight was listed only at 195 pounds—though a concrete 195.

Foxx found his way to the A's through a back door. He hooked on with a minor-league squad run by Frank "Home Run" Baker, one of Mack's old reliables from earlier in the century. Foxx made big splashes in the majors at first and third base, but Baker needed a catcher and he tried that first.

Foxx played his first games in the bigs at seventeen in 1925. He had those in-and-out-of-the-lineup moments for two more years, but was a regular at age twenty, hitting .328. By 1929, Foxx was a star with a .354 average and a .463 on-base percentage. That 1930 season was really his breakout year, beginning a stretch where he clubbed at least 30 homers twelve years in a row, and the start of a stretch where he drove in a minimum of 100 runs for thirteen years in a row.

In some youthful interviews, Foxx, who was married with a baby by the 1930 season, impressed as an aw-shucks guy. He spoke of coming off the farm to this big, wide professional sports world.

"Sure we expect to repeat this year," Foxx said upon arrival at 1930 spring training. "At least all the boys will do their best for Mr. Mack. This has really been great stuff for a farm boy with overalls and running around barefoot in the summer, pitching hay in dad's loft. But now how about a townhouse, evening clothes, motor car, gold, and a big city championship team and lots of space in the papers. Fellows, I am dreaming now!"[18]

In 1932, Foxx won the first of his three AL MVP Awards, and that season became the first challenger to Ruth's single-season home run record of 60, with 58 clouts.

Although Foxx was a keystone of the A's, Mack once again pulled the trigger, dismantling his championship club for financial reasons later in the 1930s, which is how Foxx ended up smashing 50 home runs and knocking in 175 runs for the Boston Red Sox in 1938.

Foxx worked as a minor-league manager, hitting instructor, and scout after he retired as a player in 1945, including managing a team in the All-American Girls Professional Baseball League for a season, but had a drinking problem and lost most of his money. He was only fifty-nine when he died by choking on food in 1967.

That was all later. In 1930, Foxx was a ferocious hitter who terrorized pitchers with his powerful swing as the Athletics scratched to hold off the Yankees.

7

THE WASHINGTON SENATORS

THE JOKE WAS so longstanding it became a cliché. It went this way: Washington Senators, first in war, first in peace, and last in the American League. The rubbing-it-in comment was a running insult for decades, as the Senators were a consistently bad baseball team until they left town to become the Minnesota Twins in 1961. That year a substitute team was created, becoming the Texas Rangers in 1972.

The current-day Washington Nationals are the transferred Montreal Expos, who began play in DC in 2005. So the nation's capital was without Major League Baseball during those decades.

In 1930, however, the Senators were still part of the original American League group that were founding members in 1901. In 1924, the Senators won their only World Series.

The greatest Senators player of all time was right-handed pitcher Walter Johnson, who won 417 games, second-most behind Cy Young. And in 1930, Johnson was the club's manager. Especially during the early days of baseball, many among the greats who were aging on the diamond wished to take a shot at managing to stay in the sport. Maybe, too, it was because they made less money in their playing days.

Since the Senators had such a limited winning tradition, it appealed to Johnson to try and create a championship team in a different manner. As a player, "The Big Train" was considered gentlemanly and much admired. His pitching feats of 110 shutouts over 21 seasons with 3,508 strikeouts remain impressive almost a century later.

The 1930 Senators were a good team and were in the pennant mix, hot after the Athletics and Yankees. Johnson was three years removed from the mound, but probably wished he was pitching with this team's batting support. For once, the "W" on the front of the baseball cap might have stood for winning. The team batted .302.

First baseman Joe Judge batted .326. Second baseman Buddy Myer hit .303. Outfielder Sam West batted .328. Aging outfielder Sam Rice hit .349. Backup outfielder Dave Harris hit .317. Hall of Fame outfielder Heinie Manush, acquired in a trade from the St. Louis Browns, slammed the ball at a .362 clip in 88 games.

Shortstop Joe Cronin, a .346 hitter, probably thought he obtained job security when he married Mildred Robertson, niece to Washington owner Clark Griffith. Mildred and her siblings were adopted by Griffith when her father passed away.

Cronin became a terrific player, an All-Star, a Hall of Famer, eventually player-manager of the Senators, and yet Griffith traded him anyway to the Boston Red Sox. It was a peculiar overlapping of accomplishment and rejection of family when Cronin was shipped out. However, in 1930, he was still a well-favored son on the team.

Of course, it would have been nice to have a Walter Johnson in his prime on the roster, too. There were no available Johnsons on the market, but the Senators had five starting pitchers who won either 15 or 16 games.

While the club gained Heinie Manush mid-year, they parted with one of the greatest players in franchise history by swapping Goose Goslin for him. Goslin hit just .271 in 47 games in 1930, but as recently as 1928 led the AL in average with a .379 mark and seven times in full seasons cracked the .300 mark.

This did not seem to be a guy you wanted to get rid of, even in such a trade. Born Leon Allen Goslin, in Salem, New Jersey, he broke into the majors when he was twenty in 1921 and was a regular the next year. Goslin actually began skipping school at age twelve to play ball. He was finally noticed when a visiting squad from South Carolina was tipped off when he was still pitching for his town team of Salem. The umpire was the conduit, saying, "Guarantee this boy will win games for you and that big-league clubs will want him inside of two years."[1]

The big-league club that wanted Goslin was Washington, and that appealed to him since he knew who Johnson was.

"My big thrill was to go to Washington when Walter Johnson was there," he said.[2]

Goslin's lifetime average was .316 and he played well enough to be selected to the Hall of Fame, though perhaps his greatest achievement was saving two men's lives off the Jersey Shore when they were adrift in a boat in 1936, towing them to land after they had been without power for 12 hours.

With all those positives, Goslin's 1930 campaign did not begin well. First, he battled over salary terms with Griffith, though they settled on a $10,000 paycheck. But then his hitting dropped off.

It was an intriguing swap when Washington flipped Goslin for Manush on June 13. What probably tipped it was the arrival of

General Crowder to fill in the rotation. Manush was twenty-eight years old and a few years earlier had also won a batting title with the Detroit Tigers at .378.

Johnson had no arms to match his own, but Lloyd Brown (16–12), Firpo Marberry (15–5), Sad Sam Jones (15–7), and Bump Hadley (15–11) were buttressed by newcomer Crowder (15–19). That meant Johnson and the Senators had as much throwing depth as any other AL contender.

As marvelous as Manush was as a hitter, this was the second time he was traded as a young man. He started with the Tigers, where he won his batting crown, but was traded to St. Louis when newspapers began reporting he was a correspondent in a divorce situation with a local dentist and love letters appeared between him and the man's wife surfaced. One headline in the *New York American* described Manush as a "Fence Buster Stars Also in Role of Home Wrecker." Manush denied things were as they seemed, but he was traded to the St. Louis Browns.

In 1926, when still with the Tigers, Manush edged Babe Ruth out of the batting contest by a single point, .379 to .378. The batting race seesawed over the final days of the season, but Manush clinched the title by going 6-for-9 in a doubleheader on the last day to edge out Ruth.

"I guess one of the biggest thrills I ever got in baseball was when I beat Ruth out," Manush said. "He'd get two out of four and I'd get two out of four and he'd gain a point and I wouldn't gain a thing."

In 1930, Washington, DC, was a city in turmoil—though not over baseball. As with most American cities, the Great Depression and prohibition were at the heart of the issues of the day. People were as poor and desperate for work in the nation's capital as they were in rural America. Residents could drink right there in the neighborhood to squelch sorrows if they could avoid the prohibition rules.

And, just maybe, the Senators would pay off and throw a grand party for the whole community. Sure, smart money was on the Yankees, or the Philadelphia A's, but a pennant in the nation's capital wasn't out of the question, either.

Washington could bang, and Manush's acquisition was proof the Senators owned the weapons a team needed to contend. Manush hit .362 in 88 games with the Senators, with a .406 on-base percentage. Johnson had spent two decades in the majors with only a single title, and hoped to gild his career with more championships as dugout boss. He was a revered player, but also someone the team would follow. He was well respected as a family man.

Senators supporters were still believers in late July, the team still in the hunt, after Washington completed a western swing. However, while the club was out of town, Johnson's wife, Hazel, took their five children to visit family in Kansas, though they couldn't escape the scorching summer weather. When the family returned home, Hazel was exhausted and caught a bug. The heat and dryness were beginning to conspire to construct the dust bowl that would add deviltry to the sore circumstances of the country.

At the end of July, Hazel realized her health was not improving and was admitted to Georgetown Hospital. Doctors applied their expertise, but no diagnosis was confirmed. Instead, her condition continued to deteriorate. Two days into Hazel's hospital stay, Walter was summoned to her bedside and she passed away two days later.

Theirs had been a happy marriage, and Johnson was paralyzed by the devastating, and what he called unfair, blow. He stayed with Hazel's dead body for three days, inconsolable. "I can't understand how God could do this to me," Johnson said.[3]

Johnson left the team to preside over burial arrangements. The team played on with veteran first baseman Joe Judge as the interim skipper. Johnson was popular and the effect on the team was mighty. Hazel's death turned Walter into somewhat of a zombie, his mind with his family and late wife, as opposed to the ballclub. Owner Clark Griffith put no pressure on Johnson to rush back to work, and he would miss about a week before resuming command of the Senators. They were not finished yet, and in August took off on a spree, winning 21 out of 30 games. Johnson's spirit, though, had been broken.

Johnson's wife was much admired by the rest of the team, and players knew the man who led them had been thrown terrifically off-balance.

Al Schacht, briefly a pitcher for the Senators but a keen-eyed coach and someone who made a living as a baseball clown, described the atmosphere as funereal. "This is the most terrible thing that could have happened," Schacht said. "We all love Walter and we all realize what this means to him. She was a wonderful woman. Her heart was as big and full of thoughtfulness for others as a human heart can be."[4]

This was a breakout season for young Joe Cronin. At twenty-three, he batted .346 with 126 runs batted in. Soon enough, Cronin would become the player-manager of the Senators, an All-Star, a player-manager for the Boston Red Sox, and eventually the president of the American League and a member of the National Baseball Hall of Fame.

Cronin was discovered in San Francisco and escorted across the country for delivery to Washington. This step to the majors carried him beyond his dreams. He was the good ol' American boy who dreamed of a career in baseball all right, but the limit of his aspiration was the San Francisco Seals in the Pacific Coast League. There were detours along the way for the Pittsburgh Pirates but Cronin still needed seasoning as a nineteen year old in 1926.

It seemed as if Cronin visited every minor-league port before impresario Joe Engel, one of the most innovative of minor-league operators in history, informed Griffith that this young man could help him. Engel was a spiffy dresser. Cronin was not. Before Engel brought the goods to DC, he put a little shine on the merchandise, giving Cronin one of his new suits and making sure it fit well.

The baseball writers did not select their first official Most Valuable Player Award until 1931, but in 1930, the vote unofficially went to Cronin. One reason for Senators optimism was Joe Cronin. This was a breakout season for the twenty-three-year-old shortstop, batting .346. If anyone was going to carry the Senators to a flag, it was Cronin.

"Nature gave me a good start," Cronin said of his self-analysis. "But it has taken a lot of hard work and willingness to listen to advice to enable me to make the grade in the American League."[5]

During a time across American society and in the game of baseball, when jobs were being cut and salaries slashed, Cronin signed a new one-year contract in 1931 for $10,000.

Even Walter Johnson could have thrown himself into some booze during the 100-degree days of July as relief from his troubles. Nonetheless, crushed by the worst of personal losses, the Senators did not fold. During this very odd 1930 season, good hitters kept bouncing back and swatting off the finest offerings of the American League's otherwise top pitchers.

By the rights of typical ballplayer old age, outfielder Sam Rice should not have been able to put together such numbers in 1930. The forty-year-old Rice, whose given name was Edgar, was born in Morocco, Indiana, in 1890. He was a terrific player, though hardly one of the best-known Hall of Famers. Rice, a lifetime .322 hitter, clobbered the ball at a .349 clip that season.

For all his explosive hitting, the most famous play of Rice's 20-year career featured his glove. During the third game of the 1925 World Series against the Pittsburgh Pirates, Washington led, 4–3, in the eighth inning. More of a center fielder, the 5-foot-11, 150-pound Rice, who batted left but threw right, was shifted to right field.

Pirate catcher Earl Smith smacked a pitch deep to the wall. Rice ran and the ball sailed. Rice reached the fence at the moment the ball landed in his glove. He seemed to gather it in and then fell over the wall and out of sight. An umpire hustled over. Rice popped up holding the ball and Smith was called out.

Credited with making the play that won the World Series, Rice kept mum. Pittsburgh players and fans shouted that he dropped the ball. The umpire, Cy Rigler, signaled Smith was retired and that as soon as Rice gathered it in the out was made and the play was over. The controversy lingered. Slyly, Rice wrote a letter about the play and placed it in a sealed envelope to be opened after his death.

Sportswriters tried to get Rice to talk. Magazines offered to pay him for the true tale. For years, when Rice was asked if he made the catch, he said, "The umpire said I caught it."[6] He was never tempted to break his silence and said it was more entertaining to keep the mystery alive.

Rice played coy for years, not actually writing the letter of explanation until 1965, then leaving it in safe hands.

Rice passed away October 13, 1974 at age eighty-four. On November 6, 1974, an official gathering was conducted at the Hall of Fame in Cooperstown, New York where Rice's secret letter was opened. Rice described the play and claimed he caught the ball clean and never dropped it; that Smith's smash was a legitimate out all of the way.

In some ways vivid and in others almost in pidgin English, Rice reported his case: "Going at top speed, and about 15 feet from the bleachers," Rice wrote, "[I] jumped as high as I could and back-handed and the ball hit the center of the pocket in the glove (I had a death grip on it). I hit the barrier about five feet in front of the bleachers, but couldn't stop. I toppled over on my stomach onto first row of bleachers. I hit my Adam's apple on something, which sort of knocked me out for a few seconds. At no time did I lose possession of the ball."[7] He also said he wished he had kept the ball instead of discarding it at the pitcher's mound.

In some impressive late-career hitting, Rice held on in the majors through 1934 until he was forty-four, all but the last season with Washington. Six times Rice collected at least 200 hits in a season. He took pride in producing and especially so in 1930 when observers began referring him to the "Grandpappy of the Potomac."

Rice, associated with the franchise as a player since 1915, wanted one more title for Washington, and he started the campaign with a 28-game hitting streak. There were some suggestions Rice could hit .400. "Watch our smoke," Johnson said.[8]

A knee injury, summer heat, and Rice's age conspired to clip chunks off his batting average, though.

A couple of seasons later, the Senators threw a special "Sam Rice Day" to honor their star outfielder. He was given many presents and cash gifts. "Thanks folks, this is the greatest day in my baseball career," a choked-up Rice told the fans.[9]

As part of the festivities, special note was taken of Rice's long-time service.

One Washington celebrity resident wrote:. "My dear Mr. Rice, "You have given all of us who love baseball so much pleasure that you have richly earned the honor of a 'Sam Rice Day.' I heartily congratulate you upon your 17 years with the Washington Baseball Club and with your every success in the future."[10]

The letter was signed, "Yours faithfully, Herbert Hoover."[11]

Throughout most of the twentieth century, whoever was in the Oval Office, Republican or Democrat, had a better year than the Washington Senators baseball team. Herbert Hoover stood out in the other direction for a few seasons in the 1930s.

Herbert Clark Hoover was born in 1874 in West Branch, Iowa, growing up alongside the national pastime. He was much more interested in the outdoors than team sports, and especially fishing when it came to his recreation, though it is not clear if anyone ever asked him to throw out the first worm. Hoover was passionate enough about angling that there is a complete volume written about his connection to that sport, called *Hoover: The Fishing President: Portrait of the Private Man and His Life Outdoors.*

He learned fishing in Iowa where his presidential library and burial site are now located, along modern Interstate 80. Later, he moved to Oregon where he indulged himself along such streams as the Rogue, Willamette, and the Columbia Rivers. Hoover, who lived to age ninety, treated himself to sailfish excursions and bonefish off of Florida. It might take a half-hour to reel in a hooked bonefish whereas tossing a baseball onto the field to a cheering throng might be all over in seconds.

If Hoover had much time or energy to invest in the fortunes of the Senators as banks collapsed around him and the nation became desperate, it might be said he deserved a good, solid drink. Hoover may well have been better served by some secretive nipping when times were at their toughest, but he believed in prohibition and when the law passed he and his wife, Lou Henry, reportedly dumped their fine wine collection.

8

THE CLEVELAND INDIANS

ONLY THE VERY oldest of modern-day baseball fans were around to remember Wes Ferrell, though the retroactive argument can still be made that the fiery right-handed pitcher should have his name on a plaque in the National Baseball Hall of Fame in Cooperstown, New York.

So few starting pitchers distinguished themselves in 1930, the season could be an "Exhibit A" of support for Ferrell's status. The men on the mound were almost all shunted aside in daily play all summer long. Yet Ferrell survived.

Cleveland as a team batted .304 that summer, an achievement that is to be treasured . . . only it did not help that much. The Indians finished fourth overall in the AL with an 81–73 record under the estimable manager Roger Peckinpaugh, who had played a solid shortstop for the team as a younger man. Peckinpaugh recognized the status of the best teams in the league and felt he may be able to maneuver around them with such a fine-hitting lineup.

But it was not as if oddsmakers were convinced the Indians were better than Philadelphia or the New York Yankees in that era. "It was a tough time to be in that league," Peckinpaugh said. "We were up against two great ball clubs. On the one hand, you had Connie Mack's Athletics, with [Jimmie] Foxx, [Al] Simmons, [Lefty] Grove, [Mickey] Cochrane. And on the other hand, there were the Yankees, with [Babe] Ruth, [Lou] Gehrig, [Tony] Lazzeri, [Bill] Dickey, [Earle] Combs, and those fellows. It was discouraging. You knew you were doomed when the season opened, with those two monsters in the league."[1]

Heading into spring training, Peckinpaugh knew precisely where Cleveland fit in; the Indians were coming off a third-place finish and an 81–71 mark.

Wes Ferrell, who played at 6-foot-2 and 195 pounds, and his brother Rick, born three years earlier in 1905, were from North Carolina. Wes was a hurler and Rick a receiver. They were teammates in the majors twice, but not in Cleveland. Rick played for 18 seasons, batting .281 and was inducted into the Hall of Fame in 1984. Wes won at least 20 games six times and was one of the best hitting pitchers in history, batting .280 with a major league–record 37 home runs.

There was almost no explanation for the hardiness and success of Wes Ferrell with the Indians in 1930. He was one of the best pitchers in the league who did *not* have an off-year. Ferrell, at twenty-two, went 25–13, throwing nearly 300 innings and putting up a 3.31 earned-run average, something beyond the reach of almost everyone else in the game that year.

Ferrell had confidence written up and down his approach after 1929, when he finished 21–10. The Indians liked his stuff and tried to sign him on the cheap during that season, yet Ferrell hungered for more. "I want more money now."[2] He was worth it.

In 1930, the Indians batted.304, Ferrell won 25 games, and still Cleveland finished with almost the same record (81–73) as in 1929. Ferrell was being recognized by others as one of the best throwers in the game based on 1929 and his potential.

"His teammates say that Ferrell has everything," touted the pitcher in a magazine article that appeared as spring training started. "That is a sweeping statement, but only a moderate exaggeration, at best, for he certainly has everything that he seems to require to pitch winning ball. His best ball, of course, is his fastball. But he also has a most serviceable curve, such a curve as many pitchers fail to acquire in years of patient practice. And young, and inexperienced as he is, he has developed a baffling change of pace."[3]

The Indians began the 1930 season on April 17. By the end of the month, the Indians were 8–4 and Ferrell was 2–1. On May 11, Ferrell moved his record to 5–1 after the Indians flattened the A's, 25–7, collecting 25 hits. Right fielder Bibb Falk went 5-for-5 with five runs batted in and five runs scored.

Ferrell was eager to celebrate days like that, but if his fielders let him down, or something odd occurred that cost him a decision, he could lose his temper. The Indians eased into first place briefly during the first week in May . . . for about three days, and again for another two days in mid-June after Ferrell dominated the Athletics in a 15–2 victory.

Peckinpaugh realized the A's were going to emerge on top more often, but that did not mean Philadelphia relished going against Ferrell. Once, Philadelphia tagged Ferrell for three straight home runs and he took it personally. Ferrell threw a tantrum, heaving his glove into the stands in frustration. He screamed, "That's enough!"[4] That was conduct unbecoming, made worse when fans would not readily return the mitt.

"But that Ferrell was a great pitcher," Philadelphia outfielder Al Simmons later said. "Beat us nine times when we had our great teams in '29 and '30. In Cleveland, they always wanted us to pitch Grove against him."[5]

There was great joy in Cleveland when the Indians slipped into first in the American League standings for brief moments, as the franchise had not had much success over the previous thirty years. Founded in 1894, when the team made its debut in the new American League in 1901, the signature player was the finest hitter in the sport, Napoleon "Nap" Larry Lajoie.

He was such a terrific player and so well respected that the team was called the Cleveland Naps from 1903 to 1914. Lajoie won five batting titles and in 1901, when he hit .426, his was the highest batting average of the twentieth century (and beyond). His lifetime average was .338.

After Lajoie's departure, the Naps became the Indians. One of the grandest moments in the lengthy history of the team occurred in 1920. Backed by Hall of Famers Tris Speaker, Joe Sewell, and Stan Coveleski, Cleveland beat the Brooklyn Robins to capture their first World Series title. That is only one of two world championships Cleveland has claimed, the second being in 1948. The current draught is the longest in the majors.

In 1930, there was no reason to clog the hopes of believers too early in the season, especially if the rotation could ride Ferrell. Still, while Wes was a thoroughbred, his mound partners more resembled ponies short on training. It was Hall of Fame catcher Roy Campanella who said major-league players got paid to play a little boy's game. Unfortunately, the rest of the Indians' staff seemed to pitch like little boys.

The Indians had 13 pitchers appear in a box score that season. There was Ferrell, whose shine eclipsed all the others, and practically no one else a modern-day fan would have heard of unless they were directly related.

If anyone searched the archives to determine why the Indians could not hang with other top AL teams that year, this was the revelatory box to check. Even the 1948 Boston Braves had Warren Spahn, Johnny Sain, and the option of praying for rain. The Indians had Ferrell and anonymous backups.

Most wins? Ferrell. Best winning percentage? Best earned-run average? Most innings? Ferrell. Most strikeouts? Ferrell. In fact, Ferrell was responsible for 30 percent of the team's victories, and the rest of the pitchers on staff went a combined 56–60, with a 5.32 ERA.

One other hurler perseveres in Indians lore, and that's Mel Harder. The young right-hander made a couple of cameo appearances on the mound in 1928 and 1929, and carried a 1–2 record into the 1930 season. Harder was just beginning a 20-year big-league career accounting for 223 victories. In 1930, Harder compiled an 11–10 record in 36 games with a 4.21 ERA. He showed some promise.

The 1930 season came before Harder knew it all. By 1954, when the Indians won 111 games and the AL pennant, he was the team pitching coach who did know it all. Harder had two 20-win seasons.

The Indians basically went with a four-man starting rotation in 1930. Besides Ferrell and Harder, twenty-four-year-old Willis Hudlin (13–16), and twenty-four-year-old Clint Brown (11–13) ate up innings for Peckinpaugh.

Hudlin, born in Wagoner, Oklahoma, had good genes, living to ninety-six. He was never a superstar, but possessed longevity and was a good middle-of-the-rotation man, playing 16 years and winning 158 games. At his best, he had years of 18–12 (1927) and 17–15 (1929) for Cleveland.

Brown won 89 games and only in 1932 did he record a year as sharp as 15–12. Pete Appleton finished 8–7 in 1930. The concept of the late-inning, full-time reliever had not yet taken root. Even the best starters were often borrowed in the late going, charging out of the bullpen for a couple of innings. Some starters were gung ho, while others despised the role.

Fitting with his personality, Ferrell was a bulldog who not only responded to requests, but volunteered. He innately understood he was better than anyone else around. Rather than waiting to be asked, he'd stomp around the clubhouse making the loud offer to Peckinpaugh to "Put me in, coach." He wanted to save the day.

"Any time we have a tight game, and someone else is pitching, Ferrell will come around and say, 'If things get tough, send me in there,'" Peckinpaugh said. "'I'll stop 'em!' Get that! Not, 'I'll try to stop 'em,' but 'I'll stop 'em.' What makes this important is that when you send him in, he does stop 'em."[6]

The pitching got awfully thin, but one thing that could buoy Peckinpaugh and Ferrell was gazing at the names in the everyday batting order. They had to realize they were playing in unusual times, and if the bats stayed solid just about anything could happen over the long season. They could certainly fool themselves about the team outhitting anyone on any given day.

It is definitely no small thing to bat .300 as a team, and that did make the Indians fun to watch for the 528,657 fans who showed up for home games at League Park. There are numerous songs that incorporate lyrics referring to "the days of our lives." Well, when it came to 1930, several Cleveland players could walk around the rest of their days telling people that 1930 represented the best days of their careers.

They could utter such choice phrases to grandchildren. They could tell new friends. They could tell strangers. "I remember

1930 well," they could say. "Did you know I played major-league baseball?"" "Did you know I hit over .300?" All true. So the Indians stayed in the pennant race counting on Dick Porter, Charlie Jamieson, Ed Morgan, and Johnny Hodapp. Not to mention Earl Averill, but he ended up in the Hall of Fame, and so was long-term legit.

The 1930 season was a precious gift to all those hitters . . . except, perhaps, to catcher Luke Sewell, who was a slick fielder and the brother of Hall of Fame shortstop Joe Sewell. Luke hit just .257, the prosperity of 1930 hitting pretty much passing him by, although he did enjoy a 20-year big-league career.

Outfielder Charlie Jamieson, born in Paterson, New Jersey, in 1893, could hit. For someone so little remembered outside of Cleveland (and perhaps in Cleveland, too), the man could wield some lumber. He was thirty-seven during the 1930 season and appeared in 103 games. He hit .301 on the year, far from his finest season.

Jamieson was reaching the end of the line by 1930, but the lefty swinger hit at least .300 seven times during campaigns when he played at least 100 games (.359 in 1924, .345 in 1923, .323 in 1922, .310 in 1921, and .319 in 1920).

While it took time for Jamieson to find his niche following a 1919 trade to the Indians, the Athletics boss Connie Mack lamented his own move. "One of the worst mistakes I ever made," Mack said.[7]

Jamieson's given middle name at birth was "Devine" and it was possible whoever filled out the birth certificate was projecting to his American League days. As for his nickname of "Cuckoo," that probably warranted a different discussion. Jamieson was the leading hitter during the team's 1920 World Series championship run. Later in the 1920s, Jamieson twice started triple plays from the outfield.

From a family of 10 children, Jamieson spent his teenage years working for the local silk industry. He followed a long road through the minors, including—interestingly—spending a couple of seasons as a pitcher with spot appearances in five different seasons. Jamieson may well have been able to help out on the mound in 1930 if so many years hadn't passed since his prime throwing period in 1922.

Jamieson's name does not leap to the forefront when great outfielders of the 1920s are recalled, but he did a fine job once establishing himself in the Indians lineup. In 1923, Jamieson compiled a 23-game hitting streak. After one game in which he clubbed three hits and scored six runs, the local *Cleveland Plain-Dealer* gushed over the versatile player.

"A ball is hit towards left field," the prose read. "In a far-flung arc it rides toward the bleacher fence. The sun glistens on the lenses of a pair of smoked glasses under a long-visored cap, as a stocky young man races back with incredible speed. He nears the fence, still going fast, and with his hands over his head, catches the ball. Thousands of fans shriek their approval and then settle down once more in their seats. 'The greatest left-fielder in baseball' is the verdict from the judges. Charlie Jamieson!"[8]

In some ways, first baseman Ed Morgan put together one of the greatest slugging seasons in Indians history in 1930. Any fan running a fingernail over the stats in Morgan's totals would have to take a second look, making sure their eyes weren't playing tricks on them.

Morgan appeared in 150 games, batted .349, swatted 26 home runs, 47 doubles, drove in 126 runs, and only struck out 66 times. Pitchers on other teams should have been scared to see Morgan coming. A late bloomer, Morgan did not break into the majors until he was twenty-four in 1928, when he batted .313. He followed that up with .318 the next season. After his outstanding 1930 campaign, he hit .351 the next year. At that point in his development, Morgan was on pace to become another Ty Cobb . . . yet he never batted .300 again, and was out of the majors by 1934, at the age of thirty.

One thing that did not help Morgan's longevity was his poor fielding. He could take a healthy swing at any pitched ball, but the same was true about any ground ball.

Morgan's roots were also in a well-off family in Louisiana. He attended Tulane University and was called "Tulane Eddie." Although his father was named J. P. Morgan, and was quite comfortable, he was not the world-renowned financier J. P. Morgan. This Morgan owned and operated a box factory and ultimately went into business with his son the baseball player managing investments. Ed's baseball career would have been a good investment to manage, but unlike a century later when everyone who competes in the game makes a small fortune, it was more challenging to bank a bundle from baseball then.

Morgan's terrific 1930 production, at the height of the Depression, showed him if his desire was more focused on making money than getting ahead in the sport, he needed to rethink his long-term plans. Raises came dear in the early 1930s, and Morgan received that hard hit on the head after his season failed to sufficiently advance his salary bracket.

"If that's all the money I can make after the year I had last year," Morgan said, "I realize now that I am foolish to stay in baseball when I can make so much more in business with my father."[9]

Dick Porter held down another outfield slot in 1930, and routinely hit the ball all over the lot. Porter played in 119 games, batting .350 with an extraordinary .420 on-base percentage. Sometimes gazing at those individual player numbers it is a wonder how the Indians did not average 10 runs a game (they averaged 5.78, fourth-best in the AL).

Porter, a career .308 hitter in six seasons, did seem to be one of the lesser-known names who benefited from the juiced ball of 1930. He had been a twenty-seven-year-old rookie in 1929, hitting .328 that season, and yet was out of the majors at thirty-two, but spent many more years playing minor league ball and was chosen for the International League Hall of Fame.

One thing slowing Porter's ascent was being the property of Jack Dunn and his Baltimore Orioles. Dunn sold Babe Ruth and held off selling Lefty Grove and put the brakes on a sale of Porter, keeping him out of the majors. Dunn vacillated back and forth on keeping Porter to help him win games, or to sell him to make a profit. "Porter is worth $65,000 of anybody's money," Dunn said. "He can bat like a demon, field finely, and is fast. He can help any team."[10]

The Indians wangled Porter out of Baltimore after Dunn died in 1928 in a deal for $30,000 and two players. It was said Porter brought "twitches" and "wiggles" to the plate when he settled into his batting stance, and prominent manager Joe McCarthy thought Porter would be a big hit with fans because of his charisma.

Cleveland did grow bats on trees that season. Utility infielder Johnny Burnett, who sounded as if he should have been a 1960s guitarist, hit .312 in 54 games. Another slugger for a moment, Burnett made it through nine years in the bigs with a .284 average, though, in 1932, he put together one of the most astonishing individual efforts in a single game.

On July 10, 1932, the Indians and Philadelphia A's engaged in what seemed like the Seven Years War. The final score was

18–17 in favor of Philadelphia in 18 innings. Burnett went 9-for-11, while Ferrell pitched 11 1/3 innings in relief and took the loss. On the other side, Jimmie Foxx knocked in eight runs on six hits. There were 58 hits in the game, 35 by Cleveland. No doubt Burnett remembered that day forever.

Veteran Bibb Falk lurked in the corner of the dugout with another big bat in 1930. He didn't see much action, but when shepherded to the plate he wacked the ball at a .325 clip. The Indians of 1930 were almost the Indians of *Major League*, the 1989 movie comedy. In the flick, everyone passing paused at Pedro Cerrano's locker and dipped a bat as a way of bowing to his Voodoo God, Jobu. And it worked for all of them.

Falk was another of these guys cracking the ball off the wall at League Park in 1930, then disappearing from the majors. Falk's Indians stay was the end of his major-league career. He broke into the majors a decade earlier with the Chicago White Sox, and became a longtime college coach after his playing career had ended.

When it came to one of the greatest short-term collections of great bats in a single season, one lesser-known player who might have had staying power was Johnny Hodapp.

Hodapp was born in Cincinnati, Ohio, in 1905, and hit a lifetime .311 in nine big-league seasons. Making his first appearance in the majors in 1925, at the age of nineteen, he outhit the usual second basemen as a good contact hitter and revealed notable potential. His size was an asset for a middle infielder at the time at 6-foot-2 and 185 pounds. One unique aspect of Hodapp's career was twice obtaining two base hits in one inning in the same game.

Needing more seasoning after appearing in just 37 games in 1925 and three in 1926, Hodapp came back to the majors in 1927 and he showed what he learned: how to be a regular .300 hitter.

When he hit .354 with a league-leading 225 hits in 1930, Hodapp had topped the .300 mark for four straight seasons. That spectacular year, Hodapp stroked 51 doubles (also a league high) and knocked in 121 runs on only nine homers.

The biggest fright to Hodapp and his team that season occurred on April 30. He was hit in the head by a pitched ball thrown by the St. Louis Browns' Dick Coffman. It was a scary scene, but after a club day off, Hodapp was back in the lineup, collecting three hits on May 2.

Hodapp played so spectacularly that, similar to many players at the time, he wanted big bucks from management, So he held out. His family also ran a successful undertaker business, so Hodapp could have left the game for another profession, though rare is the young man who might find more excitement as a funeral director than a ballplayer.

A knee injury followed and, soured by Hodapp's financial attitude and deeming him injury-prone, the Indians traded him to the Chicago White Sox. Just like that, Hodapp, destined for greatness in 1930, was washed up by 1933 at twenty-seven.

It was astounding how many impressive bats the Cleveland Indians wielded with such stunning results and whose days of excellence were so shortly measured. The one player of substance and sturdiness who lasted was outfielder Earl Averill, otherwise known as "The Earl of Snohomish."

Already twenty-seven as a rookie in 1929, Averill batted .332 in his first season. He spent 13 years in the majors, mostly with the Indians, with a lifetime .318 lifetime average, to go along with six All-Star nods. This aided him with selection to the halls of Cooperstown in 1975. One of Averill's children, Earl A., also played big-league ball.

For all of the bats, it was one strong arm that kept the Indians' hopes alive in 1930. The real issue is whether Wes Ferrell should have been selected for the Hall of Fame. Between 1929 and 1932, he went a combined 91–48, winning 20 or more games in each of those four seasons. Very few pitchers in baseball history have kept up such a pace. He would also hit the 20-plus win mark in 1935 and '36, both as a member of the Boston Red Sox.

Over his 15-year career, Ferrell's career mark was 193–128 with a .601 winning percentage. He was gauged as great over many individual seasons, but not necessarily great enough over an entire career. Brother Rick, the catcher, stayed in baseball as an executive (after sharing roster time with his sibling on the payrolls of the Boston Red Sox and Washington Senators). He seemed to think Wes was the better all-around player.

"There wasn't a single thing on the baseball diamond that Wes couldn't do," Rick Ferrell said.[11]

Wes Ferrell missed baseball after he left the mound in 1941, not as eager for farm life in North Carolina.

"All of a sudden, you're out of the big time," Ferrell said, "out of reach of all the glory you had. You had everything, all the time. I met so many fine people, all the celebrities. Musicians, singers, actors, politicians. Was even made a Kentucky colonel. It's great when someone comes along and tells you they saw you pitch, how good they thought you were, how much they enjoyed it."[12]

9

THE DETROIT TIGERS

THE DETROIT TIGERS were more spoilers than anything else during the 1930 season. The lineup was dominated by spectacular hitting during the 1920s and there was a resurgence, especially due to Hank Greenberg in his prime, in the 1930s.

Charlie Gehringer, one of the greatest second basemen of all time, probably woke up every day in 1930, wandered over to read the lineup card posted by manager Bucky Harris, and wondered where everyone else went.

Magnificent outfielder Ty Cobb, rated the best player ever by many, retired in 1928 at age forty-one after wrapping up his 24-season career with the Philadelphia Athletics. He retired with a .367 lifetime batting average, the best in history (although revisionist research downgraded the number by .01).

"The Georgia Peach," one of the most flamboyant and fierce of all players, won 12 American League batting titles and helped define baseball during the first two decades of the twentieth century. He was the exemplar of the scientific game, the base-by-base advancing around the infield to score one run at a time. Cobb was astonished by the evolution of the big, booming bats emerging on all teams in the 1920s, the prototype style exemplified by slugger Babe Ruth and his followers.

Cobb belittled the style because it detracted from the method he employed. But it was too late—the power game was here. The Tigers were one of the early American League standouts, winning the pennant three straight years between 1907 and 1909, although they fell in the World Series all three seasons. And despite Cobb's inescapable talent, that was it for his stay with the Tigers. Detroit's next pennant was scored in 1934.

By the 1930s, the Tigers' fortunes were dictated by Gehringer, Mickey Cochrane, and Hank Greenberg. In the 1920s, Tigers management gave Cobb a chance to run the team as player-manager, but he was done running the Tigers by the time he was done holding down a spot in the batter's box.

Cobb played the game harder than anyone else, and ownership wanted his attitude to rub off on the other men, to lift them beyond their routine capabilities, to squeeze out the full juice of their talents. While Cobb was surrounded by some tremendous individual players, the Tigers had neither the depth in the field, nor the reliability in the pitching rotation, to compete with the finest teams in the AL throughout most of the 1920s.

In some ways, Cobb has never ceased casting a shadow over the Detroit Tigers franchise, in the same manner Babe Ruth's massive ego, performance, and personality continue to dominate Yankees lore. Cobb was not all about numbers, but rather about force of personality. He was also a living, breathing mixed metaphor of a human being. There are so many baseball fans who consider him a mean, rotten son of a bitch of a racist, that there is probably no achieving clarity about the man.

He was something to behold on the ballfield. When Cobb retired, few thought his key records would be broken. He still holds on to the best average mark, though Pete Rose did ultimately surpass him in hits. With the coming and going of such basestealers as Maury Wills and Rickey Henderson, it is now overlooked that Cobb was once the greatest of all base swipers with 892.

It was not merely the stolen base he made a signature play, but rather the daring inherent in his soul when he took second, and the challenge multiplied when he stole home. It was also how he terrorized the defense on the basepaths. "When Cobb is on first base and he breaks for second, the best thing you can do really, is throw to third," said Hall of Fame catcher Ray Schalk.[1]

Cobb even acknowledged his persona on the basepaths, and how he used it to his advantage. "I [knew] I had the reputation of being a crazy base-runner who took crazy chances and I always tried to encourage that notion," he explained. "Actually, though, I never took an out-and-out chance in a close game. My craziness, if you want to call it that, came in the one-sided games. It was then that I had a chance to experiment, testing out the pitcher, the catcher, or whoever took the throw at the base."[2]

Flair was part of it. Fans showed up at Navin Field just to see what the master would do that day. Cobb's stature and meaning to the people of Detroit was broadly described by one visiting newspaper columnist who grasped the picture.

"Ty Cobb is Henry Ford's assistant in the job of keeping Detroit in the headlines," it was written. "Caruso couldn't fill Detroit's ballpark once in a lifetime. But Ty Cobb has been doing it for years."[3]

With Cobb, Gehringer, and Harry Heilmann as regulars, the Tigers had three of the finest hitters in the lineup at one time. Cobb was Cobb. Gehringer, known as "The Mechanical Man," outlasted them. Heilmann was still playing in 1930, albeit his last full season with the Cincinnati Reds (though he appeared in 15 games in 1932). Heilmann, born in San Francisco, broke into the majors in 1914 at age nineteen. His level of steadiness was so high, it is worthy of close review. This is a guy who won four AL batting titles with marks of .394 (1921), .403 (1923), .393 (1925), and .398 (1927). Yes, Harry Heilmann batted .400 once, and nearly did so four times.

His lifetime batting average was .342 and his lifetime on-base percentage was .410. This was a particularly memorable achievement because Heilmann was slow, so he did not beat out many hits with his feet, and his power game was limited.

By 1930, Cobb was gone, Heilmann was gone, and Gehringer was the mainstay. If all had stuck around, the Tigers might well have hit .320. Instead, with a much-diluted lineup, the team still hit .284, so there were reinforcements (though below the league average for the season).

Outfielder John Stone played 1,200 games in the majors beginning in 1928, splitting 11 seasons between the Tigers and Washington Senators. In 1930, he appeared in 127 games as the regular Detroit left fielder and batted .311, similar to his lifetime .310 average. John Stone? It sounds like a professional wrestler's name, or a character in an action film. The guy had a real last name of Stone, and his nickname was "Rocky."

Rocky Stone put together a 27-game hitting streak for the Tigers in July and August; something to be proud of, even that summer. With few exceptions, the comparatively forgotten player carried a big stick throughout his career and garnered enough respect to be traded for Hall of Famer Goose Goslin in late 1933. By then, star shortstop Joe Cronin was also managing Washington and appreciated the deal.

"In acquiring Stone, I think I have materially strengthened the offense, as well as the defense," Cronin said. "Stone's ability to drive in runs and his youth made him attractive to me."[4]

It is difficult to characterize Stone as a fluke since he hit over .300 for 11 seasons, but he never seemed to stand out beyond solid play. After batting .330 for the Senators in 1937, the magic seemed to run out. He coped with illness and a foot injury, and when he was checked by doctors he was diagnosed with tuberculosis.

Stone refused to accept the medical report as a career-ending sentence. Owner Clark Griffith paid Stone's salary in full while he rested in the hospital, and Stone issued words of bravado, pledging to return to spring training in 1939. "Be sure to save my uniform," Stone wrote in a note to clubhouse manager Frankie Baxter. "Maybe a lot of people don't think I'll ever wear it again, but I'll climb into it in Orlando and I think I'll be ready."[5]

For a while it seemed Stone might beat the odds. In Saranac Lake, on the outskirts of Lake Placid, New York—twice home to the Winter Olympics—was located a tuberculosis sanitorium. This was the location where famed pitcher Christy Mathewson, injured during World War I, passed away in 1925.

By the time Stone reached Saranac Lake for treatment, his lungs were in perilous condition. Yet only a few months earlier he had managed an inside-the-park home run, dashing around the bases ahead of defenders' throws. Early doctor reports gave Stone points for gumption, and there was some optimism based on that scoring dash, Stone could recover.

"Only a man with tremendous courage could have kept playing the way he has," the doctors stated.[6]

Rocky Stone was probably the best unheralded player for the Tigers in 1930, but Marty McManus wasn't far behind. The starting third baseman, McManus batted .320 and led the AL with 23 stolen bases. McManus played 15 seasons and was an established player by the turn of the decade. Except for a .333 season with the St. Louis Browns in 1924, McManus posted his highest average in 1930.

A typically built infielder at 5-foot-10 and 160 pounds, McManus recorded a respectable, but not star-turn lifetime .289 average.

McManus was an early proponent of players' rights. Twice he held out for more money on contract deals. Much later, in 1951, McManus tried to play a role in organizing professional athletes in baseball, football, and basketball through union representation in connection with the American Federation of Labor, but nothing came of it.

McManus, whose main flaw was fielding—he committed 32 errors in 1930—needed postseason knee surgery that subsequently affected his career. After his playing career ended, McManus was a very active manager, with the Red Sox, minor-league teams in Minneapolis, Denver, and Tulsa, for the Kenosha Comets and, South Bend Blue Sox, of the All-America Girls Professional Baseball League, and the Chicago Bloomer Girls of the National Girls Softball League.

For all of his erratic glove work, McManus had the remarkable fortune of simply being in the right place at the right time to be involved in five triple plays, though none of them happened in 1930.

What the heck was Dale Alexander doing with his time before 1929? Born in 1903 in Greenville, Tennessee, the hulking, 6-foot-3, 215-pound swinger nicknamed "Moose" could well have been a Hall of Fame caliber player based on his five-year body of work in the majors. Lifetime, Alexander hit .331. In 1930, only his second season in the league, he hit .326. Alexander descended from the sky and beat the heck out of pitchers with his bat.

Alexander was already twenty-six his rookie year, arriving in Detroit ready-made at first base. Before that, Alexander roamed the South, and finally Toronto of the International League, a first-rate hitter not gathering enough attention.

One of eight children raised on a 117-acre Tennessee farm that dated to 1796, Alexander's generation grew corn and tobacco. Farming and attending school at Milburn College kept Dale in the neighborhood, whereas if he had been more adventuresome he may have become a bigger baseball personality earlier.

Alexander played pro ball at low levels of the minors, making a few bucks and hitting the ball like a rocket wherever employed. This began in 1920 in the Class D Appalachian League. Throughout the mid-1920s, Alexander signed on with teams in Tennessee and then Charlotte, spending summers slugging the ball at a .320s and .330s rate.

It would have seemed likely for Alexander to attract some scouting attention, but he did not until 1927 in Toronto. That season, Alexander batted .338 against the best pitching he had yet seen. Alexander's second season in Toronto opened doors—with trumpets. He batted .380 with 31 home runs and 144 RBIs, plus 236 hits. Newspapermen sang songs of his virtues, in some cases comparing him to Babe Ruth or retired Tigers star outfielder Sam Crawford. There were some minor denigrating comments about him being a tad slow afoot.

Alexander was a supreme hitter, but never bragged. Long after he won the AL batting title with a .367 average in 1932, he was reminded of the feat and almost backed away from the achievement. "No, what I did was no more than the lady winning first prize for cornbread at the county fair."[7] Now that's modesty.

He did not appear to have any hitting secrets. "I don't look for anything except a good ball. If it looks good, I swing at it." He was once asked if he had any trouble adjusting to spitballs. "No, I would just hit it on the dry side."[8] Which of course exhibited a dry sense of humor.

Alexander was a shooting-star hitter, making a dazzling impact but fading quickly. While his slow major-league start was explainable, the bad luck surrounding his exit was unfortunate.

In May 1933, Alexander incurred third-degree burns on his leg. He was given a diathermy treatment on a twisted knee, which blossomed into gangrene and further slowed him. Alexander played in 94 games that season, but never truly recovered.

"I couldn't run and I couldn't field and when I got hurt that was the end of it," Alexander said.[9]

Alexander did continue playing in the high minors and continued hitting at a high level, batting .358 for the Kansas City Blues of the American Association. In 1935, he hit four home runs in one Class AA game. Alexander could still wield the big stick, hitting .319 for Nashville in the Southern Association and .309 for the Chattanooga Lookouts in the same circuit. When he dropped down to the Florida State League, Alexander ruined pitchers with a .345 average. Then he did it all over again in the Georgia-Florida League, batting .388 for Thomasville. No pitcher could contain him.

The Tigers, much like most of the other 15 teams, had little more depth than many Little League teams. Depending on the series it might be an eeny, meeny, miny, moe process for Bucky Harris. The Tigers had a losing record, but they had several winning starting pitchers, including some guys who could win once in a while.

Earl Whitehill, thirty-one, had the best record at 17–13, but his ERA was a shaky 4.24. George Uhle, the same age, went 12–12, though his ERA was a more respectable 3.65. Vic Sorrell met them in the middle with a 16–11 record and a 3.86 ERA. Thirty-year-old Waite Hoyt, who made the Hall of Fame in 1969, went 9–8, but his ERA of 4.78 hurt.

The 1930 season was fairly typical for Whitehill. He would win double-figure games in 13 of his 16 seasons, but also was at risk of giving up too many runs. Still, to win 17 ballgames in 1930 when the world was collapsing around most pitchers was a worthy accomplishment. Whitehill spent 17 years in the majors and won 218 games, though his career 4.36 ERA was the highest of any pitcher who retired with more than 200 victories.

The 1930 campaign was one of his best, but clearly his finest overall season was 1933 when he finished 22–8. The only problem for Detroit fans was that by then he was with the Washington Senators.

Whitehill was nicknamed "The Earl" because with his handsome looks he could appear regal. However, he had a bad temper and batters did not dig in on him. As a full-time rookie in 1924 he plunked 13 guys. Twice Whitehill threw one-hitters in the bigs. He also had one effort when he was touched for 10 doubles.

Delayed reaction to a concussion suffered in an automobile crash in 1954 killed Whitehill at the age of fifty-five.

Vic Sorrell was another late-arriving rookie, breaking into the majors at twenty-seven in 1928. His overall record was 92–101, but he somehow put together his best season in 1930.

A native of North Carolina, Sorrell attended Wake Forest University. Much later, he coached North Carolina State. He was an early big leaguer to wear glasses on the field. He apparently saw the plate well enough in 1930. We don't know what he might have accomplished in the 1930s, but just as the Tigers matured into back-to-back pennant winners, Sorrell threw his arm out and could no longer contribute, closing out his career with such seasons as 6–9, 6–7, and 0–2.

Sorrell grew up on a farm and always remembered that it was much easier to throw a baseball for pay than to pick cotton. During his first season in the minors, he was sidetracked by the mumps. "It was lost time," Sorrell said. "I was anxious to make it up. I began to work a little too soon. The result was a sore arm. It bothered me all season."[10]

Mumps, sore arm, wrecked arm. Sorrell had the right stuff and showed the goods on occasion, but could never stay healthy long enough to maintain a career. He was probably one of hundreds of almost-made-it-big league players to have dreams dashed quickly, mostly not through their own fault.

On July 26, 1928, Sorrell and Waite Hoyt went head-to-head for 11 innings, both sitting on a 1–1 standoff. Then, it was as if Sorrell's motion and concentration were blown to bits by hand grenades. The fast-deteriorating pitcher's duel saw Sorrell allow 11 runs on 10 hits to 15 batters in the 12th inning.

A symptom of Sorrell's arm problem was lack of control. He regularly walked more batters than he struck out, meaning he always had to cope with too many runners. For his 10-year career, he averaged 3.8 walks per game, topping four per game in seven seasons.

"My control is not all that I could wish," Sorrell said in rather genteel phrasing. "I bear down hard in order to get by at all, and the more you bear down, the less easy it is to put the ball where you want it."[11]

Although they were not key members of the staff in 1930, the Tigers did have young Tommy Bridges (3–2) and Whitlow Wyatt

(4–5). At twenty-three and twenty-two, respectively, they were not quite ready to make an impact. Over the years, Wyatt won 106 games and Bridges 194.

Of all the stops and all the things Waite Hoyt was known for in baseball, spending time with the Detroit Tigers was not really near the top. Born in Brooklyn in 1899, Hoyt played one game at age eighteen in 1918 as his major-league debut with the New York Giants after briefly being mentored by 373-game-winner Christy Mathewson. Mathewson liked Hoyt's approach and Hoyt liked Mathewson's style.

Hoyt was just sixteen when manager John J. McGraw found the youngster and offered him a contract as the youngest player to sign a big-league deal. For $100. Since he was too young to provide a legal signature, his father, Ad, signed on his behalf. Dad kept the payout, too.

"The Giants gave me $5 for signing and my father took it away from me immediately," Hoyt said of the 1915 transaction. "He felt it was too much money for a kid to have on his person at one time."[12]

Hoyt briefly passed through the Giants and the Boston Red Sox before taking the four-hour train ride back to Manhattan, becoming a member of the Yankees. Hoyt unleashed his best stuff on Yankees opponents during the 1920s, pitching in six World Series and winning 157 games during his stint in New York. Taking advantage of such success, he moved directly from the mound to the theatre district in 1928 to sing and dance the same autumn. New York could fete its heroes.

He was a key arm with the Yankees in the 1920s, compiling such seasons of 23–7, 22–7, 19–13, 19–12, and 18–13. Hoyt led the AL in wins with 22 and had a winning percentage of .759 when Murderers' Row blew through the 1927 season. Although he concluded his career with 237 victories and enjoyed a decades-long broadcasting career for the Cincinnati Reds before being honored with selection to the Baseball Hall of Fame in 1969, Hoyt also drifted to other big-league towns, Detroit included in 1930 and 1931.

It must be said that Hoyt was multi-talented, working as an offseason mortician and performing in vaudeville shows at other times. Going 9–8 with Detroit in '30 (after starting the season in New York, going 2–2) may or may not have been easy to fit into either of those boxes. Candid about one flaw, Hoyt later said that perhaps he would have won 300 games if he stopped drinking before retiring rather than committing to sobriety and Alcoholics Anonymous as an older man.

The superficial reaction to Charlie Gehringer's nickname was not necessarily flattering. The Mechanical Man? It does not really sing, nor convey the full nature of a compliment. The meaning behind the moniker, though, was to suggest the long-time Tigers second baseman knew what he was doing and never made mistakes.

Gehringer was born in 1903 in Fowlerville, Michigan. Inducted to the Hall of Fame in 1949, he spent just about his entire life in baseball after breaking into the majors in 1924. A left-handed hitter with a lifetime average of .320, Gehringer recorded seven seasons with at least 200 hits and finished his 19-year playing career with 2,839 hits.

It was Yankees pitcher Lefty Gomez who anointed Gehringer "The Mechanical Man" for his consistency. Gehringer was destined to be a farmer, his parents thought, but his affinity for crops was limited. He thought playing sports at the University of Michigan would be more fun. Longtime Tigers player Bobby Veach saw Gehringer playing ball in Ann Arbor and led him to Detroit. Although the Tigers sensed his talent, Gehringer showed up in just 13 box scores in 1924 and 1925 combined, before becoming a regular in '26. He was still in the learning stages, absorbing wisdom passed down from Ty Cobb.

Gehringer displayed more jitters than the average rookie in his first game, making errors, failing to make contact at the plate—an overall miserable showing—until his last chance at bat.

"I had a tough day," Gehringer said. "I booted two or three balls and didn't get any hits. On my last trip to the plate, I thought I had one. I smashed the ball to left field, but somebody jumped up in front of the scoreboard and made a great catch."[13] That flashy out made him feel good, a swing counting for zero in the statistics, but an ego booster, nonetheless.

Gehringer got into five games that season, going 6-for-13. It was a small body of work, but looked promising. As a rookie in 1926, Gehringer did not light things up, either, yet hit .277. The next year, post-Cobb, he hit .317 and impressed everyone.

He got his most serious playing chance when veteran Frank O'Rourke caught the measles, with Charlie becoming the starter at second base. "Some of us get our starts in strange ways," Gehringer said. "I was sitting on the Detroit bench wondering if I would ever get a break." Then O'Rourke got his doctor's report. "Well, Frank got sick, I went to second, and I stayed there for quite a while."[14]

By 1930, Gehringer was the best player on the team. That season he batted .330 with 16 home runs, 98 runs batted in, 19 stolen bases, and a .404 on-base percentage to go along with 201 hits and 144 runs scored. It was about as good an all-around season as one could get. His 154 games played represented an appearance in every scheduled game as well.

At the plate, Gehringer took his whacks, driving line drives all over the field. At second, he took his position and dazzled with his glove as much as with his bat. Many times ballplayers receive oohs and ahhs for making diving stops or fancy catches. Gehringer's goal was to be in the right spot ahead of time.

"That's the mechanical part you just take for granted," Gehringer said. "I never had a manager who asked me about my fielding, why I had a better year fielding this year or that. But they'd all ask you how many runs you brought in, or how many you scored, or how often you got on base."[15]

In 1930, Gehringer scored more, hit better, did more on offense than anyone else, but it still didn't matter much to the Tigers as there just wasn't enough depth in the order or support on the pitcher's mound.

There was one choice piece of irony for the Tigers in 1930. In mid-September, Detroit called up a player about to become the team's next great star. They didn't realize it yet, however, and neither did the young player.

First-baseman-outfielder Hank Greenberg, nineteen, made his major-league debut on September 14, 1930. The slugger was about to embark on one of the team's most distinguished careers, batting .313 with 331 home runs during his 13-year career (all but one of those seasons in Detroit). He added nothing to those statistics that season, mostly sitting in the dugout.

Greenberg absorbed the atmosphere, played in one game, and made one plate appearance as a pinch-hitter, popping out to second.

10

THE ST. LOUIS BROWNS

ST. LOUIS WAS an early developing major US city, founded on the banks of the Mississippi River. Countries were fighting for dominion over the port city as early as 1764, and it was the organizing center for Lewis and Clark when President Thomas Jefferson sent the Journey of Discovery West in 1803 to explain the Rocky Mountains and the vast uncharted territory recently acquired from France.

Although St. Louis has a smaller population, at 300,000, and is not mentioned among the most significant American hubs in 2020, ninety years earlier, at the time of the Great Depression and the 1930 baseball season, the city's population was 829,000. Of course, there are now 2.8 million people in the metropolitan area. Nearly a century ago, however, there wasn't much suburban territory.

By big-league baseball standards, St. Louis was always a major operator. Just as New York and Boston were felt worthy of supporting of two teams, there was pretty much always a National League and American League club anchoring the community—at least for the first half of the twentieth century.

When the stock market plummeted and the Great Depression gripped the US, St. Louis was the seventh-largest community in the country and home to the Cardinals (NL) and Browns (AL).

For all its history and strength in the national economy, the Depression hit St. Louis as hard as any significant city. In 1931, less than two years after the stock market's demise, the unemployment rate in St. Louis was 24 percent, higher even than other badly struck cities. Things got worse from there. By 1933, the St. Louis unemployment rate reached an astonishing 35 percent.[1]

Fans did not line up to watch baseball. They lined up to collect unemployment checks and meals from food banks to support their families.

Many citizens blamed President Herbert Hoover for the nation's financial woes, and when the homeless gathered in tent cities, trying to shield families from the worst of conditions and the worst of weather, the makeshift communities were called "Hoovervilles." In the modern United States, Springfield is the most commonly named city in the land. In the early 1930s, it was Hooverville. To ward off starvation, governments at all levels, and service organizations, funneled food to the hungry. In St. Louis, the Welcome Inn fed up to 4,000 people daily.

It would be redundant to say the St. Louis Browns were not contenders for the 1930 American League pennant. Between the earliest days of the AL and 1953, when the Browns were shoved out of St. Louis, leaving the fertile territory to the Cardinals, the Browns were rarely considered contenders. Ironically, in 1902, the first season of the franchise, the team was pretty decent, finishing in second place with a 78–58 record.

In reality, this was kind of the second season of the Browns. When the AL was formed in 1901, a team in Milwaukee called the Brewers (not to be confused with the present version) competed for a season, then hitchhiked to St. Louis to begin life anew as the Browns.

What a tease that was. If you were a Browns fan from the beginning, you probably were excited, likely convinced the first-year showing was bound to lead to great things to come. The next time the Browns finished as high as second, however, was 1922—twenty years later.

Not only did the Browns record a 93–61 record that season, finishing just one game out of first, but the team attracted 712,918 fans, nearly one patron per population figure of the city. For one of the rare times in its history, the St. Louis AL franchise was flush with hitters. The fabulous George Sisler batted .420, and he wasn't alone in the rare air above .300, either.

As had been the case with the franchise, this prosperity did not last. During its half-century of existence, St. Louis was the worst of all teams, one outspent and outshone by the rival Cardinals, who shared Sportsman's Park as their home field. During the Browns' fifty-two years of play, they never won 100 games in a season, and 1922 represented the only time the franchise won as many as 90. Furthermore, they amassed 1,051 more losses than wins (3,414–4,465), and were outscored by more than five thousand runs.

It was lonely at the bottom. In other seasons, the Browns lost 100 or more games eight times, 90 or more 24 times, and 111 games in a single season. The Browns never won a World Series, but in 1944, during World War II play, when roster forming and other aspects of the game were slightly off-kilter, the Browns won an AL pennant. There was no American League Championship Series, nor a division playoff. If a team won the pennant, it advanced directly to the World Series. That was the Browns' reward that season. Naturally enough, their NL foe was the Cardinals, who won the title in six games.

By 1930, the Browns' greatest season was eight years in the rearview mirror. There were no great expectations when the club lined up at the starting line, and once the games commenced, no peculiar bolt of lightning altered those expectations.

The Browns did pass through more than one ownership on the journey from Milwaukee to St. Louis. By 1916, the magnate-in-charge was Phil Ball. That was Phil Ball for short, as his more formal name was Philip De Catesby Ball. Ball was a baseball man in the sense that he wanted to run a team in his town. He had snatched control of the St. Louis Terriers during the short-lived existence of the Federal League. But when the competing league folded, he managed to walk away as owner of the Browns.

Initially, Ball was promised the chance to buy the Cardinals, despite losing $182,000 on the Terriers. He settled for the Browns, which opened a path to ownership in the majors, though saddled him with the weaker of the two hometown franchises.

Ball was welcomed into the fraternity of American League owners as part of the settlement that allowed the Federal League to drift into oblivion without causing any more trouble. Like all good owners, when he took control of this outfit, he announced he wished to bring a championship to town.

"I'll pay—well, I'll go to the limit—to get a World's Series for St. Louis," Ball pronounced. "I'm just as interested in a ball game as the kids who hand over their two bits at the windows for the bleacher seats.[2]

Family money came from his father Charles's engineering and ice business, which sold refrigeration machines the family helped develop. While Ball's father made the operation a going concern, when his dad died, the younger Ball invested $20,000, took over the business, and made the company more profitable. It also gave him the spending money needed to run a ballclub.

"It has been said that I inherited my money from my father, but I never got a nickel from anybody," Ball said.[3]

Ball, like his friends, was a cautious investor when the Federal League began business as a minor-league organization. Fourteen men threw in a thousand dollars apiece to create the team. However, in 1914, the Federal League sought to go big-time and take on the established league. Assessing the deep-pocketed competition, twelve partners bailed out. Only Ball and one other co-owner stayed to fight, attempting to make the Terriers a permanent fixture. Those bold owners did pour big bucks into their teams—particularly the Terriers' co-owners, and the Federal League won major-league status for its final two years of business. The league as a whole vanished, even if the records do count as official major-league statistics.

Ball was as serious as a heart attack when it came to trying to steal players for the Terriers. His No. 1 target was Walter Johnson, but Johnson did not jump. At that time, Philadelphia A's owner Connie Mack professed disgust with the entire greedy lot of players with eyes on the dollar sign and began dismantling his first dynasty team.

While Ball could not budge Johnson out of Washington, he did pick off southpaw Eddie Plank of the A's, a worthy consolation prize. Plank won 21 games in 1915, and the future Hall of Famer was likely the best hurler Ball employed—with the Terriers or Browns—even at thirty-nine.

Whether it was attributable to his passion, temper, or risky judgment, Ball frequently argued with his players, managers, and other AL personnel. Running the team between 1915 and 1933, the year he passed away, Ball said the only year he made a profit was 1922. Otherwise, he said, baseball was his hobby; his investment fueled by trying to bring a title to St. Louis.

St. Louis was, for a time, a one-ballpark town, with the Browns and Cardinals sharing Sportsman's Park. Baseball had been played at the Grand Avenue Ball Grounds as early as 1867. The Sportsman's Park everyone came to know opened in 1920 at 2911 North Grand Boulevard, and doubled as both big league teams' home field for decades.

Despite his grand hopes and commitment to bring home a winner, by 1930, it was probably clear to Ball that he was going to have to be the recipient of some special good fortune to win a World Series with the Browns.

Ball had engaged in a series of skirmishes with Commissioner Kenesaw Mountain Landis over a minor-league player named Fred Bennett. Landis had been a trustbuster of sorts, freeing players kept down on the farm by richer clubs. The Bennett arrangement was of the same ilk.

Ball also was not shy about feuding with his managers if they did not produce results that pleased him. So as the team struggled he, more often than not, did not get along with most of his skippers. By Browns standards, the 1929 season was quite a respectable one. They finished 79–73 and manager Dan Howley gave Ball a plus-.500 club.

Still, the men feuded, and as season's end approached, Howley blew up. Ball announced that all the "dead and dying timber will be culled." That meant a roster turnover. Howley was irritated with Ball's high-handedness. "It makes no difference where the club finishes. If we win the pennant, I'm through just the same. "I'm quitting."[4]

Ball and Howley agreed on that personnel move. Since irritation with Howley colored everything, Ball found himself a new manager for 1930. The new man in charge was Bill Killefer. Killefer, born in Michigan in 1887, joined the Browns as a player at twenty-one, though his stay was brief. After his debut campaign, Killefer was exiled to the Buffalo Bisons of the Eastern League.

The manager there was George Stallings, who led the 1914 Miracle Boston Braves. Well into the season, the Braves resided in last place, but rallied and won the National League pennant by 10 ½ games. The Braves' magic continued well into October, when they took out the Philadelphia A's in four games in the World Series.

It was Stallings who made Killefer into a first-class receiver, although he was never much of a hitter. Unlike most catchers, Killefer was a fast runner, quick enough to acquire the nickname "Reindeer Bill."

Killefer could only muster a lifetime .238 batting average, but he was a savvy pitch caller and Hall of Famer Grover Cleveland Alexander referred to him as his favorite catcher during their days with the Philadelphia Phillies. Killefer was Alexander's main catcher when the career 373-game winner won at least 30 games in a season three consecutive years. For a guy who had to make do more with his brains than his bat, Killefer did well, spending forty-eight years in professional baseball as a player, coach, and manager.

By the time Ball brought Killefer back to St. Louis to pilot the Browns in 1930 at age forty-two, he already had some managerial seasoning. Killefer ran the Chicago Cubs between 1921 and 1925, compiling three consecutive 80-plus-win seasons (1922: 80–74, 1923: 83–71; 1924: 81–72).

There was nothing wrong with Killefer's credentials when Ball gave him a chance to lead the 1930 club, but there was much wrong with the Browns lineup and they swiftly descended to near the bottom of the standings, finishing with a 64–90 record. Not much fun was had in the clubhouse, nor in the streets of deteriorating, going-broke St. Louis that summer. The Browns were destined to finish 38 games out of first place.

In the year of the hitter, the Browns had . . . well . . . no hitters. The season was characterized by sluggers, by players having the best years of their lives. However, as a team, the Browns batted .268. If St. Louis had been able to hang on to its two best guys, the franchise might have made more noise in the standings.

The Browns had two future Hall of Famers, but they were traded for one another during the season and brought more aid to others. St. Louis had Goose Goslin and Heinie Manush, who both hit well. It was just that they spent half their time hitting for someone else. Goslin played in 101 games for the Browns and batted .326, while Manush played in 49 games for the Browns and batted .328.

The only other full-time, all-season regular who hit well was shortstop Red Kress, who batted .313. Kress, born in Columbia, California, in 1905, was a solid, all-around player who hit .286 during a 14-year career, and was a popular teammate. Primarily an infielder, Kress seemed content to be deployed anywhere his manager needed him, including the outfield or behind the plate.

Kress even pitched occasionally, and stepped into the role as hurler for the Toronto Maple Leafs against the Montreal Royals in a 1945 minor-league game. He tossed a no-hitter for 8 1/3 innings before allowing a safety and losing the ballgame, 1–0, in the ninth.

Kress made this versatility pay off. Besides spending parts of 14 years in the majors, Kress competed in Canada and coached in Mexico. Big-league clubs sought his input as a coach, knowing his eagerness would help the team, and his knowledge would be spread to younger players. Of all attributes, Kress seemed to possess a rubber arm, allowing him to throw long batting practice sessions.

Coaches did not get rich but, periodically, a team found a way to show appreciation. In 1955, that's what the Cleveland Indians did, presenting Kress with a $3,000 Oldsmobile. Al Rosen, the star third baseman and later professional executive, said Kress had given so much of himself to the Indians that the club wanted to give something back. Kress worked with legendary manager Casey Stengel on the original New York Mets of 1962, and Stengel described him as "the hardest working man I ever knew."[5]

That was the kind of guy the Browns had as a regular in 1930. Unfortunately for the club, they needed eight more like him. Kress not only topped .300, but belted 16 home runs and knocked in 112 runs. He played all 154 games. Kress's average in 1930 was his big-league high, although he also hit .311 for the Browns the next year.

The one truly distinguished name on the Browns roster in 1930 was Rick Ferrell, a future Hall of Famer. It did not do St. Louis quite enough good for Ferrell to hit .268 when so many others sprinkled around the AL hit 100 points higher.

Rick Ferrell was not such a grand hitter that he had scouts drooling over his potential. He instead won them over with his mitt. Born in 1905, Ferrell was 5-foot-10 and 160 pounds, so was not an imposing physical specimen, either.

It might be said he was an acquired taste. The longer baseball men watched him, they quicker they realized that he knew what he was doing. Ferrell the catcher did the little things well and worked hard. It was that type of performance, more than slaughtering the ball, that gained him attention.

Rick Ferrell made his big-league debut in 1929, getting into 64 games before he took over the bulk of the catching the next season with 101 appearances. It took until 1931, when he batted .306, for Ferrell to make any kind of mark as a batter.

How Ferrell ended up with the Browns at all, viewed as a fate worse than the American Association, was its own tale. Ferrell had been cruising along with the Detroit Tigers organization, but things got a bit strange when the Tigers seemed likely to make him a late-season call-up. Some shenanigans came out and Ferrell learned his contract wasn't even owned by Detroit.

Commissioner Landis investigated and was unhappy to discover Ferrell's career was being impeded. Ultimately, Landis refused to permit the Tigers, the Cincinnati Reds, and a minor-league team, from bidding on Ferrell. Instead, St. Louis was the sweepstakes winner. Ferrell saw opportunity in St. Louis, plus a vacancy at catcher. He was right enough to take control within a year or so. He believed St. Louis was on the way up but, unfortunately, the team was headed the other way.

Ferrell was not a lifer with the Browns, and by 1933 was holding down the catcher's slot with the Red Sox, and later the Washington Senators. However, Ferrell did return to the Browns later in his career, spending several more seasons in St. Louis. Over the course of 18 seasons, Ferrell compiled a .281 average. He was a seven-time All-Star, including being selected for the first game ever, played in 1933.

Ferrell ended up doing a bit of everything in baseball. After retiring as a player and coach, he became a scout and then general manager of the Tigers in the late 1950s. There was some boldness in Ferrell's soul as a GM. He once mentioned in a speech how close the Tigers and New York Yankees came to sending outfielder Al Kaline and front-line pitcher Frank Lary to New York for Mickey Mantle and Whitey Ford.

"There was a lot of discussion about the trade and it wasn't our club that finally backed down on the deal," Ferrell said.[6]

If it had gone through, baseball fans would still be talking about that trade to this day.

The only way the so-so-hitting St. Louis Browns team of 1930 could have competed with the best clubs in the AL was if they owned fluky good pitching. They did not; the pitching was about as depressed as the Great Depression.

However, enter Lefty Stewart. Born in Sparta, Tennessee, in 1900, Stewart had a brief fling with the Detroit Tigers in 1920, giving up 12 earned runs in five appearances. He made his next big-league appearance in 1927, going 8–11 for the Browns.

Stewart was called Lefty because he was, in fact, a lefty. He was born Walter Cleveland Stewart, and although he was hardly the most famous pitcher in baseball in 1930, he was one of the best pitchers in baseball *that* season. It was unlikely, but true. Stewart was a 20-game winner for the Browns, finishing 20–12 with a 3.45 earned-run average.

In his 10-year career, Stewart collected a 101–98 record. It made zero sense, however, that he should have his finest season in 1930 when even the best of twirlers were getting clobbered. In this haunted season for pitchers, Stewart tied for the fifth-most victories in the majors.

How did he do it? Stewart hurled 271 innings and won with guile more than power, striking out just 79 men all season. Seventeen of his wins, however, were complete games. He did allow an AL-leading 21 home runs, which could well have spelled doom. Even more remarkable for Stewart was that, in 1927, he'd recovered from a burst appendix that nearly killed him. The state of medicine wasn't nearly as developed during that era, yet Stewart survived.

Although he lost nearly as many games as he won during his decade in the majors, and he had about as many losing seasons as winning seasons, Stewart did some good work beyond 1930. He won 14 games in 1931, and then had back-to-back 15-win seasons (1932 and 1933). If Stewart had some run support from the lowly Browns, he may well have performed better statistically.

In the early days, baseball players sported quirky nicknames. They seemed to have disappeared in the twenty-first century. Sometimes the names were merely poetic, but one might expect the Browns to be chock full of nickname guys.

The team's first baseman in 1930 was called Lu Blue. Quite melodious. As first basemen went, Blue was small, his vitals measuring 5-foot-10 and 165 pounds, and while he played one of the power-hitting positions, he was far from a power hitter. In 1930, Blue hit .235 with four home runs. During his 13 seasons in the majors, he totaled just 44 home runs, though he did manage 14 homers and 80 RBIs in 1928.

Although Blue was not known as a home-run hitter, he did get on base frequently, every year from 1921 to 1931 ranking in the top ten in the league in walks. In the same time frame, he was fifth overall in runs scored. The four men ahead of him (Sam Rice, Rogers Hornsby, Frankie Frisch, and Babe Ruth) are all Hall of Famers. Even so, his .235 average in 1930 was one of the worst hitting years of Blue's career, as his lifetime average was .281.

It is not clear if Lu Blue had blue eyes, but when he began his professional baseball career, his affiliation was the Martinsburg Blue Sox in the Blue Ridge League. When he joined St. Louis, he merely switched colors. The player pretty much came by his unusually spelled first name of Lu honestly, too, as his given name was Luzerne. It is obvious why he may have wanted to duck that parental appellation.

Overlooked somewhat in the days of Ty Cobb, Harry Heilmann, and Charlie Gehringer, Blue was a great asset at the plate for the Tigers in the 1920s. The Browns believed he would be a major acquisition at the plate, but slippage began in Blue's average almost as soon as he showed up in St. Louis. Still, the 1930 season was a turning point for him. His off-year provoked ire from owner Ball who attempted to slash his first baseman's salary by 50 percent. When Blue balked, he was sent to the Chicago White Sox.

After retiring from baseball, Blue operated a chicken farm and then a chinchilla farm. He also started one of the first baseball schools in the United States. Blue was always growing something, including ballplayers.

One name found on the roster of the 1930 St. Louis Browns looks like a typographical error. A twenty-seven-year-old outfielder who appeared in 89 games and made 254 plate appearances while batting .239 off the bench, went by the name of Red Badgro.

The reason this was so eye catching is because Badgro was primarily a professional football player. In college he played football at the University of Southern California, and then in the 1920s suited up for the New York Yankees of the first American Football League, the vehicle founded to showcase Red Grange. Badgro later played for the New York Giants— who are still the Giants of today—and the Brooklyn Dodgers football club in 1936. Quite the excellent football player, Badgro was elected to the Pro Football Hall of Fame in Canton, Ohio. He was a fair pass catcher, a tough blocker, was selected All-Pro three times, and was a member of one National Football League championship team.

After his playing days, Badgro coached football at Columbia of the Ivy League and at the University of Washington. Showing up on the roster of the St. Louis Browns seemed an indicator he took a wrong turn somewhere.

It goes without analysis that Badgro did not win a companion World Series with the Browns. He spent parts of two seasons in the majors—quite an attractive offseason job. Badgro played for the Browns in 1929 and 1930 with a lifetime .257 average. In 1930, he signed with the football Giants for $150 per game.

Badgro was conscious of making any money during the Depression. Why shouldn't he take advantage of his athletic prowess?

"A dollar was a dollar in those days," Badgro is quoted in his Pro Football Hall of Fame biography, "and ballplayers weren't worried about money. They were worrying about the game. We were grateful to have a job."[7]

He did not help the Browns nearly as much as Lefty Stewart, but tucked far down the list of semi-contributors to the pitching staff in 1930 was General Crowder. Alvin Floyd "General" Crowder, then thirty-one, was a right-handed thrower who won 167 games in an 11-year career.

Crowder won 21 games for St. Louis in 1928, with a league-leading .808 winning percentage, and 17 more for the Browns the next year. Ball was too hasty in ditching Crowder in 1930 with his 3–7 record, since he promptly finished up the season going 15–9 for the Senators. Indeed, if anyone believed Crowder was over the hill, they were fooled over and over again.

In 1932, Crowder won a major-league-leading 26 games for the Senators, and in 1933 led the majors again, this time with 24 wins, as well as with 52 appearances. Crowder kept hanging in there, seeming on the verge of being washed up, but regularly bouncing back.

The funniest thing of all about Crowder was his nickname. During World War I, Major General Enoch Crowder was Judge Advocate General of the United States Army. It was on his watch that the United States Selective Service Act of 1917 was implemented, drafting civilians into the Army.

It was Enoch Crowder who had the genuine rank of general. "General" Crowder, better known to his family as Alvin, created his own draft by blowing fastballs past batters. Keeping Alvin around a few months longer might well have given the St. Louis Browns a lift in 1930.

Still, it could be argued not very much of what the Browns did on the field during that season mattered much at all. The backdrop of the city's and country's problems overshadowed the team's woes.

And no one was really watching, anyway. The Browns operated in veritable secrecy. The total home attendance for the 1930 season was 152,088, an almost unimaginably low number and the lowest attendance mark in the American League. At times there was so much open space between fans that one could hear the wind whistling through Sportsman's Park.

11

THE CHICAGO WHITE SOX

ONE STATEMENT COULD probably sum up the life of the Chicago White Sox in 1930: they were worse than the St. Louis Browns.

Not by much, but the White Sox finished with a 62–92 record, compared to St. Louis's 64–90 mark. The White Sox finished 40 games out of first place, seventh in the eight-team American League. Yes, someone else was worse, too.

Chicago was guilty of the ultimate self-inflicted wound: conspiring to fix the result of the 1919 World Series against the Cincinnati Reds. More than a decade later, the White Sox were still being punished for this misdeed, still haunted by the most egregious team act in baseball history.

For forty years, the franchise would cope with the consequences of the rash, ill-conceived, insult foisted on the American sporting public. The baseball gods kept requiring tribute, year after year, in one fashion or another, from later generations of White Sox players—those who were teammates with the miscreants, those who never met them, and those who were not born until much later.

The sins of the fathers kept revisiting the sons, the nephews, and the most distant of relations. The White Sox of the late teens made for a great ballclub. But the worst and the greedy of the members of those teams—and, perhaps, the most naïve as well—stained the franchise name, and it took quite a bit of scrubbing over a long time, and the application of gallons of bleach, to cleanse that stain.

As each spring rolled around and each new season approached, a new-look White Sox team prepared to compete. By 1930, some eleven years had passed since the White Sox-turned-Black Sox committed their crimes. Assuredly, manager Donie Bush and his players began preparing for the season, believing what happened more than a decade earlier had nothing to do with them.

But they were wrong. They were wrong because Commissioner Kenesaw Mountain Landis had been granted supreme powers over the American League and National League by the owners when they hired him as the game's first commissioner. As such, he watched the sham of a legal proceeding in a Chicago courtroom with a critical eye. Once the eight players accused of the fix went on trial and were exonerated in what amounted to mockery, Landis stepped in.

Wielding the complete authority the owners invested in him, Landis swept aside every player who was perfumed by the scandal, banning eight talented men—some of whom were potential Hall of Famers—from the game for life. The court of law was one thing, but the dominion of Major League Baseball belonged to Landis. He was judge, jury, and executioner, expanding his old civilian job of just judge. And he also had the power to make sure they never threw another pitch that counted or swung a bat that connected with a ball.

It was the sidelining of the players, many of whom made up the heart of a likely championship team, that ruined the White Sox long-term. No franchise could immediately restock its roster with so many high-caliber contributors.

Whether stated so or not, this was also a slap at Chicago owner Charles Comiskey. While not directly complicit in the scam, Comiskey, who worked his way up from player to manager to owner, and had the ballpark named for him on the South Side of Chicago, could have been more aggressive in heading off the Black Sox maneuvers. His socks may have been clean, but it was arguable that his conscience wasn't 100 percent pure.

The team the White Sox fielded in 1930 would have been manhandled by the 1919 bunch—outhit, outpitched, outfielded. Chicago was viewed as a shady political town, a metropolis where gangsters could do their worst, advancing money-making schemes of the most brazen sort. There were often rumors about individuals not playing baseball on the up-and-up, but never before and never again has there been such sophisticated team-wide deceit. To some, the Houston Astros' sign-stealing of 2017 and 2018 is considered an extremely egregious violation of baseball protocols, but the players did not accept bribes to lose games.

The bad apples on the 1919 White Sox entered into a shaky, shady deal with prominent gamblers. It was believed the World Series would accrue such glory that no team would consider tarnishing its own reputation—or the prize—by engaging in such a despicable arrangement.

However, crime always bottoms out and the rogues who sought to win a bundle by betting on a sure thing investigated the character and behaviors of key White Sox players, and found them willing to cheat and defraud the public. The old theme was, "You don't have to lose, you just have to make it look good."

The band of White Sox in on the operation kept expanding, growing from an original handful to eight whose honesty was soiled. The planners needed the best hitters and best pitchers on their side to control outcomes. They pledged thousands of dollars to make it happen at a time when hundreds of dollars represented a good income.

Outside of the green, there really was no good reason for many of the players to participate. They had a lot at stake, from capturing a legitimate world title to burnishing their own career marks.

Right-handed pitcher Eddie Cicotte was one of those most harmed by involvement almost inexplicable, although he did collect his promised $10,000 ahead of time. Cicotte, a.k.a. "Knuckles," because he was, perhaps, the inventor of the knuckleball pitch, was a tremendous winner with a great earned-run average. If he had continued his pitching trajectory he may well have become a Hall of Famer. Instead, his name lives in baseball infamy.

Before being run out of the game by Landis, Cicotte had a record of 208–149 with a 2.38 earned-run average. He tossed a no-hitter in 1917, a season the White Sox did win the World Series. He also led the league in wins that season (going 28–12), and led all of baseball with 29 wins in 1919. Yet Cicotte is remembered for being a main protagonist in the fix. Cicotte's role was to signal the fix was on with the first pitch in Game One of the World Series. The other part of his bargain was to ease up and let the Cincinnati Reds obtain the occasional hit.

Once banned from the sport, Cicotte became a semi-recluse in Livonia, Michigan, where he worked as a state game warden, ran a gas station, and was a strawberry farmer. Few sportswriters sought him out to hear his explanation as to why he sold his soul for a few bucks.

The only time Cicotte pretended he did not participate in the scandal was during the confusing trial period in Chicago. He did blame himself, even as matters unfolded, for doing wrong.

He was supposed to lose the fourth game, but decided to try and win it, damn the consequences. He confided his thoughts in co-conspirator Happy Felsch. "I didn't care whether I was going to get shot out there the next minute," he said, thinking of gambler retribution, "I was going to win the ball game and the Series."[1]

They did not win the Series, and neither did Cicotte refund his ill-gotten payment. The train was moving and by then Cicotte's and others' consciences had been left behind at the station.

"I admit I did wrong, but I've paid for it the past forty-five years," Cicotte told one visiting sportswriter.[2]

The eight White Sox players from the 1919 team were considered innocent in a Chicago courtroom that, in terms of true prosecution and impartial judgment, was more circus than law school textbook case. The case would probably never have been brought if muckraking sportswriter Hugh Fullerton hadn't dug out the story and embarrassed the powers-that-be into charging the players.

Cicotte was important to the fix, but there were quite a few faithless White Sox. Some were underhanded planners, while some were swept up in the arrangement. The other seven of the so-called "Eight Men Out," as the crew came to be called, were outfielder "Shoeless Joe" Jackson, first baseman Chick Gandil (one of the most involved intermediaries with gamblers), shortstop Swede Risberg (another all-in guy), outfielder Happy Felsch, backup third baseman Fred McMullin, third baseman Buck Weaver, and pitcher Lefty Williams.

Weaver spent the rest of his life protesting his innocence. He said he tried to report the scam, but no one listened. The biggest cause célèbre was Jackson.

A century later, Jackson seems to be viewed as a tragic figure, an innocent led astray, an illiterate led to disaster by predatory teammates because he was too much a hitter to leave out because of his potent bat. Jackson, on a dead-straight path to the Hall of Fame, was a brilliant hitter, one of the smoothest and finest batters of all time. A left-handed hitting, right-handed throwing outfielder, Jackson was 6-foot-1 and 200 pounds.

Jackson's ability lay in the simplicity of his stroke. He managed 13 years as a player before being exiled from baseball at thirty-two, compiling a .356 lifetime average—one of the best ever. In 1911, his first full season in the bigs, he batted .408 as a member of the Cleveland Indians. In 1919, the Black Sox year, he batted .351. In 1920, as the trial played out, Jackson hit .382.

The sample size of his average was quite convincing. Jackson hit only 54 home runs, but his on-base percentage was a sterling .423. In much of the popular culture surrounding the scandal, books, and movies, Jackson comes off as a bit of a confused bumpkin, someone only vaguely aware of the seriousness of the events. Determining the accuracy of his role and emotions is a daunting task. Jackson picked up many partisans as he aged, and even in death. They urge Major League Baseball to reinstate him based on a belief he was not an evil participant, but more an innocent tool of the real bad guys.

The great Ted Williams took up Jackson's cause over a many-year period, ending with his own death in 2002, lobbying for Jackson to be accepted back into baseball's good graces. Essentially, beyond the symbolism of the action, Jackson would presumably become eligible to be placed on the Hall of Fame ballot.

When the eight players were cleared by a Chicago jury, they spent the night celebrating, convinced they had nothing more to worry about. Not so, as Landis controlled their baseball fates.

His swiftly issued statement read: "Regardless of the verdicts of juries, no player that throws a ball game, no player that undertakes or promises to throw a ball game, no player that sits in confidence with a bunch of crooked players and gamblers where the ways and means of throwing games are planned, and discussed, and does not promptly tell his club about it, will ever play professional baseball."[3]

There were pleas for reinstatement, especially on behalf of Weaver and Jackson, but none ever legitimately played for pay again. Jackson, it was said, roamed small country areas playing semi-pro ball and collecting cash.

Unfortunately for the White Sox, it seemed as if they had been relegated to being a semipro team themselves. In the 1920s, teams did not have multiple minor-league affiliations. So the White Sox were not in an easy position to restock the team. Chicago won the World Series in 1917 and should have won it in 1919, but the 1920s were a fallow period.

The guilty players competed in 1920 before Landis booted them. But by 1921, the White Sox were losers. They finished seventh in the eight-team league with a 62–92 record. Comiskey could not have guessed how common such poor showings were about to become.

The White Sox were as good as fifth in 1922 (77–77), but seventh in 1923 (69–85), 30 games out of first place. It was last place for the White Sox in 1924 (66–87). They seemed to have descended to Dante's circles of hell.

An accident happened in 1925—the Sox rose to fifth place and recorded a winning record of 79–75. Eddie Collins, the Hall of Fame third baseman and later general manager of the Boston Red Sox, managed the team to respectability. There were few famous, or recognizable, names in the everyday lineup, but there were a few .300 hitters, such as Bibb Falk. Hall of Fame catcher Ray Schalk called the pitches behind the plate.

The 1926 White Sox were almost a rehab club. Collins was still in charge, and the team finished in fifth place (81–72). After the bitterness of 1919 and 1920, the White Sox showed signs of wooing fans back. Either spectators had short memories, their lifelong grudges against the Chicago Cubs from the North Side were too ingrained, or there were hints of a thaw. The White Sox attracted 710,339 fans. That was third most in the league. Although they did not win often during the 1920s, the White Sox still compiled respectable attendance totals compared to the rest of the AL, regularly third or fourth.

By 1927, Schalk was the manager. Chicago may have placed fifth in the AL, but the won-lost mark was not terribly flashy at 70–83. Schalk did not last out the 1928 season, as the team went 32–42—the bulk of those losses blamed on him. Lena Blackburne took over in the dugout and went 40–40 over the rest of the season.

It was the same-old, same-old in 1929, except the team had returned to the grim days of yesterday, finishing in seventh place (59–93) while attendance dropped by about 250,000 fans from a couple of seasons prior.

This brought the hapless White Sox and their lost decade to the 1930 season, with really no more reason for optimism than they'd had since 1920. Lifetime White Sox fans could look at the 1930 lineup and ask, "Who *are* these guys?"

While there was much teeth gnashing and frustration throughout much of the 1920s, one stalwart player could be called on for rescues on the mound.

He may well have been the loneliest star of all.

The righty throwing, switch-hitting Ted Lyons was born in Lake Charles, Louisiana, in 1900, and threw his first pitches for the White Sox in 1923 at the age of twenty-two. He did not throw his last pitch for the club until 1946. In parts of 21 seasons, Lyons won 260 games. There were an awful lot of sketchy 1920s seasons when Lyons was all the White Sox had. He was their best and most—or, perhaps, only—reliable hurler, a future Hall of Famer.

He would win 20 or more games three times, and pitched a no-hitter to beat the Red Sox on the road in 1926.

Lyons led the American League in wins and innings pitched twice, once leading the majors in innings—plus led the majors in complete games twice. Since he pitched for so many bad teams, he also lost a lot of games—230 of them. But he was a gamer, and threw 4,161 innings for his career. It was a very tough role, being the perpetual ace on a team that offered little consistent support. Fans did appreciate Lyons, seeing as he was as popular as any player for as long as any player performing his yeoman service act for the White Sox.

As Lyons aged, he and the White Sox came to an interesting arrangement. He began starting games just once a week, and gained the nickname "Sunday Teddy." In 1942, following this schedule, Lyons finished 14–6 in just 180 1/3 innings, but he led the AL in ERA at 2.10. There may have been a message about rest in there somewhere.

Famed manager Joseph McCarthy, keenly watching how Lyons kept extending his career, took a close look at the pitcher's achievements and observed that if Lyons had been pitching for the Yankees during the 1920s when they were winning pennants and World Series, he may have won more than 400 games. Only Cy Young, at 511, and Walter Johnson, at 417, ever won that many.

It did not bother Lyons to shift his pitching to once-a-week status because he made the most of his opportunities.

"A good pitcher is a pitcher who has the ability to go the distance in a lot of games and to hold opposing clubs to low scores and infrequent hits," Lyons said.[4]

Lyons was discovered playing ball on the campus of Baylor University in Waco, Texas, and never played in the minors before joining the White Sox straight from college ball.

The knuckleball was also used to good effect as one of Lyons's large assortment of weapons. Many latter-day knuckle pros used the pitch 90 percent of the time, and never even thought of throwing genuine fastballs.

Lyons used it more later in his career after a sore arm slowed him down, but he had it on call for a while. His education with the knuckler began by reading a story in *The Sporting News* about the knuckler's strange movement properties.

"I started working on that sort of freak delivery that very day," Lyons said of his absorbing the magazine article.[5]

Whether Lyons gained respect from fellow players because he endured so much with the White Sox, that he was just a good pitcher, or a combination of the two, he did reach such status. Tris Speaker, Hall of Fame centerfielder for the Boston Red Sox and Cleveland Indians, held Lyons in high esteem.

"If I had a choice of any pitcher for a clutch game, the guy I would pick would be Ted Lyons," Speaker said.[6]

The Ted Lyons of 1930 was still by far the best pitcher on the White Sox. The team really did not even have a starting rotation. The pitching was so thin, it was Lyons at the front of the line and then a guess who might be ready to throw in the rest of a series to give the club a shot to win.

This might have been different if Red Faber was not nearing the end at forty-one and a shadow of himself at his best. Faber was still present on the roster for the 1930 season, but finished 8–13. This was the same guy who won 20-plus games four times in his career (1915: 24; 1920: 23; 1921: 25; 1922: 21) in a 20-season career.

Born in 1888, Faber spent his entire big-league career with the White Sox. Intriguingly, he won games with a spitter, and when the Deadball Era concluded in 1920 and Major League Baseball banned trick pitches, he was grandfathered in for the rest of his career, still permitted to employ the spitter.

Faber did not develop his spitball until 1910, when he was in the minors, but his bosses affiliated with the Pittsburgh Pirates forbade him from using it at first.

"When I was with the Pirates," he said, "they wouldn't let me throw no spitters. I don't know why, but they wouldn't let me do it."[7] Perhaps they were more hygienic than other organizations.

Faber's grandest stretch of pitching took place for Chicago during the 1917 World Series when the White Sox defeated the Giants. Faber started four games, winning three, and the White Sox captured their only world championship between World War I and 2005.

Manager Kid Gleason appealed to Faber to pitch on short rest, and the request was a no-brainer.

"Heck, I never heard of anybody refusing to pitch unless they knew something was wrong with 'em and they couldn't help the ball club," Faber said. "I'd rather be pitching than sittin' on the bench." There was always more of a strain for me on the bench than pitching, especially in a tight spot."[8]

Faber faced some challenges after the glory of the Series victory, going 4–1 in 1918, as he had enlisted in the Navy for World War I. Later, he was one of the millions worldwide who contracted the Spanish flu in 1919 and lost 15 or more pounds, though he still managed an 11–9 record. Weak from his battle with the disease, Faber did not throw as crisply. He also had some sore arm problems.

Gleason wanted to rest Faber more, but ended up rushing him into service a little hastily because he had his own shortage of pitching talent as the White Sox tried to clinch the pennant. The White Sox captured the flag near the end of September, and even put Faber on the postseason roster, though Faber said he could only last four innings at a time.

When the World Series fix of 1919 was being contemplated, Faber was out of commission. Citing his temperament, desire to win, respect for the game, and take-charge personality, some said if Faber was active and taking on his usual role when the scam was being plotted, the scandal never would have happened—putting a kibosh on the discussions before they had a chance to evolve. Perhaps.

Faber refused to retire and still took a frequent turn on the mound in 1930, although Lyons had surpassed him. Faber did not quit until after the 1933 season, though he never had another winning season after 1928's 13–9.

Lyons was the stalwart of the 1930 staff. Faber was the fading stalwart of a bygone era. It may have made sense for Faber to hurl once a week, too, maybe on Saturdays.

Outside of the duo, and Faber being what he was, the White Sox had no pitching to count on—neither starters nor relievers—Gleason could plan around. These were the rest of the strangers Gleason, Lyons, and Faber were surrounded by: Pat Caraway (10–10), Tommy Thomas (5–13), Garland Braxton (4–10), Dutch Henry (2–17), Hal McKain (6–4), Bob Weiland (0–4), Jim Moore (2–1), Ted Blankenship (2–1), and Biggs Wehde (0–0).

There was also a guy on the staff named Ed Walsh. As it so happened, it was not Big Ed Walsh, one of the greatest pitchers who did wonders for the Sox in the past, but Little Ed Walsh, as in the original's son. The younger Ed Walsh went 1–4 as a twenty-five-year-old.

The Ed Walsh who broke in with Chicago in 1904 was a Hall of Famer. He won 195 games, including an astronomical 40 in 1908, and owns the modern record for the best career earned-run average at 1.82.

Little Ed Walsh, on the other hand, compiled an 11–24 record with the White Sox over four seasons. People called him Ed Jr., because it was a handy thing to do, but technically the younger Ed was not a junior because he had a different middle name. He really wasn't Little Ed, either, as he was about the same size as his father, the same height at 6-foot-1, though a bit lighter at 180 pounds instead of 193. In 1930, the younger Ed was just about as good or bad as anyone else the White Sox had beyond the couple of fellas at the front of the rotation.

Alas for the White Sox of 1930, the depth on the rest of the field pretty much resembled the quality and reliability of the pitching. As mediocre as Chicago's results were, the team still managed to hit .276, proving even the worst group could still sting the ball.

Not that there were players of enduring fame populating the lineup. Even the guys who played well in 1930 were, for the most part, players with no lasting fan base. A few are remembered by baseball historians for shooting-star contributions during their careers.

First baseman Johnny Watwood, born in Alabama in 1905, managed a .302 average in 1930. Watwood enrolled in what became Auburn University, with the aim of developing his farming skills. He was pinpointed as a good ballplayer, though, and it turned out a job he was given as a cotton inspector in Jackson, Mississippi, mostly entailed playing semipro baseball for his company.

"I discovered my principal duties were to make base hits and play the outfield for Jackson's leading 'amateur' baseball team,"

Watwood said.[9] His semipro status led to professional minor league status, which led to a contract with the White Sox in 1929.

Watwood was a steady major-league hitter, though he committed too many errors in the field. "There is one of the most natural hitters I ever saw," said New York Giants manager John J. McGraw.[10]

Fielding may well have held back Watwood, but a mishap immediately after the 1930 season did not help him at all, either. Starting in 1903, the White Sox and Cubs played an exhibition City Series. That year, the teams met as soon as the regular season ended. Watwood took a pitch to the head from Cubs hurler Pat Malone and suffered a fractured skull. He would spend three weeks in the hospital, recovering.

A backup first baseman that season was John "Bud" Clancy, who hit just .244 in 68 games. His claim to fame in 1930 was something that happened in the field—or, rather, did not happen in the field. On April 27, against the St. Louis Browns, Clancy played the entire game at first base without having an assist or putout. Only a few players at that position have gone through an entire game without a fielding chance.

The primary catcher in 1930 was Bennie Tate, who appeared in 72 games and batted .317, the team's second-best average. Tate was mostly a backup throughout his 10-year career, but contributed to the Washington Senators' back-to-back pennants of 1924 and 1925.

The White Sox could not hide Smead Jolley in the field. The outfielder couldn't catch, and made so many errors he survived only four years in the majors despite swinging a very solid bat. Jolley played in 152 games for the 1930 White Sox and batted .313, though he averaged an error in one of every nine games played.

Before becoming a professional, Jolley and his brothers made up much of a local town team in Arkansas, managed by their farming father.

"We were pretty good if I do say so myself," Jolley said. "We had to be. My daddy didn't like to lose. You lost and you didn't get fed."[11] It was not clear what daddy thought about Smead's constant violation of the fundamentals in the field.

White Sox manager Donie Bush praised Jolley's prowess at the plate and did his best not to cringe over his erratic nature in the field, while suggesting he made for a good teammate and a player managers would like to have around.

"He's a wonderful hitter," Bush said. "But no fielder. He has a fine baseball disposition. He never worries, frets, alibis, or cuts up. If all players were like him, managers would have fewer gray hairs."[12] Perhaps, since one might wonder about the color of Bush's hair after watching Jolley field for a week or so.

Jolley's distinction was playing brilliantly in the Pacific Coast League, where he was enshrined in that top minor league's Hall of Fame. He hit .397 in 1927 and .404 in 1928 for the San Francisco Seals. Jolley played 16 seasons in the minors.

Given his poor fielding percentage, Jolley may well have been one of the worst fielders in big-league history, perhaps born to be a designated hitter. After a while, Jolley made jokes about his own fielding, a recognition of how hopeless he was. Once, after missing a fly ball, he said, "There's a bad sky today. Not an angel in the clouds."[13]

While Jolley hit .313 in 1930, he was not satisfied with the mark since he had put together such outsized statistics in San Francisco. "I feel like I've been in a slump all year," Jolley said. "When I was a cleanup hitter with the San Francisco Seals, my normal gait was .380 or better." Jolley made it seem as if a hitter had to cope with an endless army of throwers coming after him. "The pitchers in this circuit are not so much better than they are on the Coast, but there are more of them. If you drive one from the box, another one just as good will take his place."[14]

The undisputed hitting champion of the 1930 White Sox was outfielder Carl Reynolds, who batted .359 with 202 hits, 22 home runs, and 104 RBIs, to go along with 16 stolen bases. No complaints there. Like many batters in 1930, it was his finest year at the plate. Reynolds batted .302 lifetime in 13 big-league seasons split between the White Sox, Red Sox, and Chicago Cubs, while topping .300 six times.

Reynolds, the victim in a nefarious play where Hall of Fame catcher Bill Dickey punched him in the face, breaking his jaw in an apparent misunderstanding, was deemed to have great potential in 1930. Umpire George Moriarty described him as an aggressive hitter who went to the plate with that "I'm-here-to-knock-it-down-your-throat look at the pitchers."[15]

For many years, post-Black Sox Scandal, the White Sox had very few players who made a significant impact. Although it was little noticed, and of little importance in the big picture of the season, in 1930, Chicago introduced a fresh face to the roster who would become one of their greatest players.

That season, a twenty-three-year-old rookie named Luke Appling began his 20-season Hall of Fame career with the team. Appling did tease the future with a .308 average in six games before compiling a lifetime .310 average in 2,422 games.

Above all, with his 22 wins and his rock-solid dependability, it all came down to Ted Lyons, just as it did for two decades.

"It's true that I spent a long time with a team that was in the second division most of the time," Lyons reflected after retirement. "But I didn't find it frustrating. I would have liked to have won more, but I'll say this: My ball club always hustled for me. I never could find fault with a ball club that put out.

"Sure, you'd have liked to have finished higher. It would have been more pleasant once in a while. And if we could have won a pennant, just one, to see what it was like, it would have been nice."[16]

12

THE BOSTON RED SOX

TO GET A feel for the performance of the Boston Red Sox pitching staff of 1930, it's clear to see how the team finished 52–102, behind the lowly St. Louis Browns and Chicago White Sox.

Milt Gaston, 13–20. Danny MacFayden, 11–14. Hod Lisenbee, 10–17. Jack Russell, 9–20. Ed Durham, 4–15. George Smith, 1–2. Ed Morris, 4–9. Frank Bushey, 0–1. Red Ruffing, 0–3. Ben Shields, 0–0. Bill Bayne, 0–0. Frank Mulroney, 0–1. Bob Kline, 0–0.

Not a single pitcher compiled a winning record, and as a group this gang's cumulative earned-run average was 4.68. Right-handed or left-handed, young or old, these Sox could not get anyone out. There were veterans in their thirties and novices in their early twenties, but it mattered not who manager Heinie Wagner sent to the mound, as the club played in a world of its own, finishing 50 games behind the Philadelphia Athletics in the standings.

By 1930, a decade had passed since the Red Sox and owner Harry Frazee had been flimflammed out of Babe Ruth by the New York Yankees, essentially changing the balance of power in the AL forever. But in the intervening decade the Yankees brass revisited Boston's roster and duped the Red Sox into trading away more prospects and more talent.

Boston owner Harry Frazee wanted money, and the only commodity he had that the deep pockets Yankees coveted were ballplayers. In later years, depending upon who was in charge, a commissioner of baseball may have stepped in and prevented Frazee from even speaking to Barrow for his own good.

By the time Yankee management got through with Boston management, you had the emperor running through the streets of the Hub with no clothes. The Yankees ran one hustle after another on Boston. The heist of Ruth was the biggest robbery of them all, but other Hall of Famers changed teams, too, shifting from Boston's roster to New York's.

It was difficult to remain a Red Sox fan when player after player paraded from Boston to New York, jumping on a fast train before the outcry could echo.

Ruth, who helped Boston win the World Series in 1916 and 1918 from the mound, was about to become a full-time legendary swinger who revolutionized the sport with his power, and become baseball's greatest gate attraction of all time. Many consider Ruth-to-New-York for cash to be the worst exchange ever made.

Iron man shortstop Everett Scott, who played in 1,307 consecutive games, broke into the majors with the Red Sox in 1914 at age twenty-one. By 1922, he was a member of the Yankees. Right-handed pitcher Waite Hoyt spent two seasons with Boston in the early 1920s, then four times won at least 19 games for the Yankees later in the decade. Two years in a row, pitcher Red Ruffing led the American League in losses for the Red Sox, but before the end of his career had won 273 games and was selected for the Hall of Fame—thanks to the Yankees.

Submarine thrower Carl Mays was a big winner with the Red Sox, then won 27 games for the 1921 Yankees. Hurler Herb Pennock won his share for Boston, and then got better with New York, winning even more frequently. Sad Sam Jones won as many as 23 games for the Red Sox in one season and, before he could blink, was wearing pinstripes.

Still another pitcher who rode the trails to the big town from Beantown was Ernie Shore. Babe Ruth was once thrown out of a game after protesting a first-inning pitch, and was relieved by Shore. Shore pitched the equivalent of a perfect game after that, setting down everyone else.

While many had the same thought, Shore once said of the Boston-New York pipeline, "They talk about the Yankee Dynasty, but I still think of it as a Red Sox Dynasty in Yankee uniforms."[1]

Never mind Lisenbee, Durham, and Russell, what type of results would Ruffing, Pennock, Jones, and Mays have produced in Fenway Park? Probably the same kind of results they produced in Yankee Stadium, leading their team to pennants and World Series championships.

It is easy enough with the hindsight of a century for a devoted Red Sox fan to dismiss Frazee as stupid. Frustration may lead to such a conclusion, but Frazee was more indifferent to the results of his team than committed to bringing a winner to Broadway. He concentrated more on his shaky finances and his favorite mode of entertainment for the masses was producing plays, not watching baseball.

Frazee owned the team from December 1916 to 1923, and the Red Sox did win a World Series crown in 1918 under his watch. By the time he sold the club in mid-1923, he had wrecked its long-term prospects. Frazee did send hit show after hit show to Broadway, making a fortune on some of them. The ingrained story goes that he took the profits from selling Babe Ruth and poured them into the production of the extremely popular show *No, No, Nanette*. While it is accurate that show became a mega-hit, the connection between Ruth's sale and the bill for that production was nil. Ruth was long gone, and *No, No, Nanette* was not even in the works until after Frazee sold the Red Sox.

A bit more confusing, and carrying a whiff of conflict of interest, was that Frazee had a deal going with Ruppert whereas the Yankees' owner held the mortgage on Fenway Park. Maybe that's where Boston fans should have focused their outrage. For sure, there seemed to be an unhealthy, incestuous relationship between Frazee and Ruppert.

It was only much later that anguished Red Sox fans who suffered through tense, close loss after agonizing big-game loss, began to speak of "The Curse of the Bambino," assigning Frazee's sale of Ruth to the Yankees so long before as a critical failure in franchise history. Spookily or not, they connected the Ruth mistake to clutch losses and the eighty-six-year-long drought between World Series titles, from 1918 to 2004.

The Red Sox of the 1920s were not about to win a Series, an AL pennant, or even make a serious run at a championship. The talent drain, from Ruth to Scott to the pitchers, was too much to overcome. From 1920 to 1930, the Red Sox were extreme also-rans.

This is how it went for the Boston Red Sox between 1921 and 1929 in the immediate aftermath of the sale of Ruth. In 1921, Boston finished 75–79 and attendance was last, with 279,273 fans buying tickets.

The next year the Red Sox record went 61–93, and attendance was 259,184, also last. In 1921, Ruth hit a record 59 home runs, the Yankees reached the World Series, and saw 1,230,000 fans click the turnstiles. A quick assessment of how good business was led Yankee management to invest in a massive new concrete and steel ballpark, which opened in 1923. That Yankee Stadium's nickname was "The House That Ruth Built" because Ruth's popularity advanced the idea of constructing it.

While the Yankees reached the World Series again and again, drawing more than a million fans, Boston's attendance continued to decline. Some 229,688 fans showed up to watch the 1922 61–91 team flounder. It was more of the same for the Yankees each season. They wooed in more than a million fans, won more than 90 games, and regularly clobbered the competition. Ruth created so much fanfare with his muscular swings that not only did home fans in the Bronx come out to see what he would do next, but he became a road gate attraction, spectators clamoring for tickets to see the Bambino bam down the ballpark walls.

Although Red Sox attendance improved by about 200,000 in 1924, the club was still last in the league and next-to-last in the standings with a 67–87 record.

It was not perceived the Red Sox could get any worse on the field, but in 1925 they did just that. While seeming to conspire to drive fans away completely, Boston's record was a dismal 47–105, while just 267,782 spectators paid their way into the park.

No pitcher really came close to posting a winning record, Jack Quinn's 7–8 being the only final record threatening .500. Twice a World Series champ, Quinn had one of the longest pitching careers of all with 23 seasons in the majors. Quinn won 247 games, and threw his final big-league pitches a week after his fiftieth birthday.

Quinn, who was born in Hungary, was a fourteen year old watching a semipro game when he retrieved a foul ball and accurately threw it back to the field. A manager signed him on the spot. Quinn, who pitched for eight teams, including the Federal League's Baltimore Terrapins, was better for Boston, in three other seasons winning at least 12 games.

The Red Sox were about equally as horrendous in 1926, going 46–107 with a team batting average of .255. Veteran Baby Doll Jacobson, who split his season between the Browns and Boston, hit .305 for the Red Sox in 98 games. Jacobson was the biggest offensive weapon for the club that season.

It is not clear if Jacobson's teammates called him "Baby Doll" to his face, but he did have a sweet swing, hitting over .300 in seven straight years (1919–25). He concluded with a lifetime .311 average in 11 seasons while also being a sophisticated, record-holding fielder.

A powerfully built 6-foot-3 and 215 pounds, he actually received his odd nickname by accident. Long ahead of the trend, when major leaguers have specifically designated walk-up music as they approach the plate, Jacobson was serenaded by a band in that situation. It was opening day of the Southern Association season for the Mobile Sea Gulls in Alabama, and the song played was "Oh, You Beautiful Doll." Jacobson never shed the "Super Glue" nickname of the immediate moment.

Born William Chester Jacobson, the player was a bit surprised to receive a new nickname out of nowhere.

"Everybody called me Bill until that day in Mobile," Jacobson said. "Well, I led off with a homer on the first pitch and a lady sitting behind the plate jumped up and shouted, 'You must be that beautiful doll they were talking about!' The name stuck with me, and that was it."[2]

When Jacobson died in 1977, *The Sporting News* suggested he should have received more support for possible inclusion into the

National Baseball Hall of Fame than several other players who had been inducted.

The long Boston Red Sox nightmare continued. In 1927, it was another season, another disaster going into the record books, with Boston finishing 51–103. So few players on that club are significantly remembered, longtime fans could probably not even collect more than a dime apiece for their baseball cards.

In the last season of his 13-year career—mostly spent with the St. Louis Browns—thirty-five-year-old outfielder Jack Tobin batted .310 for Boston, a performance that almost completely dovetailed with his lifetime .309 average. For a few years, Tobin, who was a lightweight and slightly built 5-foot-8 and 142 pounds, might well have been one of the best hitters in the American League.

Between 1919 and 1923, Tobin never hit lower than .317 and hit as high as .352 in 1921 with a league-leading 18 triples. Tobin's final two years were with Boston, but he was gone by 1930 when his bat would have been quite welcome.

The headaches continued in Boston and at Fenway Park in 1928, as the Red Sox kept ringing up the losses in comparative anonymity. The team went 57–96, though attendance did increase into the 300,000s. There was actually no hint the Red Sox problems would end any time soon in 1929, either, when the team record read 58–96.

There it was, a complete, thorough record of futility for the 1920s after Babe Ruth left town, year-by-year terrible marks without a moment's contention for a pennant and only short bursts of weekly or monthly play keeping Boston out of the cellar. Pitching doesn't grow on trees, but even if the Sox owned a nursery they would not have had a cluster of throwers strong enough to put up winning records.

So there was no particular reason for fans to get excited during spring training leading to the 1930 season. The decade may have changed, but 1930 lined up suspiciously like 1929 and the rest of the 1920s.

One pitcher who rose to semi-prominence with the Red Sox in the late 1920s was Ed Morris. He went 19–15 with a 3.53 earned-run average in 1928, which was such a good showing that the front office began thinking of trading him. A year later he finished 14–14, which by Boston standards made him an All-Star.

Morris followed with seasons of 4–9 in 1930 and 5–7 in 1931; he was bottoming out before Boston could obtain value. Then, the worst followed. The 6-foot-2, 185-pound righty was murdered on March 3, 1932 while attending a fish fry. Stabbed to death, he was only thirty-two years old. Morris was spending the offseason in Florida and was about to depart for spring training. The fish fry was conducted in a bar and a man in attendance whipped out a knife and stabbed the guest of honor in the chest. Despite medical treatment administered at a local hospital, Morris died from the wound.

So even when there was a possibility of a redemptive player, bad luck intervened.

Danny MacFayden was born in Truro, Massachusetts, on Cape Cod and moved to the Boston suburb of Somerville as a child. Some called him "The Somerville Scot." In an extraordinary performance, MacFayden went the distance in a 17-inning high school game and struck out almost everyone on the other team. Statisticians needed a calculator to figure out how many strikeouts he accumulated, the conclusion being either 31 or 32. In a single game! Remarkably, MacFayden actually lost, 2–1.

Being a local, the Red Sox did not want such a young man of potential to get away. They signed MacFayden and brought him right to the majors, talking him out of attending Dartmouth College of the Ivy League. MacFayden was an early major-league player to wear glasses on the mound, as well as the first in the American League.

In MacFayden's debut in relief, two of the first three hitters he faced—Heinie Manush and Harry Heilmann—were future Hall of Famers. In MacFayden's first start he went head-to-head with Walter Johnson and the Washington Senators.

Johnson, the second-winningest pitcher of all time, paused to give the youngster a pep talk, saying, "Take your time, son, and get the ball over. Good luck."[3] MacFayden always remembered Johnson taking the time to give him a little boost.

MacFayden was on his way to a 17-year career in the majors, finishing with a 132–159 record. During that 1930 season, he went 11–14 with a 4.21 ERA. In 1931, also with Boston, though, he went 16–12—one of his best seasons.

Playing for the Red Sox bad teams took a toll on righty Milt Gaston's record, although he did spend the bulk of his career with other teams. Gaston's career mark was 97–164, with a best year of 15–14 in 1925. But he led the American League in losses twice, once with St. Louis and once with the Red Sox. There was no mercy if you were a starter for those hapless teams that could not score runs and almost always ended seasons near the bottom of the standings.

It was a good news, bad news season for Gaston with the Red Sox in 1930. His 13–20 mark did lead the AL in defeats, but he was a mainstay worker, hurling 273 innings with a not-bad 3.92 ERA.

"I pitched my best ball in the sandlots," Gaston said of getting a late start in professional baseball. "They didn't know it, but I was twenty-eight when I went into the majors. They thought I was twenty-three. I had a brother, Alex, who was with the Giants. He put me wise to all the tricks of the trade. They would have got rid of me long before if they knew how old I was."[4]

Gaston was born in New Jersey and, when he broke into the majors in 1924 with the New York Yankees, was the roommate of Lou Gehrig. Gaston, traded around the American League to half the teams, lived to be one hundred years old.

Many years into retirement, Gaston was blunt about the Red Sox leadership and abilities of the 1920s to 1930s time period when they struggled. Bill Carrigan kept losing 100 games a season as manager and didn't really want the job. Gaston said Heinie Wagner didn't have anything to work with, either, as the Sox went down the tubes regularly.

"Heinie wasn't a particularly good manager," Gaston said, "but he was a nice fellow. Everybody liked him. He didn't have the goods to manage, but he didn't have anything to manage."[5]

The talent shortage on the 1930 Red Sox was acute. Just about the only serious hitter was outfielder Earl Webb. Webb was born in White Country, Tennessee in 1897, and made his major-league debut with the New York Giants in 1925 at age twenty-seven. As it was, Webb only showed up in four games that year, with the restraints still on from John J. McGraw.

It was not until 1927, now with the Chicago Cubs, did Webb receive a true chance to make an impact. He appeared in 102 games and batted .301 with 14 home runs. By 1930, Webb was property of the Red Sox. He was also already thirty-two, which meant he had to hurry up and do something if he wanted a steady job.

The Red Sox let Webb alone to just play his game, and he batted .323 with 16 home runs and 66 RBIs in 127 games. Although Webb hit .306 lifetime in a seven-year big-league career, it did not even seem as though the lowly Red Sox worked that hard to keep him.

However, it was in 1931—one of his three seasons in Boston—when Webb produced one long-lasting statistic of note. In 151 games, among his 196 hits, Webb cracked 67 doubles. That performance set an American League and major-league record that stands to this day. Webb batted .323 with 103 runs batted that season, too.

"Earl Webb was the only hitter we had on the Boston ballclub," Gaston said of the early 1930s squads.[6]

Whether it was the nature of the Red Sox' awful pitching or inconsistent hitting in 1930, the baseball world pretty much passed them by.

It was not until 1933, when young millionaire Tom Yawkey bought the Red Sox and began investing in his team with the sole aim of bringing a championship to Boston that the Red Sox began reviving, contending for pennants with the likes of Ted Williams and Bobby Doerr, and later Mel Parnell and Carl Yastrzemski.

Just as the Chicago White Sox repeatedly found themselves on the outside as they recovered from the mistake of becoming embroiled in the Black Sox Scandal, the Red Sox spent years recovering from the giveaway of many of their best players, including committing the unforgiveable sin of parting with Babe Ruth.

As such, the Boston Red Sox worked to become the worst of the worst in the AL in the 1920s and in 1930.

13

LEFTY GROVE UNTOUCHABLE

HE WAS GRUFF and ready. Lefty Grove did not ease into his starts. He growled his way to the mound, viewing the batters lining up against him as the enemy. There was no fraternizing between Grove and members of other clubs. He was all business, with the sole goal of mowing them down.

Grove was grumpy on the days of his starts—even to his own teammates in the clubhouse before he began throwing. He could be irascible after he left the game, too, especially if one of his teammates made a costly error.

There is no doubt that Grove was all about winning. He possessed a mean streak and did not want anyone to get in the way of his mental game plan. He liked being in charge on the mound and wanted to remain in charge once a game began.

Robert Moses "Lefty" Grove was left-handed all of the way. Not only did he pitch southpaw, he batted left-handed, and off the field he behaved a bit on the left-handed side, as well, an individual who acted very individually. He cared more about winning than making friends—actually, he cared more about winning than anything else. He came up the hard way, barely reaching his ultimate pitching goal, but walked away from the game with greatness stamped on him and as an obvious Hall of Famer.

Although he is not readily mentioned that way, it could be that Grove can be considered one of the best pitchers of all time. Certainly, compared to his peers over a 17-year career, Grove shone. The only reason his lifetime statistics were not better than they were is the manner of how he was held back as a young man and was exiled to the minors longer than he should have been.

Grove was born on March 6, 1900, in Lonaconing, Maryland, coal country. Grove was one of the many top ballplayers of the era who emerged from the nation's farmlands and hardscrabble working class towns where the choices for a young man were stark. They either hustled their way out of the neighborhood by succeeding in sports, or they engaged in backbreaking work for decades, with sometimes that work eventually killing them at a young age.

In Grove's case, he was one of eight children (four boys and four girls), and his father and brothers wore the skin-coating dust of the coal mine while the pitcher toured the nation as a famous athlete who came to be regarded as a star, even if he did not adopt the trappings of celebrityhood.

At the top of his game in and around 1930, Grove was indisputably the best pitcher in baseball. So many of the other top hurlers in the sport faltered in 1930 that any pitcher who had a solid season was a rarity. Grove outdid them all. Not only did he perform at his usual high level, but he was as good as ever, standing out so clearly that his showings left opponents gasping with astonishment. That season, they all wondered what gave Grove the right to be so good when most quality pitching had evaporated. For the most part, the other seven teams in the American League had no chance against his best stuff. His level day in and day out was so high, it seemed almost impossible.

As one measurement of how good Grove was between his rookie year of 1925 and his retirement in 1941, was that his statistics were at least the equivalent of Babe Ruth's hitting numbers. He may have been pitching during the Great Depression, but Grove threw so well that his home teams of the Philadelphia Athletics and Boston Red Sox earned the right to charge a bonus fee on the days he was scheduled to start. Of course, no such thing happened, but anyone who purchased a ticket for a day Grove was on the mound could well have been charged a premium and thought the cost worth it.

Over the course of his major-league career, Grove was tops in the American League in victories four times (leading all of baseball three of those times), first in strikeouts seven times (and the league four times), and won the earned-run average title nine times. The latter represents an all-time record. In other words, Grove was just about the best of anyone, almost all of the time.

In 1930, when Grove was thirty years old, he compiled a 28–5 record with an ERA of 2.54. In addition, he led baseball in appearances (50) and strikeouts (209). He was not really a relief pitcher, but manager Connie Mack found work for him—as needed—as the A's battled the New York Yankees for the pennant. So as a side statistic, Grove picked up nine saves, another major-league–leading number.

Rather amazingly, Grove's 1930 season did not even stand out as especially special for his career. His 1929 and 1931 seasons were just about the same, meaning he was that great for Philadelphia three years in a row. In those three seasons, he went a combined 79–15. In 1931, Grove won 17 games in a row. He broke the previous record of 16 consecutive wins shared by Boston's Smoky

Joe Wood and the Senators' Walter Johnson. The season after Grove's stupendous 1930 season, his ERA was a lower 2.06 and his win total was a higher 31–4. As such, he was almost unanimously named the league MVP.

When he was active, Grove exhibited the confidence that, in his mind, he was the best pitcher in the game—and perhaps a dissection of his lifetime numbers indicates he was right. His circumstances were humble in the beginning, but he had little reason to be humble upon retiring from the game.

Sometimes, it was suggested Lefty Grove was confused with Lefty Gomez, another Hall of Fame pitcher, though for the New York Yankees, and a man who was much more congenial and entertaining. Also, unlike most pitchers in today's game, Grove did not sport a particularly impressive athletic build. He had an angular look, standing 6-foot-3 and perhaps weighing 190 pounds if that is to be believed—and certainly did not look it. If anything, he appeared much thinner.

"They look at me and my skinny arms and think maybe I'm some kind of magician," Grove said of how his fastball was viewed. "I don't know any more about it than they do. The other guy hasn't got it. I have. That's all there is to it."[1]

Grove grew up hard in Lonaconing, and the community was beginning to fade when he was at his peak in the majors during the Depression. The Depression made nothing easy on anybody, anywhere in the country. Grove had escaped to play a game while others stayed and tried to cope, while others fled, looking for a new home in a new place as the United States seemingly imploded on itself on those years between 1929 and 1933.

Some of Grove's ancestors used the name Groves when they emigrated from Wales to Virginia in 1726, and some of the earliest newspaper clippings about Grove did refer to him in that manner.

By 1920, Grove had gravitated to baseball over coal. He was fortunate that one of best minor-league clubs in the land was located in Maryland: the Baltimore Orioles of the International League. By 1919, Grove was playing for his town team, which was a hobby, but one that could showcase his skills. He made an impression right away, overpowering most batters. The Baltimore & Ohio Railroad planned to hire Grove in some capacity for the summer of 1920 so he could pitch for the company squad.

It was a solid idea, but before that could happen, word spread across the state and Grove came to the attention of Orioles owner Jack Dunn. Dunn was one of the most famous minor-league team owners of the period. Born in 1872, he wanted to be a ballplayer. A childhood accident, when he was run over by a train boxcar, causing permanent damage to his left arm did not stop him. He still managed to play parts of eight seasons of big-league ball for a group of National League teams around the turn of the century.

By 1909, Dunn owned the old Orioles, not to be confused with the current major-league franchise, dishing out $70,000 for the club. He became a savvy magnate who scouted and developed quality players and, sometimes, cautiously held them back from the marketplace to maximize his profits.

When the Federal League came around to challenge the American League and National League, Dunn supervised the Baltimore Terrapins. The upstart league only lasted three seasons, including one as a minor-league outfit.

Dunn fielded a respectable team, and one of his key players was Babe Ruth. Ruth grew up in Baltimore and was a natural fit for the Orioles. Dunn wanted to hang on to the promising Ruth longer, but he was losing money and after moving his minor-league squad to Richmond, Virginia, sold him for $10,000, which was an attractive price in 1914. Dunn's other players referred to Ruth in conjunction with the deal as "Dunn's $10,000 Babe."

The owner moved his team back to Baltimore in 1916, where it thrived. He plowed money into signing players and recruited several excellent prospects while fielding a perennial winner. At one point, the Orioles won seven straight International League titles. Grove arrived in 1920 and pitched for Baltimore through 1924.

Grove had no business being kept down on the farm so long. He was just too good. Dunn held his rights, however, and held out for his price. It was obvious Grove could pitch in the majors and big-league teams wanted him, peppering Dunn with offers. But Dunn frustratingly kept Grove on his own roster.

The southpaw went 12–2 in 1920, 25–10 in 1921, 18–8 in 1922, 27–10 in 1923, and 26–6 in 1924. Grove won four International League strikeout titles, too. Overall, he won 108 games for Baltimore. It was almost as if he was being held prisoner. In the end, Dunn coaxed a payment of $100,600 from Connie Mack and the A's. It could have ruined Grove's career, for sure, and it definitely did harm his lifetime totals. By then Grove was twenty-five and had little time to waste getting started.

While Grove was hard to hit, once in a great while he threw a clunker. In one game with Baltimore, he issued 14 walks. His fastball was a firecracker and his curve knew how to dance. But when he was on, he was really on.

One day, Dunn asked him, "Who taught you how to pitch?" Grove replied, "Nobody. Learned myself." Dunn thought that over and weighed the results against the occasional faltering and said, "Well, learn the rest yourself."[2]

Apparently, he did so, topping the decade in most wins (199), and ranked second in ERA (2.91) and strikeouts (1,313).

Dunn was a benevolent owner; as long as his men produced and kept winning, he didn't care what they did away from the ballpark, whether that was drinking or playing cards. Show up on time and do your job. As long as you did your job, you were OK in his book.

That made playing in the minors palatable. If you were going to be stuck in the minors, Dunn made it as enjoyable as it could be.

"See, we had an easy-going club," Grove said. "It was a good life. I've seen the ball club sitting up in the hotel playing cards all night. No night games then, see. And we'd have a Pierce Arrow limousine hired waiting for us at the hotel at a certain time and around one or two in the afternoon we'd go downstairs and pile into that son-of-a-gun car and get to the ballpark just in time to start the game."[3]

The more time passed, the better Grove pitched, and the more attention he garnered from the big-league teams. Several located so close by like the Washington Senators, Philadelphia Phillies, and Philadelphia A's, that scouts could take a mere afternoon train trip to watch him twirl. The teams threw out offers to Dunn to buy Grove, but he rebuffed them time and again. Even if he wished to make a good deal on Grove's services, it seemed obvious Dunn enjoyed playing this game somewhat. His favorite word to the suitors was, "No."

"He's pitching for me," Dunn declared.[4]

As an aside, even though he was barred from the majors, Grove was actually making good money. Dunn paid him $750 a month, plus bonuses for pitching in playoff games and exhibition games. Grove, who was married and had a baby girl at the time, needed the money.

In 1924, when Grove went 26–6 and really had outgrown the International League, the Orioles played a contest against the

Yankees and Ruth. Ruth, acting a bit imperially, reacted strongly when a Grove inside fastball brushed past his jersey. He insulted him by claiming he was just another minor leaguer who didn't know where he was throwing the ball.

Grove took none of that from the Babe.

"I'll know where I'm throwing the next one when you come up," Grove directed at Ruth. "It will be right at you, Ruth. I'm not afraid of you."[5]

Babe Ruth, Ty Cobb, Rogers Hornsby, or any of the others in the game in 1924, by then Grove wasn't afraid of any batter he might face.

Grove finally got his big-league opportunity with the Philadelphia Athletics in 1925, but he was not an instant sensation. Grove was a regular pitcher from the start, but his record was 10–12 with a 4.75 ERA. Apparently, despite Dunn's recommendation, he had not yet taught himself everything else he needed to know when he became a regular at Shibe Park. Although his 116 strikeouts led the league, a low total, Grove reverted in his wildness and also led the AL in walks with 131.

The pitcher did need a bit of an adjustment period, but none of what he showed with Baltimore was a fluke, either. Grove finished 13–13 his second season, but while the numbers were not so special, his earned-run average was. His 2.51 was the best in the league. Now if Grove could capitalize on run support from the improving A's, limit opponent run-scoring at the right time, he could run up some victories. And that is what followed. In 1927, he was a 20-game-winner (20–13), and on his way to becoming the Lefty Grove that is remembered.

By then, some of Grove's bad humor seeped through at inopportune moments when teammates committed costly errors that led to runs and threw him off-balance.

One game Max Bishop and Jimmy Dykes both made errors in the infield, Grove lost his concentration and gave up some deep swats off the fences by the Indians. The players seemed to think Grove let up on his tosses and gave him some grim looks. Sensing the tenseness of the situation, Mack told everyone to cool it. He needed Grove to be his usual self. He did not want to have to yank him from a game because he lost his temper.[6]

"Stop muttering," Mack ordered the regulars. "Do you want him out of there?"[7] They did not particularly want that. They knew they were better off most games with Grove on the mound rather than fuming in the locker room.

Grove said he was initially misjudged in Baltimore and his reputation for having a wider assortment of stuff wasn't accurate until he was with Philadelphia.

"I won all those games with fastballs," Grove said. "Didn't have a curve then. Didn't know what a curve was. They tell you I was tough to get along with in those days? Well, maybe. I was going my work. That's where I was tough. You've got to remember that a lot of those guys against me were tough, so why shouldn't I be, too?"[8]

Whether he had mellowed or not, talking in older age, Grove said if the Athletics thought he was an ill-tempered cuss in Philadelphia they should have seen him with Baltimore when he believed he should have been pitching in the big-time.

Grove was aware when the New York Giants offered Dunn $75,000 for him and the Baltimore owner turned it down. He had to wonder if he would ever get a big-league chance.

In 1928, though, after a few years with the A's under Mack, Grove led the American League in wins with 24 for the first time. Then he went 20–6 and the next season was 1930 when Grove completely dominated. By 1930, Mack, who had been in the game for more than three decades, and was in his sixties, considered Grove the fastest thrower he had ever seen.

"Did you ever see speed like that in a human arm?" Mack asked out loud during spring training in Fort Myers, Florida. "Why, it gives you a sore arm to watch him, doesn't it? The next pitch came so close to infielder Max Bishop's chin it could have shaved him. "Look out!" yelled Mack. Bishop took the scenario calmly. "Don't worry, Mr. Mack," Bishop said, "I am looking out. I don't want to get killed by a pitcher on my own team."[9]

This byplay continued around the batting cage and in the dugout. Jim Keesey, a backup first baseman, wandered over to Mack. He expressed concern he had made the staff ace angry.

"Mose is mad at me because he says I didn't offer at three fast ones right over the middle," Keesey said of Grove becoming peeved because he felt he was wasting batting practice throws. "But honest, Mr. Mack, they were by me before I could get my bat around."[10]

Grove was the most expensive purchase Mack had made and yet he did not regret it. He reminded listeners of the $100,000 sale—those first reports about the deal with Baltimore are the ones that sported headlines reading "Groves," the old family name. As for Mack, he usually, but not 100 percent of the time, called Grove "Robert."

"One of the biggest satisfactions of my baseball life is that I bought Grove for the Athletics," Mack said. "I certainly would be in hot water whenever Bob was in the park if he was pitching for an opposing team."[11]

Mack was a legendary baseball figure. He built dynasties and knew talent. Above all, Mack was known as a gentleman. Instead of doing the same as almost all managers in history sporting team uniforms, he wore a suit and tie and often a straw boater. He moved his players around in the field by waving his scorecard.

Although Mack sometimes displayed a temper, he was known for treating his players like men. As often as Grove could explode, he always maintained a solid respect for Mack.

"I got along fine with him," Grove said. "He was just like a father to everyone."[12]

14

PENNANT RACES

WHETHER IT WAS the "Year of the Hitter" or the "Year of the Pitcher," there were going to be teams that were favored and teams that were hopeless cases. Even though they all have the same record, never does a season begin with every team dead even. By the time spring training is over, it is clear some teams are going to be better than others; that some teams are going to be in the hunt and some teams are going to be doomed by mid-May.

Most interestingly in 1930, of course, was that none of the teams realized it was going to be an historic year for hitting, a season when the most astonishing things happened at the plate, and the most ridiculously awful pitching performances showed up on the mound.

The season opened a little later in April than it does now, but trends became evident early. Yes, there are fast and slow starts, but often enough the way a team plays in the first month of the season defines how it plays the rest of the year.

The Washington Senators got off to the best start in the American League, going 10–3 by April 30. The last-place team was the New York Yankees, not one used to such a spot in the standings. In the National League, the Pittsburgh Pirates were hottest earliest, going 9–3, while the Cincinnati Reds ending the month at 4–8.

By the end of May, the American League standings seemed to make more sense. The Philadelphia Athletics and Senators were tied for first place at 27–14. The four teams at the bottom of the standings were the ones that would fight it out for the last four spots the rest of the summer: the Detroit Tigers, St. Louis Browns, Chicago White Sox, and Boston Red Sox.

The Brooklyn Robins had a two-game lead on the St. Louis Cardinals with their 25–15 mark by the end of May, and the Phillies, at 12–22, were beginning to sink into sole possession of last place.

It is often said that the team that leads the pack by July 4 will be the team that wins the pennant by the beginning of October. That is not an absolute, but there had been a shakedown by the end of June in the American League.

The A's, riding high in recent years, were at 46–25, a record that represented a two-game lead over the Yankees and Senators, so things were sorting themselves out. On June 30, the White Sox and their 24–40 record were in last place, some 18 ½ games out of first. The Red Sox were 26–42, the equivalent of being just as far behind. Philadelphia was the defending World Series titlist and the Athletics took out the Cubs in five games in 1929.

Fans sometimes forget the Chicago Cubs were a power team in the National League during this era, even if they did not take home a World Series crown. For a stretch of more than a decade, the Cubs reached the Series every few years between 1929 and 1945. At the end of June, Chicago was in front in the National League with a 43–26 mark, one-and-a-half games ahead of the Dodgers. The Phillies were last at 24–38, beginning to slip below the horizon.

It was taking some time to unfold, but was gradually becoming apparent that the baseball season of 1930 was shaping up as an unusual one; one where the hitters were supreme against pitchers whose fastballs seemed a few mph slower than normal and whose curves did not break.

Fans might not have been able to name them, but all eight of the St. Louis Cardinals' regular daily starters were .300 hitters. The Phillies hit terrifically, yet pitched awfully (their .315 batting average was second in the NL, yet their ERA was last at 6.71).

For the time being, attendance was holding up, though with the Great Depression gradually infecting every aspect of daily life, baseball would soon start suffering its own ills. It was one thing to joke about Babe Ruth having a better year than President Herbert Hoover, but when swells began losing their jobs altogether, interest in tickets became shaky.

Athletics leader Connie Mack felt good about the club's 1929 title, but felt it more important that his team repeat to show its true mettle. "We've proven we're a fine ballclub," said Mack, "but I have always maintained that no team is entitled to call itself 'great' unless it repeats. By that I mean we won a pennant and a World Series last year. If we take the Series, then my boys deserve to be ranked as a great team."[1]

It was obvious the Athletics had the talent to repeat and that certain teams were more suited to win at the moment than others. Whether it was a propaganda speech for parity or not, Commissioner Kenesaw Mountain Landis declared the pennant races were wide open—as open, he said, "as a beggar's hand."[2]

Future Hall of Famer Red Ruffing, who was still stuck on the Red Sox before his transforming trade to the Yankees, discussed the matter of facing Philadelphia's future Hall of Famers Jimmie

Foxx and Al Simmons in the same batting order, sluggers extraordinaire who provided nightmares for hurlers.

"Jimmie Foxx was a pain," Ruffing said, "but Al Simmons was a plague."[3] That was a vivid description, but it wasn't clear which hitter bothered him the most.

It seemed clear that Lefty Gomez, who was just starting out in 1930, shook to his toes when he went against Foxx, given how many humorous stories he told about the difficulty of getting the big man out. Foxx, Gomez said, "hit a home run off of me that broke seats in the third deck at Yankee Stadium. You can't walk that far in an hour-and-a-half."[4]

Simmons was a holdout throughout the spring, sparring with Mack over money right up until the moment the Athletics were poised to start the season against the Yankees. Then Simmons came out and batted .432 in April.

Whether Landis departed from his neutrality quietly, or Hoover even had time to do any rooting for the team playing two miles from the White House, there was probably some sentiment favoring the Senators. Walter Johnson had his fans, and although the Senators had at long last broken through with some first-rate seasons in the 1920s, their victories had been rare enough to remain novelties.

The Senators of the era did field some of the best players in club history. No one was better than Johnson, even though he had become the manager, but several hitters had a lot to say about how Washington fared.

Having guys like forty-year-old Sam Rice around still producing was not the type of blessing usually afforded the Senators. But there he was, appearing in 147 games, batting .349 with an on-base percentage of .407. Those were the kinds of things that made supporters believe Washington had a chance.

At that age, there were skeptics about whether or not Rice could keep up such batting for an entire season. It has rarely been done. But whenever anyone pointed out a guy of forty should not be able to better guys half their age, Rice played on, oblivious. "Rice is beginning to feel the effects of his long service," one account read, "and cannot be counted on to play through an entire season at top speed."[5] Wrong.

Babe Ruth had gained weight and coped with bellyaches and numerous training violations that could have sidelined him for games at a time, but he kept coming back and bashing the ball with the same fervor as always. The difference being in 1930 that Ruth was not the only power hitter in the game. Now he had company.

He was thirty-five years old, yet hit as if he was in his prime. In fact, he led all of baseball in on-base percentage (.493), slugging (.732), and walks (136), and was top ten in numerous other categories. Never mind the usual stratospheric batting average, home run, and RBI totals, Ruth still owned this game. The Babe had refashioned baseball in his own image, and to review his year-by-year totals for the decade leading up to 1930 and inclusive, it is impossible to truly catalog how great he was. No emphasis can be so highly placed on his record to make the point.

The thing was that Ruth had dragged an entire sport in his wake. He had been ahead of everyone as he bashed the ball over fences, off walls, into the stands, and each of those players who hit so well, who defied the circumstances in 1930, should have sent him personal thank-you cards.

As Ruth clubbed his way to a record 714 regular-season home runs, one of the things that was apparent to fans, teammates, and all of baseball supporters was how much he reveled in it. Ruth loved rounding the bases. One could basically hear him chortling as he minced his steps after taking some bold, challenging pitcher deep. Sometimes Ruth shook his head as if to say he did not even know how he did it. Other times he was so cocksure, so full of confidence, that the whippersnapper on the mound was bound to get what he deserved by delivering the pitch in the wrong location.

When he first joined the Yankees after the Red Sox trade and attended his first spring training with New York, he said, "I was big news."[6] He noted that thirteen newspapers showed up to greet him, more than the team had drawn before.

Not even Ruth knew how many homers he could hit, but he scoffed at critics who suggested he would never hit more than he did near the end of his stay with Boston.

"There were a lot of people in 1920 who didn't think I'd ever again approach my 29 homers of 1919," he said. "It was the same in 1921. They thought my 54 of 1920 was such an unheard-of accomplishment that no one again could ever push it up that high."[7]

Ruth was still royalty in 1930, a man whose batting line could make most readers faint just by glimpsing them.

Maybe Goose Goslin didn't derive as much pure joy from swinging a bat as Ruth, but he said he did. By 1930, the Washington Senators outfielder was a star. But about one-third of the way into the campaign his old team gave up on him. Rarely do teams swap players who are destined for the Hall of Fame for each other, but Washington gave up Goslin, then twenty-nine, for the twenty-eight-year-old Heinie Manush, on June 13, although the Browns obtained pitcher General Crowder in the deal as well.

Washington probably felt Goslin was losing it because he was batting just .271 through 47 games. As soon as Goslin was shipped to the Browns, he snapped out of his funk and hit .326 for the rest of the year in 101 games. Also in those games, Goslin smacked 30 home runs and knocked in 100 runs, giving him 138 RBIs for the season. There was no way a Hall of Fame hitter should slump in 1930.

Goslin brought confidence with him to baseball when he came out of Salem, New Jersey, to join the Senators as a twenty year old, confident he could hit any pitcher alive. He was either too immature to know the difference between hurlers with the best stuff, or he was just that good. Since his lifetime average was .316. it just may well have been the latter.

"Heck, let's face it, I was just a big ol' country boy havin' the time of his life," Goslin said. "It was all a lark to me, just a joy ride. Never feared a thing, never got nervous, just a big country kid from South Jersey, too dumb to know better. In those days, I'd go out and fight a bull without a sword and never know the difference.

"It was just a game, that's all it was. They didn't have to pay me. Listen, the truth is, it was more than fun."

After twenty years in the majors, Goslin said, he'd had enough. "Goose, ol' boy, it's time to go fishin'."[8]

Not in 1930, though. Not yet. Goose still had some base hits in him, especially when pitchers were practically giving them away that year.

15

THE PHILADELPHIA PHILLIES

WITHOUT MINCING WORDS, the pitching staff of the 1930 Philadelphia Phillies was atrocious. It may have been the worst of all time, the most embarrassing in the history of baseball. If a student of the game thinks the simple explanation offered by the use of the word atrocious is unkind, unfair, or an exaggeration, such person should be invited to consult a thesaurus and review synonyms.

Many would be suitable. Feast on such choices as awful, barbaric, heinous, lousy, scandalous, shocking, bad, beastly, desperate, diabolical, fiendish, flagrant, godawful, grody, gross, hairy, monstrous, nefarious, villainous, wicked. Some of those listings seem a bit far afield, unless perhaps you were the manager.

The casual fan might well vote for awful, lousy, rotten, or godawful. Though grody may not have been in popular usage in 1930, a Merriam-Webster definition of disgusting or revolting seems to fit as neatly as a tailored suit.

The 1930 Phillies gave away runs like a street-corner Santa passing out gifts. They could not get anybody out. It almost seemed as though the pitchers went out of their way to assist the team in having a horrendous record, bad enough to finish last in the National League. The team's earned-run average was 6.71. That was not one particularly egregious individual, that was an aggregate, a group effort.

That resulted in a record of 52–102 and dead last in the NL. The truly astounding aspect of the Phillies' godforsaken season was that Philadelphia was stocked with excellent hitters. As a squad, the Phillies batted a ridiculously good .315. Few position players were famous sluggers, but some could hit with anyone and lived up to their reputations as the pitchers lived down to their reviews.

Five members of the starting lineup hit .300-plus, as well as three heavily used substitutes. Hall of Fame outfielder Chuck Klein recorded the statistics of a lifetime, yet couldn't lift his team out of last place. Not even with the aid of sweet-swinging Lefty O'Doul, who but for some oddities in his career would also have been a Hall Famer, could lift the club out of the cellar.

What a combination the dichotomy between pitchers and hitters for the Phillies. A pitching staff with an ERA of 6.71 counterbalanced by a batting average of .315. Apparently, good pitching is more important than good hitting.

One astonishing thing is that, as poorly as many throwers performed, manager Burt Shotton kept sending his hobo staff to the mound to take shellackings. That suggested the Phillies had nowhere to turn, no aid to summon to the rescue. The club may have provided hitting entertainment at the Baker Bowl, but the fans wised up, recognizing the scalding mixture provided heartburn. Just 299,007 paid to enter the home grounds.

There was one born survivor on the Phils' pitching staff, one stalwart who somehow eclipsed all the bad karma. Righty Phil Collins, a second-year man at twenty-eight, went 16–11. This was tantamount to impossibility. Still, Collins's 4.78 ERA was not to be highlighted for praise.

The rest of his compatriots, however, produced one horrible outing after another, one skyrocketing ERA overwhelming another. Collins was the only one with a winning record, while the others were either scarred by too much sunburn, too much opposing bat burn, or found their way to the saloons and taverns that surreptitiously served willing imbibers in defiance of Prohibition. If anyone could use a drinink during the summer of 1930, it was Phillies pitchers.

Much like the gangsters controlling the New York and Chicago liquor flow, Philadelphia and the nearby Jersey Shore, considered an easy port of entry for smuggled booze, made that mid-Atlantic area a wide-open receiving area for bootleggers. It was once said that Philadelphia was "soaked in alcohol" during Prohibition.

Although there was no indication that members of the Phillies were involved in the manufacture or transport of moonshine or other liquor, there is every reason to believe the players were just as easily wooed into such drinking sin as the everyday businessman.

Ironically, another local sporting figure, boxing promoter Max "Boo-Boo" Hoff, was heavily connected to the rackets. His nickname, after all, was "King of the Bootleggers."

Visiting players took note of how much room there was in the stands when they faced the Phillies. Cincinnati star pitcher Bucky Walters once said, "Sometimes there were so few fans in the park that you'd say, 'Where is everybody? They must all be down at the shore.'"[1] That may have been the milk and cookies interpretation of where they were.

Prohibition, or the 1920 Volstead Act, had to be one of the most dismal government policy enactments in the history of the country. For the teetotalers who opposed drinking on religious grounds and other moralistic motives, everything turned out wrong. The drinking and wild behavior associated with speakeasies and the wild parties of the Roaring Twenties seemed to encourage more drinking, not less.

"Prohibition . . . made liquor more appealing and helped increase its social acceptance among both men and women," one author observed of the time. "People clustered in speakeasies to imbibe illegal drinks, leading to disrespect for the law and growth of organized crime. Before Prohibition, respectable women did not drink, smoke, or wear provocative clothing. After Prohibition, however, these customs became socially acceptable, as young, cigarette-puffing, short-skirted 'flappers' and 'jazz babies' ushered in the Roaring Twenties."[2]

Drinking aside, some of the Phillies' steady clientele were gamblers. Certainly, those oddsmakers did not often set numbers favoring the home team. Sometimes they reduced the gambling to the offbeat, taking bets of 10 cents on whether or not the next pitch would be a strike. In 1930, odds were that the next pitch spun by a Phillies hurler was not going to be a strike, as the team averaged 3.6 walks per game, yet 2.5 strikeouts per game.

The Baker Bowl was more the size of a soup bowl. Constructed in 1887 and used as a big-league ballpark through 1938, the cost was just $80,000 and the original seating was only 12,500. That meant the Phillies did not have to create much excitement to fill the place even after later expansion to 20,000 in 1929, just in time for the miserable 1930 season. And that's what they did. They did not create much excitement.

Effects of the Depression began taking hold early in Philadelphia because of challenges to the textile industry. By 1930, Philadelphia was coping with 135,000 unemployed and a year later that number reached 250,000. Not unemployed, though it could easily be argued they deserved it, were the Phillies' pitchers. Yet they were no doubt suffering through a Great Depression of their own.

Phil Collins the pitcher never became as famous as Phil Collins the singer. The Windy City was the heart of the meatpacking industry, and Collins's father operated a meat market. Born in the city in 1901, he dreamed of running his own butcher shop, though it's unknown if that was because he simply loved eating steak or was inspired by his dad.

Actually, while Collins diverged from this early dream, other members of the family kept the business going long after his father passed away. Originally signed by the Cubs, Collins was just twenty-one when he started his first career game, on October 7, 1923. He pitched five innings and took home the win.

Collins bounced around Rockford, Illinois (where he went 17–4), Terre Haute, Indiana, and New Orleans before he got a second chance at the majors, this time as Philadelphia property. Although he struggled through an unhealthy season (he had his tonsils removed at the end of it) at twenty-seven, he finished 9–7 for the 1929 Phillies.

Despite his limited record, he struck many observers favorably. The National League Service Bureau highlighted Collins as a potentially rising player, noting "he has a cool head and a brave heart and a most baffling screwball. It is not hard to understand why he is so hard to hit when he takes his place on the pitching hill."[3]

Predictions were made Collins might pitch the Phillies out of the cellar in 1931, but he finished 12–16. A year later he finished 14–12, on his way to an 80–85 record in eight seasons.

Collins acquired the nickname "Fidgety Phil" because of nervous tics. He constantly pulled up his pants, stamped around the mound, pulled at his cap, and swung his arms frequently. His windup was also described as herky-jerky.

There was also no secret when it came to deciphering what Collins was all about, though. Meat.

"Now I love my baseball," Collins said, "and I am proud and glad to be a big leaguer, but I guess I am different from most boys about my ambitions. My brother and I grew up with the one main idea to carry on a butcher shop like the old man did in the same neighborhood. He wanted to build up the business and he has been on the job all the while I have been away more than half the time. We may not ever build up any Swift or Armour butcher business, but you can bet we will cling to the old man's lines and build it up as big as we can. I put my savings from baseball right into the old meat market."[4]

Collins only partially fulfilled his desires. He died in 1948, at the young age of forty-six.

The rest of Philadelphia's pitching got lumped under atrocious all over again.

Ray Benge, 11–15, had a 5.70 ERA. Les Sweetland went 7–15 with a frightening 7.71 ERA. Claude Willoughby recorded a similar ERA at 7.59 with a 4–17 record. Shotton also took chances on anyone else who came along, like Hap Collard (6–12, 6.80 ERA) and Hal Elliott (6–11, 7.67 ERA). The next tier was worse off.

Snipe Hansen finished 0–7 and was battered all over the Baker Bowl and other ballparks, compiling a 6.72 ERA, as was Harry Smythe (0–3, 7.79 ERA).

There was more than one Chet Nichols in major-league history. The earlier Chet pitched for parts of six seasons, including his 1930 adventure with the Phillies. He made it through the year 1–2 with a 6.79 ERA (and his only major-league win). In three games with the New York Giants in 1928, Nichols's ERA was 23.63—probably as close to infinity as possible without being there. In three games with the Phillies in 1931, his ERA was 9.53, all contributing to a lifetime ERA of 7.19.

This Chet Nichols was the father of the latter-day Chet Nichols, whose career record—from 1951 to 1964—was 34–36 with a much snazzier earned-run average of 3.64. Players on the 1930 Phillies would have killed for an ERA like that.

Right-hander Benge was a workman who battled through 12 seasons in the majors, never reaching stardom. In 1930, he threw 225 2/3 innings for his 11 victories. He was hit particularly hard though, permitting 305 hits. Benge's lifetime mark was 101–129 and though he won at least 10 games six times, he never won more than 14 (which he did twice).

Later in life, Benge said he received many snippets of mail seeking autographs from young baseball fans who didn't know anything about his career, only that he played.

"If they send it, I sign it," Benge said. "Most people, not all of 'em, don't know the meaning of all of it. They see the losing record and think, 'Just another ballplayer.'"[5]

Benge said lack of team range in fielding haunted him. Furthermore, the squad had the most errors (239) and the lowest fielding percentage (.962) in baseball.

"Now, if you really want horrendous results, couple poor range with poor hands and arms," he said. "Not only do the fielders not get to as many balls as their counterparts on other teams, those they do reach they can't handle."[6]

Benge spent his career hurling for teams that were buried in the second division.

"I just wished I could have been with a better club," Benge said. "Everybody does that. There wouldn't be any baseball clubs if everybody was on the best. Even the bottom club, when you come right down to it, they're a heck of a ball club. They're not a bad ball club. You got to be good to play in the major leagues."[7]

In an interview, given at age ninety, Benge was asked how bad the Phillies of 1930 and that era were, but in his reply was somewhat diplomatic.

"Well, they were good in some places, but most of the players didn't come up to par with the other teams. They just needed two, or three, or four players in different places here and there and they'd have a good ball club. I always felt if I pitched like I did and had been on a better ball club I'd have won a lot more games."[8]

Another non-All-Star member of the 1930 Phillies pitching staff was Les Sweetland, who would have been happy to obtain mortgage rates lower than his earned-run average of several seasons, not only this eye-opener of a career-worst 7.71.

Born in St. Ignace, Michigan, in 1901, the 5-foot-11, 155-pound southpaw broke into the majors for the Phillies in 1927. He finished 2–10 in 103 2/3 innings, and was rocked for a 6.16 ERA, hinting at things to come. His control was a problem from the start, and even though pitching coaches determined his repertoire could fool many batters, they could not tame his stuff.

Results were similar in 1928, when Sweetland was crushed for 6.58 runs a game and finished 3–15. Somehow, Sweetland survived for another invitation to Phillies camp, and in 1929 went 13–11. Even though his ERA improved from the previous season, it was still an embarrassing 5.11. Still, that gave Sweetland a slot for 1930—and he made the least of it. His final line in the majors was 33–58 with a 6.10 ERA.

Uncharacteristically, even the National League Service Bureau essentially declared him a puzzle too difficult to solve, writing, "Sweetland just went bad last year [1930] and his case merely goes to swell the list of pitching mysteries that have cluttered the league records for the past half century."[9]

Almost anonymously tucked into the middle of the list of 1930 Phillies pitchers is a last name, "Alexander," that blinks like a neon sign. It was a shame such a personage blended with the cast of misfits.

This was the end of glory for one of the finest pitchers of all time. This was how it ended for Grover Cleveland Alexander, winner of 373 games and once, when younger, the sparkplug thrower for this same Phillies club. Alexander was forty-three and ending his 20-season run in the majors, trying to add a few more wins to his victory total. He couldn't, unfortunately, finishing 0–3 . He only threw 21 2/3 innings, yet gave up 22 earned runs.

The right-handed Alexander was born in Elba, Nebraska, in 1887, and stepped off the plains right into the Phillies' rotation in 1911, winning 28 games as a rookie. Nine times Alexander won at least 20 games and, for a three-year stretch, 1915 to 1917, dazzled the baseball world with seasonal victory totals of 31, 33, and 30,.

Dodgers Hall of Fame hurler Burleigh Grimes once said about Alexander at his best, "If anybody was ever a greater pitcher than that guy, I wouldn't know what his name was. It was just a pleasure to watch him work, even though he was beating your brains out most of the time."[10] And this is coming from a contemporary who won 270 games during his 19-year career.

In the days leading up to the 1930 season, Alexander was repeatedly in trouble regularly because of incidents related to drinking. He was arrested for such offenses as drunkenness and disorderly conduct. Alexander could not stay off the bottle long enough to whip his body into shape for a final attempt with a big-league team.

Shotton believed Alexander was going to crank his arm up and take the team and his own highlight machine back in time to lead the 1930 club to a pennant. So much ballyhoo had been attributed to Alexander's second wind that he was forced to hold a press conference to explain an off day.

A newsman boldly asked if he intended to follow the team's training rules. Alexander recognized the euphemism in the guarded question. "I guess you mean my drinking, don't you?" he responded. "Well, I admit I drink. But I'm not the playboy you read about. I never have painted myself as an angel with one of those halo things, but it's physically impossible for any one man to hold all the liquor accredited to me."[11] As a reminder, this was during Prohibition, and Alexander wasn't being secretive.

Whether it was booze or an aging body, Alexander tried to explain his lack of consistency.

"Tricky things, legs," Alexander offered. "For the first three or four innings everything will be rosy, when all of a sudden, your legs go dead. If I can get my legs in fairly good shape I ought to be able to fool my share of batters next year."[12]

This was poignant oratory from one of the game's best pitchers. From a baseball standpoint, it didn't really matter anymore what he said. It was over. After those cameo showings for the last-place Phillies, Alexander never threw another major-league pitch.

He hooked up with the House of David touring team as an exhibition attraction, though. Alexander was not a natural showman. He came, he threw, he got paid, he left. That was the deal.

Alexander was a big enough name for fans in rural America who had never seen him pitch in person, clamoring for the chance to see him in the flesh. Inwardly, though, Alexander cringed. Yes, it was baseball. Yes, it was pitching. But even the last-place Phillies were more big-time because they were still part of "The Show."

"I was advertised like an elephant in the circus," Alexander said, "and had to pitch an inning or so every game. I always picked the eighth or ninth inning and prayed for rain."[13]

Grover Cleveland Alexander was elected to the National Baseball Hall of Fame in 1938, and was only sixty-three when he died in St. Paul, Nebraska, in 1950.

If Alexander represented what could have been for the 1930 Philadelphia Phillies' pitching staff, even if that thinking erred on the side of the fanciful, Philadelphia did possess hitting to beat anyone.

It was a shame Alexander had to be associated with such a ragged bunch, but the credentials of this pitching staff as one of the worst on record, and the worst of the worst, is supported by statistical evidence.

Many baseball experts consider the 1899 Cleveland Spiders the worst team of all time, finishing the season 20–134. The Spiders' team earned-run average was 6.37. Two pitchers endured stupendously awful seasons. Frank Bates's record was 1–18 with a 7.24 earned run average, while Harry Colliflower finished 1–11 with an 8.17 ERA. Also note that this was more than three decades before these Phillies.

The 1915 Philadelphia Athletics finished 43–109 and recorded total home attendance of 146,223 at Shibe Park. But the A's ERA did not approach a level of true disgrace, topping out at 4.29. To illustrate how desperate Connie Mack was for pitching that year, though, twenty-seven throwers appeared on the mound at least once.

The 2006 Kansas City Royals were probably the most forgettable collection of pitchers in franchise history. Compiling a 62–100 record, the pitchers' group ERA was 5.65. Mark Redman was practically a hero, going 11–10, but he was just one of thirty-one different guys who threw at least one pitch for the team that year.

The stunning overall performance of the 1930 Phillies' pitching staff endures. There have been individuals, however, who began big-league careers with optimism who were drummed into retirement with brutal bludgeonings on their resume.

Righty John Van Benschoten received a few chances with the Pittsburgh Pirates in the 2000s. Twice, he was anointed the best prospect in the team's minor-league system. But in 26 games, distributed over parts of three seasons, he ended up 2–13 with an ERA of 9.20. It is not clear if an enemy put a curse on him. In college at Kent State, Van Benschoten was a star power hitter. Although Van Benschoten also had serious of arm problems, maybe the worst mistake of his career was turning from hitter into thrower.

Between 1996 and 2000, righty Andy Larkin received chances to shine for the Florida Marlins, Cincinnati Reds, and Kansas City Royals, but he was lit up like Broadway theatre marquees, finishing 3–11 with an 8.86 earned run average. Rather stunningly, during one of his short seasons, Larkin made as much as $170,000.

Southpaw Jeff Kaiser, who drank coffee with the Oakland Athletics, the Cleveland Indians, Detroit Tigers, Cincinnati Reds, and New York Mets, got 50 chances totaling 52 innings but never won a game, going 0–2 and spread over seven seasons, Kaiser built a 9.17 earned run average.

So pitching did its part to make the Phillies a loser in 1930. Philadelphia basically found the only way to undermine its own sterling hitting with the beyond-belief horror show on the mound.

Outfielder Chuck Klein was just twenty-five, and cobbled together the finest season of his Hall of Fame career, batting .386 with 40 home runs and 170 RBIs. He was one of the hitting monsters of the 1930 season . . . and yet he barely led the team in average. The remarkable Lefty O'Doul, author of a unique career, batted .383 that season. Those were the two linchpin contributors to Philadelphia hitting .315 as a team.

Pitcher Ray Benge did not blame Klein or O'Doul for lack of run support.

"He was a good one," Benge said of O'Doul. "As far as I'm concerned he does [belong in the Hall of Fame]. Chuck was an extra good hitter. What I mean, if the ball was over the outside of the plate, or something like that, it would be almost the same as if it was right down the middle. He'd hit it."[14]

Klein and O'Doul were deadly together that season, but the Phillies had even more oomph in the lineup.

Just as the club trotted out pitchers of little distinction who have faded in memory, so too did some of the hitters whose batting averages deserve to be remembered.

Virgil "Spud" Davis was the main catcher for the club, and he wielded a solid stick, batting .313 with 14 home runs in 105 games. In a 16-year career, with a .308 lifetime average, he was not merely a 1930 wonder. Davis put up seven straight seasons of .300 hitting (1929–35). He is probably the best-hitting catcher no one knows about.

First baseman Don Hurst did Davis one better, batting .327 with 17 home runs. Hurst attended the University of Ohio and then turned pro in the Blue Grass League. He had been a catcher, but shifted over a base. Only a dramatic slump in the last of his seven seasons dropped his lifetime average below .300 (.298).

In 1928, the 6-foot, 215-pound Hurst set a Phillies rookie record with 19 home runs. The next year he clubbed 31. That was after trimming down from 230 pounds, which was his playing weight as a collegiate football player.

"He was a big, strong guy, a pretty good all-around ballplayer," said Fresco Thompson, who was a teammate. "He was not solely a Baker Bowl hitter. He hit 'em out of the big parks, too."[15]

Hurst used to debate the best approach to his own swing. Hit in uppercut fashion, or not?

"There are plenty of cases when meeting the ball fair doesn't get you as good results as when you're a little off on your swing," Hurst said. "Naturally, I hit up a little at the ball so when I'm really meeting the ball the best, I'm likely to hit up in the air. That's not so good [because of fly-ball outs]. So I've told some of the fellows that I'm not so good when I'm at my best. And that's the truth, though it sounds rather foolish."[16]

Who's on first?

The best season of Arthur "Pinky" Whitney's career was 1930, when he ripped the ball at a .342 clip while manning third. His nickname came from an old comic strip character, Pinky Thompson, because they both wore baseball caps.

Whether old-time memories just grow sweeter with time, or get massaged later in life Whitney remembered Phillies fans as being loyal even when the team was bad.

"They'd ride the umpires and the visiting ball players," Whitney said. "We'd get beat 14–0 and 14–2 in a doubleheader and they'd still be cheering for us."[17]

Whitney was also praised by fellow ballplayers for his stellar defense. "[Pinky] Whitney is the greatest third baseman in baseball," said Grover Cleveland Alexander in 1930. "It's a shame he couldn't have gotten with a winning club. That boy is a wonderful fielder and one of the most dangerous hitters in the game."[18]

Probably the best player in baseball history not in the Hall of Fame is Lefty O'Doul, who could hit in a telephone booth, underwater, or anywhere a cocky pitcher lined up.

Francis Joseph O'Doul was a San Francisco guy, and his unique ties to the city kept interfering with his performing his best in the majors. He spent too much time involved with the San Francisco Seals of the Pacific Coast League.

When not managing the Seals, or another top minor-league club, O'Doul acted as a baseball ambassador, becoming one of the most popular post-World War II American figures in Japan.

Over 11 seasons, O'Doul batted .349 and twice won batting titles. He hit .383 for the 1930 Phillies with 202 hits, which was a drop-off from his 1929 campaign when he won the NL batting title by hitting .398 with a .465 on-base percentage. He also stroked a stunning 254 hits that year, with 32 home runs and 122 RBIs. O'Doul scored his other batting title with Brooklyn in 1932, hitting .368.

O'Doul was personable, entertaining, a jokester, and a public speaker. A sportswriter also once noted he was perfectly named, commenting, "The name Lefty O'Doul is a precious thing, a name that could not have been invented. Anybody named Lefty O'Doul could not possibly be commonplace, or fail to make his mark in some direction. Lefty O'Doul is a finer name than Rocky Moore or Tam o' Shanter."[19]

O'Doul always respected superstitions surrounding the act of hitting, especially if a streak was involved. His wife once recounted how she tried to convince him to change a shirt. He refused. "I can't," he said. "That's a hitting shirt."[20]

O'Doul was also known to frequent the same restaurant for dinner before a game and sit at the same table. He did not want to disturb his karma.

"I am always looking around for a lucky locker on the road," O'Doul said.[21]

Although the title seems to have informally passed to Mike Schmidt, the greatest Philadelphia Phillies player of all time, before the third baseman's arrival, it was outfielder Chuck Klein. Klein's most memorable year was 1930, when he did everything with the bat except pound nails.

It takes a deep breath to assess Klein's season and more than one turn exhaling. He batted .386, slugged 40 home runs, and knocked in 170 runs, while collecting 250 hits—59 of them doubles. The RBI and doubles totals are still team records. So are Klein's 1930 marks in slugging percentage(.687) and total bases (445).

Klein's lifetime average was .320. He led the National League in home runs four times, and won the Most Valuable Player Award in 1932 before being selected for the Hall of Fame in 1980. Klein was not an exceptionally large man, though good sized at 6-foot and 185 pounds. Indeed, a bat was manufactured with Klein's name on it, and future slugger Ralph Kiner owned such a model as a kid.

"I didn't know if he was a right-handed hitter or a left-handed hitter," said Kiner, who batted right and led the NL in homers seven consecutive years. As it so happened, Klein batted lefty.

In an era when weightlifting was nonexistent, muscles were developed through jobs. Klein was from Indianapolis, and the iron he built in his arms that translated into power, stemmed from work he did when younger.

"I worked in the steel mills in Indianapolis," Klein said. He emphasized the word *work* to explain how he gained his strength. "You'll come out with shoulders like mine and these muscles. That's all there is to it. It stands to reason a big fellow with the [physique] is going to drive a ball farther than a little man. "While in the mills, I could carry beams from 100 pounds and up. I could barely make it the first month, but gradually I felt myself getting stronger."[22]

Eventually, Klein said, he could tote the beams around as if they were baseball bats, which were weighed in ounces, not pounds. On July 10, 1936, Klein hit four home runs in one game against the Pittsburgh Pirates in spacious Forbes Field. Many players equaled the feat, but none have broken that record.

Klein could explain what made him as powerful as Samson, but when it came to scientific baseball analysis, he was not in the same category as Ty Cobb.

What did the pitcher throw him?

"Damned if I know," Klein said. "I just swung."[23]

And connected.

16

THE CINCINNATI REDS

IN A SEASON rich with subplots, fascinating individual stories, unusual baseball developments, and when even the worst teams (like the Philadelphia Phillies) could enthrall fans, the main sin of the Cincinnati Reds was being boring.

In 1930, the Reds were neither good nor bad. They featured no superstar hitting like so many other teams. There was no one to point to on the pitching staff as capable of dominating other opponents.

There was little to hype up Reds fans that season. The 1930 group happened to be located precisely in the middle of the franchise's intermission of success. The 1919 Reds had won the World Series, even if with a boost from the Chicago White Sox. The next time the team mattered was 1939, when it won the National League pennant, then repeated and won the World Series in 1940.

In between? Well, the Reds fielded several teams like the 1930 group seeking to entice fans into Crosley Field. Mostly, the fans were not fooled. That year, as Cincinnati finished 59–95 in seventh place in the NL pennant race, just 386,727 spectators came out.

In the "Year of the Hitter," the Reds batted .281, OK, if not terrific. In the "Year of the (Bad) Pitcher," the staff earned-run average was 5.08. In neither case were the players spectacularly good enough to provoke comment, or spectacularly bad enough to provoke disgust, although that 5.08 was borderline.

The manager assigned to squeeze success out of the Reds was Dan Howley. Nicknamed "Dapper Dan," Howley was the kind of player who was a grunt worker, a catcher who became a coach, who became a minor-league manager, who reached his dream to run a big-league team . . . only to be saddled with no-talent clubs.

In six seasons at the helm of big-league teams, four of Howley's squads suffered through years well under .500. But he did lead the St. Louis Browns to two winning seasons (1928: 82–72; 1929: 79–73), the type of success with a perpetually bad team that could earn a manager a war service medal.

It seemed to work for Howley. Those two solid seasons with the Browns earned him a job with the Reds. Owner Powel Crosley Jr. could reasonably review Howley's performance and figure he would only produce better results in Cincinnati.

Who knew the Reds of that season would be as lousy as the average Browns team?

In the 1930s, owners of baseball teams were wealthy individuals—not mega-corporations ranked high on the list of rich Fortune 500 companies or the like, but wealthy nonetheless. They were basically baseball men, mindful of their money, but very much men of the sport, lovers of the game, who viewed themselves as civic-minded contributors in it for the glory of winning more than making the big bucks.

Crosley was an inventor who sold cars and radios, was a broadcast pioneer, and ran a radio station. While some baseball executives find their way into the Baseball Hall of Fame, Crosley is a member of the Automotive Hall of Fame and the National Radio Hall of Fame. Perhaps he could not hit the curveball.

The Great Depression led to Crosley becoming the Reds' owner. His predecessor was Sidney Weil, but Weil lost his wealth because of the stock market crash and sold out to Crosley. It was a gradual demise for Weil. He began bleeding money in 1929, his first season as president of the team, yet didn't want to let go. But the Depression ate at his finances and at last, in 1934, Weil capitulated to Crosley.

The problem was that, in 1930, the team was starting to tiptoe toward bankruptcy because of Weil's woes. Crosley became the community rescuer and had to infuse cash to save the operation and rebuild it.

The 1930 season was a beginning-of-the-end year for Weil. He was under siege because of the new reality across the country and had to concentrate on balancing his financial books more than acquiring talent. So he did have an excuse for putting a fairly lame team on the field.

Crosley was better for the team. He was a visionary who disagreed with fellow owners on several topics. While most owners did not favor radio broadcasts or television airings of games, feeling no one would buy tickets if they gave the product away for free, Crosley understood the radio audiences would be teased and have their interest piqued and TV showings later the following decade would work likewise. If fans liked what they saw and heard, they would want to come out to the park to see it all in person.

To his credit, after Crosley inherited a weak team, he hired front office help that knew what it was doing—one person in particular being Warren Giles—and turned the Reds into a winner down the line.

But not in 1930, though. He was still on the outside, and not more than an interested fan who had to endure what the other fans put up with that summer.

Cincinnati coped with the Depression better than many other cities because it experienced a resurgence in river trade. As for Prohibition, the residents of the Queen River enjoyed their alcohol as much as others elsewhere.

On one occasion, after a court case, police officers destroyed $10,000 worth of booze by hurling it into a river. Members of the local media periodically had fun tweaking the Volstead Act. One article asked if everyone who lived in the city with the last name of "Beer" would be required to change it.

In any case, there was no one in the Reds lineup with such a name. On the other hand, there were few players in the lineup with more famous baseball names, either.

Like many teams in 1930, the Reds were not burdened with large numbers of top-tier players. Guys who never became famous. Guys who just did their job. Guys who took advantage of the fluke beat-on-pitchers season.

Of all people, Cincinnati's leading batter was outfielder Harry Heilmann. Some thirty-five years old and nearing the end of his career, Heilmann was a refugee from the Detroit Tigers, where he had been a mainstay for 15 years.

The Tigers no longer had him, the Reds did not have much, but Heilmann still had it. His swing never deserted him, and he batted. 333 that season. It may have been a hasty deal, but the Tigers did not even receive a player for Heilmann when they sent him to Cincinnati the previous October. The price was cash.

At twenty-two, third baseman Tony Cuccinello, who had a 15-year playing career and a long career as a coach, appeared to be a budding star his rookie year, hitting .312. He did it all over again, batting .315 the next year, but although he occasionally sprinkled in a few other .300 seasons, his hitting fell off and he rarely reached a high level again.

Once he ceased playing, Cuccinello was one of those baseball lifers who managed in the minors and coached in the majors for decades, including a return stint in Cincinnati as a big-league coach.

While he was less remembered, and 1930 was his last of his 12 big-league seasons, lefty-hitting outfielder Curt Walker produced a .307 season for Cincinnati. Although fame eluded him, Walker swung a reliable stick, batting higher than .300 seven times while playing in at least 85 games, once reaching .337, and concluding his time in the majors with a .304 average.

Walker was precisely the sort of workmanlike roster man who was bound to hit well in a season when there were bargain sales on base hits. He was an excellent contact man, difficult to strike out (never striking out more than 46 times in a season). During a season when pitchers could not find home plate without radar, that provided a bonus attribute.

He later had a long career as a justice of the peace in Beeville, Texas, which at that point in the century may have paid better.

Proving .300 hitters *did* grow on trees that season, Cincinnati installed Joe Stripp at first base, and he hit .306. It was his first full season in the majors, but he proved 1930 wasn't a fluke, batting .300 five more times in his career. He was not a power hitter, collecting just 24 homers lifetime in 11 seasons, but if you wanted a base hit, Stripp was your man.

In a trivia item that had less to do with Stripp than his opponent, in 1934, the third baseman became the last major leaguer to record a legal at-bat against a spitball pitcher. The sport had banned such pitches, but grandfathered in players who were already using the weapon. Stripp was the final batter to face Burleigh Grimes, striking out.

Of course, only the naïve believe that was the final time a pitcher threw the spitball. This was, technicality, the last "sanctioned" spitter. Presumably, the ball has dried by now.

The Reds had a reserve outfielder named Evar Swanson who hit .309 while being used in 95 games. Swanson was such a terrific athlete in his younger days, he seemed capable of hitting .300 without practicing. At Lombard College, he excelled in basketball, football, and track, as well as baseball. He was like the fictional Chip Hilton, the boys' book series sports hero.

In those days, Swanson was a pitcher who threw a no-hitter as a collegiate star. Although it seemed as if, perhaps, he could have helped the Reds as a pitcher in 1930, his season was actually cut short because of an arm injury.

A switch-hitter with exceptional speed on the bases (a career high 33 steals in 1929—though thrown out 20 times, which led all of baseball), Swanson had his moments. After college, Swanson made a stopover in the National Football League with the Milwaukee Badgers and Chicago Cardinals, running, punting, and place kicking.

Adding to this somewhat intriguing cast of Reds characters was catcher Clyde Sukeforth (who hit .284). Sukeforth gained his greatest fame about a decade and a half later when Brooklyn Dodgers general manager Branch Rickey gave him the assignment of scouting for the first African American player to break baseball's twentieth-century color barrier. Sukeforth, who served Brooklyn as a coach and scout, played a major role in the signing of Jackie Robinson.

When it comes to Leo Durocher, he is known for being a shortstop on some of the great New York Yankees teams of the 1920s, and as a member of the St. Louis Cardinals' "Gashouse Gang." His often stormy tenures as manager of the Dodgers, New York Giants, and Chicago Cubs are well remembered.

But playing shortstop for the Cincinnati Reds for three-plus years? Who remembers that? Just a footnote in Durocher's colorful career, including 1930 when he hit .243. That was the usual batting territory for Durocher, who was never much of a hitter, but led by force of personality and with his fielding.

If the Reds did not have to worry about pitching—which is something most teams had to worry about in 1930—they might have demonstrated more survival skills. But Cincinnati pitching was as anonymous and weak as any team in the league that season.

The Reds staff can be summed up as Eppa Rixey, Eppa Rixey, and Eppa Rixey. Alas, for him and the team, by that point in his career that was by reputation only. Rixey won 266 games in a 21-season career and through grit and tenacity was voted into the Baseball Hall of Fame.

Beginning his big-league career in 1912, Rixey was the National League's winningest left-handed pitcher from 1933 to 1959, when Warren Spahn broke his record. Born in Culpeper, Virginia, in 1891, Rixey's entire career was spent with the Phillies and Reds.

He struggled representing some poor teams, but won more than 20 games in a season three times, including 25 in 1922 for the Reds, but also led the National League in losses twice.

By 1930, Rixey was thirty-nine years of age and just hanging on, trying to add a few more wins to his lifetime total. He finished 9–13 and wiggled through parts of a few more seasons before retiring in 1933. His compatriots on the Reds staff offered little aid and comfort. Weil was lucky that group of arms didn't rocket him into bankruptcy.

Right-hander Charles Frederick "Red" Lucas, who at least had the right nickname to play for the Reds, went 14–16, skirting the suburbs of respectability but spoiling the teasing look with a 5.38 earned run average. For a solid pitcher, who won 157 career games and a lifetime ERA of 3.72, that one-year aberration was ill-timed and embarrassing. Lucas, who posted seasons of 18 and 19 wins, was better than that.

Lucas had first tried to make the majors as an outfielder, but that didn't take. He was regularly listed as a pinch-hitter, and of three career home runs he stroked, two of them were as substitutes. While Lucas may not have been the Angels' Shohei Ohtani, he was used 505 times as a fill-in hitter and recorded 114 pinch hits. The double duty suited him, as Lucas batted .281 for his career.

Speaking of players who could mix and match: before he ever thought of becoming a pitcher, Rixey planned to become a chemist. For many years he successfully mixed his good stuff, and despite his ups and downs with wins and losses, his ERA was a sharp 3.15.

Rixey was chosen for the Hall of Fame thirty years after he retired. Once, on a vacation to Cooperstown, New York, home of the Hall, he sent postcards to friends in Cincinnati saying, "I finally made it."[1] When he did truly finally make it into the Hall, Rixey kept joking to sportswriters, saying, "They're really scraping the bottom of the barrel, aren't they?"[2]

The announcement was made in late January 1963, but barely a month later Rixey died from a heart attack and he could not experience the firsthand joy of the induction ceremony.

17

THE BOSTON BRAVES

BY GEORGE SISLER'S standards, the 1930 season was nothing special. If someone else batted .309, it might have been a career year. But then, Sisler, a.k.a. "The Sizzler," was thirty-seven, so merely hitting that well was acceptable.

Once again, with one of the mediocre teams of the National League that year, the good news was all written by the bats and the bad news was spelled out by the arms. Boston finished 70–85, in fifth place. No one was giving out prizes for fifth place, but no one was sneering at a team that could still place higher than three other clubs.

No matter what name was in use for what season, the easiest thing to do when dealing with this franchise is call it the Braves. Currently, it is the Atlanta Braves. For a while, it was the Milwaukee Braves. Before that it was the Boston Braves. Then, for a little while in the middle, the team was known as the Bees. Between 1936 and 1941, a new owner tried to spiff up the team's image and separate its history from past financial difficulties . . . but the Bees didn't stick.

At least in 1930, it was pretty certain the team was the Braves—the same Braves that won a miracle pennant in 1914, yet had hardly won anything ever again while located in Boston.

Sisler was the most famous player on the 1930 team. One of the game's greatest hitters, the first baseman who shone most of his career with the St. Louis Browns was thirty-five when he moved to Boston for the final two and a half years of his illustrious career.

Sisler, born in Ohio in 1893, was one of those ballplayers who seemed to be a natural with a bat in his hands. At 5-foot-11 and 170 pounds, he was no giant, but when he swung his lumber the ball always seemed to land where he wanted it to go.

Playing just 81 games as a rookie in 1915, it took half a season for Sisler to master the big-league game. After hitting .285 during that apprenticeship, he batted over .300 for nine years in a row on his way to a lifetime .340 average. During that time he also batted over .400 twice, capturing two batting titles.

He was the rare player to top .400 more than once, hitting .407 in 1920, and hitting a stupendous .420 in 1922, one of the highest averages ever compiled. Most players cannot even put together an on-base percentage of .420. It probably seemed as if Sisler never made an out in 1922.

"There never was a greater player than George Sisler in 1922," declared Branch Rickey, the Hall of Fame executive who was spellbound by Sisler's performance that season.[1]

He may have been aging, but the Braves didn't have to worry about Sisler doing his job. The team brought in a new manager of some repute to correct some serious problems, and Bill McKechnie set out to build a pennant winner.

The one-time third baseman led the Pittsburgh Pirates to a World Series crown in 1925, and the Cincinnati Reds to the Series title in 1940. That made McKechnie the first manager to take two teams to the pinnacle of the sport. The Braves opportunity came along in between and Boston did not win a Series title with McKechnie in the dugout. He wanted to think they were improving, but he got the chance to move to Cincinnati for more money and with more of an investment philosophy for the future, since Giles gave him carte blanche to lift the Reds where they needed to go.

McKechnie, nicknamed "Deacon," won 1,872 career games as a manager. The Braves were not particularly good under McKechnie, but they overachieved by threatening the first division. Not so in 1935, though that year Boston was a landing spot for Babe Ruth at the tail end of his career.

But 1930 was McKechnie's first season in Boston when everything was fresh and seemed rosy, the way it is in spring when flowers bloom and everyone forgets those flowers won't last forever. Boston owner, Emil "Judge" Fuchs, who invented ladies day to woo women to the ballpark for games, did not make promises about the roster brimming with talent. McKechnie mixed and matched, and definitely had some respectable hitters to call upon in 1930.

One was the irrepressible shortstop Rabbit Maranville, who was impish, clever, and a savvy player who seemed destined to compete forever. Then thirty-eight, the 5-foot-5, 155-pound Maranville barely averaged more than one home run per season for his 23 years in the game (ending at forty-three in 1935), but he did many other things well. In fact, at such an age Maranville still had it in him to play 142 games.

Playing upon the old comment about a fighter being the best pound-for-pound boxer regardless of weight class, a sportswriter once commented that Maranville was, pound-for-pound, the most notable jokester of them all. New York Yankees owner Jacob Ruppert said Maranville was the funniest man he ever knew.

Once, when managing the Cubs, Maranville passed through a train car and woke up all players who were sleeping by pouring ice water on them. Another time, when exiled from a game by Hall of Fame umpire Bill Klem, he stood outside the park, imitating a newsboy and shouting, "Extra! Extra! Read all about Maranville and that big baboon Klem!"[2]

Another time he played dead so convincingly during an intra-team wrestling match that his opponent rushed into the street to find a police officer to confess to manslaughter. In St. Louis, Maranville dove into a water fountain with all of his clothes on and when he surfaced displayed a goldfish in his teeth.

Once, Maranville had a minor disagreement with the great Jim Thorpe, who had taken time out from his gridiron and Olympic fame to play major-league baseball for the New York Giants. Thorpe was not going to banter with Maranville—he was much stronger and found it easier to extract revenge by hanging Maranville out the window of a sixteen-story hotel by his ankles than debating.

If Maranville showed fear, he did not let on, saying, "Let go, you big bum. You haven't got the guts to drop me."[3] Since Maranville lived to tell about it, apparently Thorpe chose to spare his life.

Maranville contributed 157 hits in 1930. Though it was clear he was slowing down somewhat, with 19 big-league seasons already under his belt, he was sure McKechnie was going to make the Braves a success all over again so many years after they earned that come-from-behind pennant and World Series, and he wanted to be part of it. The Braves never did get rid of him; he spent the last five-plus years of his career with them, after playing his first game for Boston in 1912.

A sparkplug of a player, Maranville was the heart of the 1914 Braves championship team, and was elected to the Hall of Fame in 1954, nineteen years after his playing career had ended. Maranville received the nickname "Rabbit" when just a child, having it bestowed by another kid because he was always jumpy and hopping around.

Late in his career, although still several years from the end, Maranville wrote a package of stories for the *American Legion Monthly* magazine about his experiences in baseball and reflected on the changes he saw between the Deadball Era and the 1920s home-run era.

"In those days," Maranville said of when he started playing in 1912, "two or three runs put a game on ice. Those were the days when earned run averages were low. Anybody who doesn't waste a ball now and then is just telling the good hitters to lay into it, and even a fairly bad ball nowadays is liable to go sailing into the next county."[4] From 1914 through 1919, MLB teams averaged less than four runs scored per game.

In another piece, Maranville stressed that one of the most important things keeping him in the game for 23 years was an ability to maintain his enthusiasm about the sport. And others who acquire longevity did as well.

"I've seen Babe Ruth stop at the roadside on his way to a park to watch kids play in the street," Maranville said. "I've seen him when he was so tired he could hardly lift his head when he still had enthusiasm enough for baseball to show a small boy how to swing a bat. I was his roommate when he was with the Braves and I've seen him sit down in the morning to sign a thousand or more cards or trinkets that kids sent him to autograph.[5]

Maybe the same spirit kept catcher Al Spohrer going, too, even though he had one millionth of the name recognition of Babe Ruth. In 112 games in 1930, Spohrer batted .317. No doubt, he had more fun in 1930 than he did in his other seven big-league seasons. He was one of the poster boys for 1930, his finest hitting year by far. While he batted .272 in 1929, his career average was .259. For one year, though, it seems a sure thing Al Spohrer felt like royalty.

Outfielder Lance Richbourg hit .304 that season but, unlike Spohrer, was used to such results. The little-known eight-year player batted .308 lifetime and topped .300 four times, something he could proudly tell his kids—including all about that 1928 season, when he smacked the ball at a .337 clip. Never mind his own children, Walton High School in DeFuniak Springs, where he hailed from, was so proud of Richbourg that school officials changed the team mascot's name to Braves simply because he played for that club.

Not even George Sisler gave the fans the thrills generated by a newcomer to the team and league, though. Outfielder Wally Berger was the man from nowhere whose name became synonymous with the home run in 1930.

Berger was born in Chicago and was a twenty-four-year-old rookie when he arrived at spring training. Not only did he bat .310 with 119 RBIs, but one of his other statistics captured the attention of the masses. He blasted 38 home runs, a mark that remained a rookie record for fifty-seven years. This was precisely the type of hitting mark one expected to emerge from the 1930 season.

Berger became an instant sports celebrity and established a reputation that remained for his lifetime. It took until 1956 for Frank Robinson of the Reds to tie Berger's record, and until 1987 for Mark McGwire to eclipse it with 49 for the Oakland Athletics.

"I didn't know it was going to take so long," Berger said when McGwire took over.[6]

The Braves sputtered along in 1930, but Berger created excitement. Rookies were not supposed to be so precocious. In later years, Berger admitted he was fortunate to come along during a season when hitters had the upper hand, even using the word "juiced" to explain the extra pep balls seemed to have when they flew off the bat. But Berger felt the dimensions of Braves Field did not favor him, nor did the local winds. "An east wind often blew in off the Atlantic and pulled a lot of my drives foul at Braves Field because I hit them so high. As far as I'm concerned, it was the biggest and toughest park to hit in."[7]

By 1930, it was apparent that, for teams to succeed, they had to somewhat rely on the home run as part of their offensive repertoire. Ruth and the New York Yankees had shown that. Jimmie Foxx with the Philadelphia A's also demonstrated the need for power. Yet for their above-average batting averages, the players in the Braves everyday lineup seemed to have little aptitude for slugging.

While Berger powdered his mighty 38 home runs, the rest of the team hit a combined 28 homers. No one else was in double figures. The next highest total came from Buster Chatham, with five. In fact, Berger accounted for 58 percent of his team's homers, a percentage no player has come close to since. It was almost bizarre. Berger should have given home-run-hitting lessons at the batting cage.

Berger spent 11 seasons in the majors, but his auspicious start did not herald a superstar career, though a solid one. In 1935, Berger hit 34 homers with 130 RBIs, which both led the National League. He was selected to four All-Star teams.

As an analyst of power hitters, Berger gave Ruth the nod as the best. The men were briefly teammates with the Braves, and Ruth was so close to retirement he no longer seemed like the same guy. Berger still admired him, though.

"His legs were gone when he came to us," Berger said. "But in his day, he used to hit even the balls he was fooled on so high that it was like catching a meteor. He found nothing difficult about hitting a pitched ball."[8]

Like most teams, the Braves had sufficient hitting and deficient pitching. For every .300 hitter there was someone with a 4.00-plus or 5.00-plus earned-run average. That was far from an equal trade. The pitchers were the losers, both figuratively and literally. Winning records were at a premium. The thrower who produced the most pleasant surprise was Tom Zachary.

Zachary, a lefty who went 186–191 in a 19-year career, was 1–1 with the Yankees before being cut loose and joining Boston. From there he went 11–5—by far the best mark on the team—though he still had an unhappy 4.58 ERA. Zachary is best remembered as the pitcher who served up Babe Ruth's record 60th home run, on September 30, 1927.

Fred Frankhouse, who had some better and more distinguished winning years later in his career on the way to a 106–97 record, was another pitcher on the club with a winning record, at 7–6. Bill Sherdel, also a somewhat successful journeyman with a lifetime 165–146 mark (including a 21-win season in 1928) was 6–5 that season.

The rest of the hurling gang: Socks Seibold (15–16), Bob Smith (10–14), Ben Cantell (9–15), Ed Brandt (4–11), Bruce Cunningham (5–6), Ken Jones (0–1), and Burleigh Grimes, the former Dodgers star, at 3–6. Johnny Cooney and Bob Brown went 0–0. Possibly those were great escapes since Cooney's ERA was 18.00 and Brown's 10.50.

Fans were surely most excited over the explosiveness displayed by Berger, who gave them something to talk about throughout the season. But the discerning, knowledgeable fan must have relished the sight of Sisler at bat. They may not have seen it coming, but 1930 was the end for him; the final season of his marvelous career.

Despite his advanced age, and his most prestigious seasons already in the books, Boston Braves fans were lucky enough to watch Sisler every day for almost three complete seasons. His .309 for 1930 was not a bad way to go out, but the two preceding seasons offered fuller samples of his great capabilities, with his hitting .340 and .326, respectively. The man was just always a gifted hitter. Only Sisler and Ty Cobb twice hit over .400 in the twentieth century. Of course, that spoiled some fans who then figured they could do it any time they wanted.

One season some friends predicted Sisler would bat .400 again, but if he did not outright scoff, he did say, "Whoa."

"Some ambitious friends hint of a possible .400 batting season," Sisler said in 1929. "I appreciate their good opinion, but I cannot agree with their prophecy. A .400 batting season is rare in any batter's career. In order to hit .400 everything must go exactly your way from the start to finish of the season. There can be no important slumps anywhere. Why shouldn't I expect to hit .400 again in what remains to me of my Major League career? I have already crossed that mark twice. Is that not enough? This late in the game I can hardly expect to do so."[9]

In 1920, Sisler smacked 257 hits. In 1922, when Sisler batted an absurd .422, he recorded a 41-game hitting streak. In 1925, he became the first baseball player with his picture featured on the cover of *Time* magazine.

"Except when I cut loose at the ball, I always try to place my hits," Sisler said. "At the plate you must stand in such a way that you can hit to either right or left field with equal ease."[10]

Sisler did place those hits, more than 2,800 of them, with equal ease.

18

THE PITTSBURGH PIRATES

IT WAS IMPOSSIBLE not to love the dual nicknames of brothers Paul Waner and Lloyd Waner, "Big Poison" and "Little Poison." Any way you looked at it, as a joke, as a catchy phrase, even if, as some said those were corruptions of "Big Person" and "Little Person" by a Dodgers fan with a Brooklyn accent, the bats told quite a story.

Then you had Harold Traynor, who was much better known by his nickname "Pie." So the Waners could poison the enemy pitching and then you got a pie thrown in your face when you confronted the other stud in the Pittsburgh Pirates batting order.

In 1930, the trio showed the rest of the National League why they all became Hall of Famers. Men who wielded big sticks and feared no pitched balls, Waner, Waner, and Traynor (which could have made for a catchy automobile bumper sticker if people were dreaming them up in that decade) were at the forefront of an offense that batted .303.

That season teams had to outscore the Pirates to beat them, though just enough did so to keep Pittsburgh from being a major factor in the pennant race. The Pirates finished 80–74, respectable, but not good enough to provoke too much excitement at Forbes Field. Indeed, the fans never truly got the message that some of the finest batting they would ever see could be viewed for 72 home games.

It was likely the discerning Pirates fan also recognized the team possessed a pitching staff roughly the equivalent of a Class AAA team, so no matter how hard the locals hit the ball, they were not going to score sufficient runs.

Same old story of 1930, a surfeit of hitting, a shortage of pitching. Attendance for the season in Pittsburgh was 357,795, optimists, but not enough to rank higher than seventh out of eight teams.

In those days, Pittsburgh and Western Pennsylvania lived and died based on anthracite and bituminous coal mining. The central city was surrounded by one-industry towns and they felt the brunt of the earliest days of the Great Depression. Worse, the coal industry had delved into a slump by the late 1920s, so ominous storm clouds were massing even before the stock market crash took down so much investment.

Jewel Ens was the man handed the reins and tasked with sorting out a marvelous hitting lineup while seeking to coax just enough quality hurling out of a staff that not long before had given Pittsburgh National League pennant winners in 1925 and 1927. Pittsburgh won the World Series in '25, a team Ens helped as a player and a coach. A .290 hitter lifetime, Ens played for, coached, and managed the Pirates.

When the Pirates faltered under Donie Bush after their earlier 1920s success, Ens was right there on the bench, someone who appealed to owner Barney Dreyfuss as a fresh voice.

Ens was installed as Pittsburgh manager at thirty-nine in 1929 with 35 games left in the season. The Pirates won 21 of them to place second.

"This is the chance that I have been looking for," Dreyfuss said when he promoted Ens. "I have been watching Ens for a couple of years with the idea that some day when the chance bobbed up, I would make him the manager. I am not putting him in the job to wind up the year. He is the manager."[1]

Neither Dreyfuss nor Ens realized if Ens was going to produce another winner for Pittsburgh he was going to need a magic formula to manufacture pitchers.

The Pirates were well-enough stocked with some arms to make a go of it on many days of the week, but it was a thin front line of starters backed by players who should not have been collecting big-league salaries. The staff earned run average was 5.24, bad enough to negate much of the hurricane-force scoring velocity on offense.

The statistics don't lie, so merely by perusing the list of the handful of the least active Pirates pitchers of the season, it is easy enough to read Ens's mind. The front office was willing to try anybody, thus accounting for five different guys whose records were 0–0 in limited viewing. That handful of hurlers appeared in 11 games combined. If anyone felt they showed potential to help, they would have been called on more frequently.

There were others thrown into some innings whose performance was similar. Percy Jones finished 0-1 in nine appearances and Ralph Erickson finished 1–0. The mark would be something Erickson could forever point to since it was his lifetime record. Alas for him, accompanying the 1-0 record in baseball annals was another statistic reading 7.07, his 1930 earned-run average. Ericson's lifetime ERA was 8.40.

In 1930, Jesse Petty went 1–6, 8.27; Leon Chagnon went 0–3, 6.00. Glenn Spencer was 8–9, but with a 5.40 ERA, and Heine Meine went 6–8 with a 6.14. There was no escaping the hard evidence. When Pittsburgh hurlers were handed the ball by Ens, the best advice for their fielders was to get out of the way.

Right-hander Erv Brame got his major-league opportunity late, in 1928 at twenty-six, and whether it was through smoke and mirrors or not, compiled some worthy won-lost records while never compiling a favorable earned-run average. The best season of his five-year major-league career was 1930 when he finished a sterling 17–8. He also went 16–11 in 1929. But his earned-run average was still a shaky 4.70 in 1930 and 4.76 lifetime despite a contradictory 52–37 record and career .584 winning percentage.

Actually, Brame did have a secret answer to the question of "How did he do it?" He was a pitcher who could hit the hell out of the ball, amassing a lifetime average of .306 in the majors. In 1930 alone, Brame batted .353, propelling him towards Waner territory. Now that's helping yourself in a pinch.

Southpaw Larry French was just twenty-two in 1930, but was a regular member of the rotation as he sought to establish himself in the big leagues. French, born in Visalia, California in 1907, was probably greatly encouraged by what he accomplished that season, perhaps believing he was starting a Hall of Fame career.

After gaining a look-see from the Pirates in 1929 while going 7–5, French showed enough promise to become a regular starter. As inexperienced as he was, he was probably initially ignorant of how weird the new season was setting up to be. French was more likely just happy to be there.

French finished 17–18 for Pittsburgh in 1930. The 18 defeats led the National League, a little bit surprising given how many pitchers suffered so egregiously that season. Year after year he turned in solid seasons, accumulating victories, though he never quite had that one great big season to win him general acclaim.

French three times won 18 games and five other times won at least 15 times in a year. He was selected for the 1940 All-Star Game. Those solid win seasons included his final big-league year of 1942 when he totaled a 15–4 record at thirty-four for the Brooklyn Dodgers. French had his finest earned run average, 1.83 that year, as well. After coping with some throwing problems stemming from a broken and dislocated thumb he kept quiet, French had developed a knuckleball and that helped him late in his career. French could have pitched on, but the United States entered World War II and French joined the Navy.

Managers appreciated French's work ethic. When it was his turn, he took the ball, throwing 274 2/3 innings in 1930, 275 2/3 the next year, 274 1/3 in 1932, and a career-high 291 1/3 in 1933.

"I don't have a lot more stuff than I had in the minors," French said during the 1930 season, "but I have learned how to use it better. The difference between a great pitcher and a poor pitcher is just about one line drive a game. If they catch it for you, you're a great pitcher."[2]

He didn't strike out many, and opposing batters got wood on the ball often. For three consecutive years, beginning in 1930, French probably gave his managers ulcers for allowing first 325 hits and then 301 and 301. The knuckler may have baffled, but his velocity was low, so French still permitted more than the average share of hits.

It may be throwing slower stuff to the plate cost French in reputation because he didn't blow hitters away. But he didn't walk many, either.

"He was a better pitcher than a lot of people thought he was," said Phil Cavarretta, who was a teammate with the Chicago Cubs, "because he didn't throw hard. He had a real good screwball, a pretty good curve. He would never beat himself. You had to beat him. So many hitters went up and faced him and would say, 'Jesus, with that garbage you're throwing, how the hell can you get anybody out?'"[3] Much the same was often said about knuckleball artists over the decades.

It was Leo Durocher who came to appreciate just how masterful French could be with his knuckler late in his career.

"This fellow is truly a great pitcher," Durocher said in 1942. "The knuckleball he developed this season has increased his effectiveness tremendously."[4]

French did not envision retiring from baseball after the 1942 season. When he entered the Navy, he was stationed at Brooklyn Naval Yard and thought he would be able to pitch part-time for the Dodgers in 1943. He owned a 197–171 pitching mark and wanted to collect three more wins. Only when French asked the Navy for permission to pitch part-time, the request was turned down.

Instead of being able to obtain those few opportunities to chase 200 wins, the Navy became French's second career. Not only did he serve during wartime, French remained in the Navy for 27 years, rising to the rank of captain, earning the Legion of Merit, and also serving aboard ships in the Korean War.

Blame the Pacific Coast League and lack of vision by scouts, but it is possible Ray Kremer might have been a Hall of Famer if someone had cared more when he was younger.

The mainstay of the Pirates' 1930 staff, there is even a dichotomy within Kremer's season. The same reliable hurler who finished 20–12, extraordinary given the year, leading the National League in triumphs, with 38 games started and 276 innings pitched, also posted a frustrating 5.02 earned run average and gave up an irritating league-leading 366 hits. Somehow, it seemed, Kremer was the good, the bad and the ugly personified within the same body.

During a 10-year career, Kremer recorded 143 wins, including two no-hitters. He also went 20–6 in 1926 and led the National League in earned run average twice, with 2.61 and 2.47 marks. In other seasons, Kremer won 18, 17, 19, and 18 games. Yet Kremer was overlooked much of his prime. After failing a tryout with the New York Giants in 1916 because of an onslaught of debilitating rheumatism, Kremer found employment in the Pacific Coast League.

Kremer excelled, but couldn't get noticed, or at least taken seriously. He threw roughly the equivalent of 10 seasons worth of innings (more than 2,100, mostly for the Oakland Oaks) before he broke in with the Pirates in 1924.

Winning 25 games and hurling 357 innings for Oakland finally got Kremer some attention and a big-league contract. "I thought I was doomed to stay in the minors forever," Kremer said. "I won and won. Scouts came and went."[5]

Kremer condensed his big-league greatness into a smaller window, but by winning twice when it mattered most he helped the Pirates capture the 1925 World Series and helped lift Pittsburgh to a second pennant in the 1920s. He spent his entire major-league career with the Pirates. Since he got such a late start, and so much of his history was spent in the minors, Kremer had to compensate as his fastball diminished and he added more science to his approach.

"I have a clearer understanding how to handle opposing batters," Kremer said as he pitched well into thirties, "a confidence in what I can do, and recognition of the limits of my ability."[6]

Besides the Big Three of Paul Waner, Lloyd Waner, and Pie Traynor waving heavy lumber, manager Ens and his always-hopeful pitching staff were aided by other dangerous bats in 1930, even if the stick-holders were not nearly as notorious.

Second baseman George Grantham batted .324 with 18 home runs and 99 runs batted in during the 1930 season and he was also a lifetime .302 hitter over 13 seasons. He was no Rogers Hornsby, but seven other times Grantham hit over .300 during his career. He played in two World Series and stole as many as 43 bases in one season.

Outfielder Adam Comorosky batted .313 and also slammed a league-leading 23 triples in 1930 and knocked in 119 runs—his best season. Along with the Waners he gave Pittsburgh an all .300-hitting outfield. He had introduced himself to Pittsburgh fans in 1929 by batting .321. However, those two seasons turned out to be the only ones in his 10-year career Comorosky hit .300.

Not that he would ever have complained. A native of Swoyersville, Pennsylvania, Comorosky went to work in coal mines at age twelve. Playing baseball must have seemed to be a breeze after that.

Six of the eight starters topped .300 for the Pirates in 1930, including another player edging towards stardom. Shortstop Dick Bartell was just twenty-two and at the front end of an 18-year, big-league career that saw him called "Rowdy Richard."

Bartell, born in Chicago in 1907, made a cameo debut with the Pirates in 1927, appearing in one game as a nineteen-year-old. By 1930, the player who really would make more of an impact as a fielder and leader than hitter, was into his third season as a .300-plus hitter.

Despite his long career and .284 lifetime average, 1930 was actually Bartell's finest season at the plate, including 75 runs batted in. Bartell scratched out five .300 years, but he was mostly known for scratching out every hit possible, playing hungry, and trying to squeeze out every advantage on the field. Bartell was twice selected to All-Star teams.

Bartell once called being a rookie in spring training the lowest form of life. He was eager to exempt himself from that status and did so quickly with the Pirates, playing in 77 games as a twenty-year-old in 1928 and then becoming the Pirates' starting shortstop.

"The Pirates were no bums," Bartell said.[7]

Bartell went into the last two seasons of the 1920s barely old enough to vote or drink (though it was Prohibition), but more than anything anxious to prove himself as a big-league ballplayer who mattered.

"Once I got in the lineup, nothing could get me out of there," Bartell said. "I knew there was somebody else waiting to take my job and I didn't want to give them the chance. That was my attitude for the next eighteen years. They had to carry me off the field."[8]

Although things started well for Bartell, he ended up feuding with owner Barney Dreyfuss over money. But that was not until after his .320 average of 1930.

"But 1930 was the year it seemed almost every hitter had a good year," Bartell said. "It wasn't just the lively ball because the ball changed several times in its rabbit qualities during my playing days. It's probably just as lively today. And it certainly wasn't poor pitching. No, I think it was just one of those bumper crops of hitters the likes of which we haven't seen since. We might argue that all night."[9]

Bartell was one of those hitters and he stuck up for his own kind. But labeling the fluke of 1930 attributable to just too many good hitters was being overly kind. There was also very much a collection of "poor pitching."

Actually, an asterisk is needed for the Pirates' trio of batsmen who hit so high they might all have been in the top ten in average.

Lloyd Waner batted .362, but didn't qualify for the batting crown. He played in just 68 games with 274 plate appearances.

Older brother Paul, who was more established, hit .368, and incomparable third baseman Pie Traynor hit .366. That is a murderers' row of a sorts, though not of home-run hitters.

The Waner brothers made for an intriguing pair. Paul was twenty-seven in 1930 and Lloyd was twenty-four. It was common knowledge Paul was an avid imbiber of alcohol, legal or not, and sometimes carried a flask in his uniform pants pocket that supposedly affected how he slid into second base. Lloyd was a milk drinker, never touching booze.

The dangerous duo of hitters came from the same farm background in Harrah, Oklahoma. Oklahoma was a still a territory, not yet a state, when Paul was born in 1903. The spread was a substantial 400 acres, but his experience at East Central State Teachers College, where he excelled, convinced him he could become a professional player. Originally, he thought of being a pitcher since he went 23–4 with a 1.70 earned run average. It turned out he was at least as good a hitter.

His route took Waner through the Pacific Coast League to the San Francisco Seals. In three seasons by the Bay, Waner batted .369. .356, and .401. San Francisco sold him and one other player to the Pirates for $100,000.

Paul broke in with the Pirates in 1926 and played his first 15 seasons with Pittsburgh. A brilliant practitioner of hitting balls to gaps in the outfield, Paul Waner won three National League batting titles, collected 200 or more hits in a season eight times, and finished with a .333 lifetime average, all of which helped carry him into the National Baseball Hall of Fame.

It only took until 1927, Waner's second season, for the NL to recognize how potent a player he was. That year he hit .380 to win the batting crown, stroked 237 hits, knocked in 131 runs, and as a bonus led the league with 18 triples. He was voted Most Valuable Player of the National League.

He may have been best known as "Big Poison" (there was no doubt he was that to opposing pitchers), but Paul Waner was not a big person. He was 5-foot-8 and weighed 153 pounds, so he was an unlikely candidate to knock too many balls into the next county. He accumulated 113 home runs in 20 seasons of play, though, so Waner was not all bunting, with a high of 15 in 1929. His line drives could also bring runners home. For his career, Waner drove in 1,309 runs, and twice he topped 100 in a season.

In 1932, Waner clubbed 62 doubles, a mark hardly ever approached in the modern game, making sure he had a nice mix of hits among his 215. He worked in 10 triples, too. The combination of a variety of hits contributed to Waner totaling one of the best on-base percentages, too, each year.

Waner was twenty-seven in 1930, and his showing that season fit right in with the rest of that stretch when he was doing everything well on the diamond. He batted .368, which he topped three other times, hit 18 triples and accumulated 217 hits. Surrounded by other reliable hitters, Waner reached base often enough to score 117 runs, as well.

Paul Waner was readily known throughout the sport as one of the finest active hitters and sportswriters scurried his way asking how he accomplished what he did. Sometimes it was like bees drawn to honey, those thirsting for an elixir figuring he could provide the secret of life itself.

"What's the secret of hitting, Paul?" the esteemed syndicated columnist Grantland Rice once asked Waner. "Just what I'm doing now," Waner responded somewhat enigmatically as he sat with the scribe in the dugout. Pause. "I mean relaxing. You have to be relaxed before you can hit. You know how it is in golf because you play so much of it. Well, I play golf too—and the same thing goes for both sports. When a fellow is tense and tight, he can't do any good for himself—at the plate, on the tee or the green.

"Here's the way it works. When you can relax at the plate, you have a terrific advantage. Your stance is easy, your arm and shoulder muscles are loose and free, and your eye is clear and you can time your swings."[10]

More than once Waner expounded in such straightforward terms, as if anyone who could understand his thought process could hit like Paul.

"It is simply doing the right thing in a perfectly natural and unconscious way," Waner said another time. "To hit .350, you must hit the ball squarely eight times out of 10. When you are fouling balls off, you are not hitting them right. My first tip to the young batter with the very essential stroke is not to be too choosy. If a ball is close enough to the plate to be called a strike it is close enough to be a hit.

"Ty Cobb said that no pitcher ever should throw three consecutive balls over the corner of the plate. That may be true, but you never know when an umpire is going to draw a fine line. The good batter never guesses."[11]

Other players were great admirers of Waner's swing. Fellow Hall of Famer Heinie Manush, a contemporary, was one and he employed a popular boxing description, saying Paul Waner was "pound for pound" the greatest of hitters.

There were some oddities about Waner's meticulous hitting. It was known he was a drinker and it was once suggested if he ceased he might hit .400. Later, it was determined Waner was nearsighted and needed glasses. He was reluctant to make a change because he generally saw the ball in triplicate coming towards the plate, the ball in the middle appearing as large as a grapefruit to him, and the one he chose to swing at. Why tamper with success? Still, he did experiment with glasses as he approached his 3,000th career hit. He complained the glasses made the ball look smaller, not larger. In all, Waner collected 3,152 hits and batted over .300 14 times.

Maybe that vision story was true and maybe not. Waner, it seemed, enjoyed embellishing baseball tales. "If they're good stories, why bother to spoil them?" he said.[12]

The stories of Waner's hitting prowess did not need exaggerating and the first sentence of his obituary in *The Sporting News* included the phrase, "One of baseball's great batsmen." When Paul and brother Lloyd were at the height of their stardom, one frustrated National League pitcher said, "Every time I look up, a Waner is rounding second base."[13]

In mid-career, after it was apparent Waner had mastered the short game of hitting the ball where fielders chose not to stand, a sportswriter with a fanciful imagination asked him to picture the someday distant super hitter of the future, one who might bat .500.

Waner took up the discussion for sport. Yes, maybe such a tremendous player would appear one day. Waner, with his dimensions of about 5-foot-9 and 153 pounds, said the .500 hitter would not only be larger than him, but bigger than the 6-foot-1, 215-pound Babe Ruth.

"He'll be a big fellow," Waner said, "this guy who can bust 'em at .500 or better. Yeah, bigger than the Babe. He'll have to be because the main thing the .500 hitter will have will be the size and strength enough to murder the ball like it was never murdered before. Every time he connects the ball must do one of two things—knock infielders down or go out of the park." This mythical player would be thirty-five to forty years old, because "it takes a long time to learn how to hit."[14]

Some 83-plus years later, baseball is still waiting for its first .500 hitter, though many powerful hitters, who lifted weights, or unfortunately enhanced bodies with drugs, have come along and displayed the strength to knock the ball out of the park as often as Waner pictured. Really, though, over those decades since his speculation, the lost art of hitting is more of the precision Paul Waner brought to the game, a knack for placing the ball where no one can catch it.

Younger brother Lloyd was the same type of player. Lloyd Waner was the sibling for whom the old joke about talented brothers being back on the farm was virtually invented, as in, "If you think I'm good, you should see my brother." Lloyd was not better than Paul, but he was Hall of Fame good.

At 5-foot-9 and listed as 150, three pounds less than Paul, Lloyd was built very similarly. He was just twenty-one in 1927 when the duo helped the Pirates win an NL pennant. Rookie Lloyd burst into the game with a .355 average that season and led the league in runs scored with 133. The man belted 223 hits as a rookie. The best summation of Lloyd's introduction to the bigs was to say, "As advertised."

During his 18-season career, also spent mostly with the Pirates, Lloyd Waner batted .316 and struck out only once every 45 times up. In the 1930 season, even though he was slowed by injury, Lloyd was in his sixth straight season of batting over .300. Promising players wanted to attend summer camp in Harrah, Oklahoma in hopes they too, like the Waners, might emerge as magnificent major-league hitters.

The quiet Lloyd came off as a little less confident than his brother, but he never shrank from a pitched ball. No one ever called Lloyd arrogant, but no one ever felt he was not in command in the batter's box either.

The Lloyd of 1930 was his usual self for a time, a guy who kept hitting 'em where they ain't until he could no longer hit at all. He missed a chunk of that season because of an appendicitis attack and surgery. Imagine if both Waners and Traynor hit in the .360s for the entire campaign. Pittsburgh might well have finished better than six games above .500.

Lloyd did not expect to succeed Paul as a selectee to the Baseball Hall of Fame and when it happened in 1967 he was caught off guard. "It was the biggest thrill and the biggest surprise I ever had," Lloyd said.[15] He was only saddened that Paul had already passed away and could not attend the ceremony in Cooperstown, New York.

Lloyd joked that some of Paul's late hours viewed at 8 a.m. in hotel lobbies on the road followed the younger brother around accidentally in the retelling.

"We looked quite a bit alike," Lloyd said, "and these tales kept coming back to me. Finally, I asked him if he impersonated me. He said he didn't, but he did admit that if anyone called him Lloyd, he said hello."[16]

Although Lloyd's overall numbers were not as good as Paul's, some thought his long wait for Hall induction by the Veterans Committee was unfair. One outspoken supporter was Traynor.

"He should have been in the Hall of Fame a long time ago," Traynor said. "He's unjustly lived and played in Paul's shadow. Paul was a great ball player, but so was Lloyd."[17]

As was Traynor.

The No. 1 question that followed Harold Traynor around throughout his seventy-three years was how he got the nickname "Pie." Yes, it was because he liked pie. A lot. He used to show up at the grocery store so frequently in his hometown of Somerville, Massachusetts, asking for a different flavor of pie that the owner called him "Pie Face." The diminutive shrunk and stuck throughout the player's 17-year major-league career with the Pirates, and beyond, through his managing and broadcasting days.

For much of his career and life, Traynor was regarded as the best third baseman ever, although in recent decades there have been several excellent players considered challengers for that title.

Traynor earned his Hall of Fame stripes by batting .320 lifetime, knocking in at least 100 runs in a season seven times and by blossoming into an exceptional fielder of great range. Traynor retired in 1934 due to an arm injury and almost immediately took over as manager of the club for five seasons.

As solid a hitter as he was at all times, Traynor's top batting year was 1930 with that .366 mark. Only once did he drive in more than his 119 RBIs of that season, too. His on-base percentage of .423 was a career high also, all of this indicating that the established star hitter gained from the weakness of baseball's pitching that year as much as some otherwise non-descript players.

Traynor was elected to the National Baseball Hall of Fame in 1948 and because of his ongoing and close connection with Pittsburgh baseball, partially through his broadcasting career, Traynor remained in the limelight in that city. Periodically, fans and supporters honored him, once with an elaborate testimonial dinner in 1971, organized by the Pittsburgh Baseball Writers group. Somehow the meal planner missed the boat, choosing such items for inclusion as tropical fruit, tender tournedos of beef filets, rolls and butter, capped by a desert that included ice cream bombe and assorted cookies. But no pie! What an oversight.

Traynor was always heralded as a great player and a gentleman. He was also popular as a storyteller about the decades of baseball past. One thing Traynor was known for in certain circles, even if his public was not always aware, was how he casually switched bats. He often swiped bats belonging to other players instead of relying on his own.

"Any I could pick up that pleased my fancy," Traynor said of his bat choice of the moment. "I stole most of them. Sure. You know how the clubs lay out the bats in front of the dugouts. Well, I'd just stroll around and pick them up and try them. If I came across one I liked, I'd take it. I wouldn't exactly steal it. I'd tell the manager or somebody else on the club that I was taking it. Many a hit I'd make against a club with one of its own bats."[18]

Ironically, in 2017, a story surfaced from a twenty-four-year-old student browsing a Pittsburgh area Goodwill store who stumbled across an old baseball bat. It was a leftover, an item being sold as part of a group of things sold by the pound. Translated, the young man paid $2.22 for the bat.

It was said to be a Harold "Pie" Traynor model. A sports memorabilia expert checked it out and announced, "Pie Traynor used that at Forbes Field. At the end of the season, or the end of the game, or whatever, he gave it to somebody. He gifted it."[19]

The funniest aspect of this possible transit from Traynor's hands to the Pirates clubhouse to some fan's attic to the creative buyer's ownership is that perhaps Traynor never swung it at all. He may well have been busy employing a bat belonging to an opponent that game day, one stolen before the first pitch.

Traynor never learned to drive a car and often took very lengthy walks. Regardless of which bat he used he demonstrated familiarity with the wood, batting over .300 10 times and finishing with that eye-catching .320 average. He was definitely among the most admired and beloved Pirates for the decades he invested in the team, including twenty-two years behind the microphone.

Traynor broke in with the Pirates in 1920, just when baseball's Deadball Era was concluding and the lively ball era was ushered in with the home run. Later in life when he reflected on how the sport had changed, he found it easy to pinpoint and summarize.

"With the dead ball," Traynor said, "any time a team got the first man on base in any inning, it was standard procedure to bunt him down to a scoring position. Today, with the lively ball, and the home run, they hit away for the big inning. The eras of Ty Cobb and Babe Ruth present a study in contrast."[20]

19

THE BROOKLYN ROBINS/DODGERS

THE TEAM FROM Brooklyn representing the National League often seemed to have an identity crisis. One year they were called the Robins, another year the Superbas, and at other times they were known by the Dodgers—short for the Trolley Dodgers, a trait residents of that New York borough felt was needed when it was wise to be nimble. Of course, there were the times people referred to the baseball team as the Bridegrooms, too.

Sportswriters played a role in these varying nicknames for what technically was called the Brooklyn Base Ball Club. While Dodgers was ultimately settled upon, and the name has adhered to the franchise without fail since the team moved to Los Angeles in 1958 (where there are no trolleys), during the 1930 season one of the three major-league teams located within the confines of New York were most often called the Brooklyn Robins.

The robin may be a popular bird, but these Robins were so named as a tribute to beloved manager Wilbert Robinson, a generous salutation it can be said, especially since managers often wear out their welcomes and get fired. Rarely, though, do they take the team name with them.

Although 1930 was not to prove the Robins' year to win a pennant, for the most part it was a favorable season. Brooklyn finished with a solid 86–68 record, and attendance at Ebbets Field topped 1,097,000 fans, the second-best total in the NL.

It can safely be said Wilbert Robinson was still feeling the community love that summer. Born in 1864, the native of Boston had a respectable big-league career, hitting .273 spread over 17 seasons. On the field, Robinson was the catcher for the 1890s dynastic Baltimore Orioles, where some of his famed associates were Ned Hanlon, John J. McGraw, "Wee" Willie Keeler, and Hughie Jennings.

Fondly referred to as "Uncle Robbie," Robinson served as Brooklyn's manager from 1914 through 1931. He retired with a mark of 1,399–1,398, but his accomplishments got him voted into the Baseball Hall of Fame in 1945 as a manager.

Brooklyn suffered as many agonies as ecstasies with Robinson at the helm: to the good (capturing two pennants), to the questionable (somehow often coming close, but losing out). The club was viewed as an outfit that was often its own worst enemy, making ill-timed, costly mistakes, though the reputation seemed to exceed fact.

Babe Herman was a great hitter, but was often zinged for his poor baserunning. He was said to triple into a triple play, although that was myth. It was said Herman was blamed by an official scorer for being hit on the head by a fly ball he should have caught, which caromed over the fence for a ground-rule double—except that a substitute, Al Tyson, was the victim. Herman *was* hit on the shoulder by a fly ball that bounded safely away. These types of incidents led to the Robins of the era being called "The Daffiness Boys."

Presented as the all-time example of how the Robins could shoot themselves in the foot is the story of how they shot themselves in three feet during an August 15, 1926, game versus the Boston Braves. Brooklyn had the bases loaded in the seventh inning with Herman at the plate (he had to be involved somehow).

The NL Babe hit a screamer off the right-field wall in Ebbets Field. Hank DeBerry, in at catcher, scored easily from third base. Pitcher Dazzy Vance was on second, but did not run all out because he feared Herman's smack might be caught and he would be doubled off second.

Belatedly, Vance dashed around third base and ran for home plate. He saw the throw from the Braves sailing in, so he turned around and headed back to third. But Chick Fewster, who had been on first, believing the coast was clear, also ran to third. Herman belted the ball so hard he figured all he had to do was keep running and he would have a triple. He caught up to Fewster at third, meaning Vance, Fewster, and the optimistic Herman created a traffic jam there.

Vance and Fewster were tagged out, the fielding play for Boston going right field to second base to catcher to third to second. Officially, Herman doubled into a double play.

That news was established in Brooklyn lore by 1930. The Robins of that season, with a variety of such evidence having mounted against them over the years, were not in a position to complain about anything. While Dazzy Vance's record of 17–15 could not match American League star Lefty Grove, his earned-run average nearly did. Somehow, Vance compiled a 2.61 mark, one so good no one else in the National League was within hailing distance.

Since the Robins finished 18 games over .500, it can be said that every time Vance took the mound, he gave his team a chance to win. Unlike the staffs of the losing clubs, the Robins produced a true rarity that season. Not only did they feature someone as solid as Vance, but actually put together a whole pitching staff.

Members of the 1930 Brooklyn pitching group did not have to be ashamed for their efforts. Four of the regular starters in the rotation recorded winning records, and the fifth finished at .500. Also, two backups had winning marks, too. This seems like a typographical error given the season, but it was as if that year the Robins were put on earth to make up for the Phillies.

Vance was thirty-nine that year, hanging on and making up for his late start. Despite several tryouts, Vance never got a team to take him seriously—until 1922. He was thirty-one before he won his first big-league game, a frustratingly long journey to recognition and the top.

He was so spectacular in 1924, the league was agog. The man nobody wanted finished 28–6 with a 2.16 ERA, pitched 30 complete games as part of his 308 1/3 innings, with 262 strikeouts—all but the innings leading all of baseball. Vance was voted the NL's Most Valuable Player, an exceptional rarity for a pitcher. He deserved every accolade he received after his plod through the minors.

As early as 1915, Vance got a chance with both the Pittsburgh Pirates and New York Yankees, going 0–1 and 0–3, respectively. Three years later, the Yankees tossed him into two more games, totaling 2 1/3 innings. Four more long years passed before Vance got his breakthrough opportunity with the Robins.

Vance was a late comer to baseball in more ways than one. His upbringing was so rural, he never saw a game until well into his teens when he was starting to pitch in them. He said he and his brother Fred invented their own way of participating. "We built a backstop out of chicken wire and marked off the foul lines," Vance said. "We never went out to play without taking a needle and thread along to sew up the ball."[1] There were no other boys in their neighborhood to help flesh out teams, though.

Just about every team had a shot at Vance, but he failed to stick because the right arm that would prove so valuable later let him down repeatedly; when the opportunity arose, he always seemed to come down with a sore arm. For a time, Vance was the king of rubdowns, a player brimming with potential who could never stay healthy long enough to earn the trust of a ballclub.

Occasionally, he gave people reason to remember him. Based on an early tryout, Hall of Fame shortstop Honus Wagner referred to Vance as "a nervy big chap for a pitching experiment."[2] He also recalled being picked off base by the same fellow, an achievement given that Wagner stole 723 bases for his career.

Generally, Vance was a fun-loving guy and acquired the nickname "Dazzy" early in life, replacing his birth name of Charles Arthur. Once in a while, fooling around, he reversed the two names. And for a time, goofing around even more, Vance told people his real name was Clarence.

Born in Iowa, raised in Nebraska, for years Vance maintained his belief in the power of his arm—when it was healthy—trying to prove himself in minor-league stops in cities all over the United States.

He won 26 games for two teams combined in the minors in 1914, but mostly had a mixed record trying to get well. It was not until 1921, when Vance won 21 games for the New Orleans Pelicans in the Southern League, did Brooklyn commit to him. He ended up winning 133 games in the minors during his apprenticeship.

Vance realized how peculiar his journey was when he arrived with the Robins at age thirty-one. He felt as if he knew everyone in baseball because he had been everywhere. "I'll bet a hundred bucks that if I dropped in on every minor league club in the country—and I wouldn't care how small the league was—I would know at least three men on every one of them," he said.[3]

Pretty soon, he knew everyone on the Robins after winning 18 games as a rookie.

In 1930, Vance was the stalwart. He threw 258 2/3 innings, appeared in 35 games, and hurled 20 complete games. Once Robinson gave him the ball, Vance was his man—win, lose, or draw. He also helped himself by striking out 173 batters. One thing about 1930: keeping runners off the bases was to a pitcher's advantage. So many regulars hit so well they were bound to bring them around to score.

That happened to be one season Vance did not lead the NL in strikeouts. Previously, he led the circuit seven times in a row, from 1922 through 1928, with a high of 262 in 1924. The league could not catch up to Vance's fastball.

Vance's mere presence elevated the Robins. Many years the lonely Vance had only a minimum number of helpful throwers keeping him company. The exception was his longtime partner, Burleigh Grimes, the last of the legal spitballers. But Grimes was gone by 1930, finishing off his long, Hall of Fame career elsewhere.

Robinson once evaluated baseball in such an analytical way he saw how a team could win a pennant when it was not a juggernaut. "Give me three fellows that can pitch that ball and four that can hit it and I'll win the pennant," he said.[4]

Unlike several other managers during the 1930 season, Robinson actually had the arms besides Vance. Ray Phelps finished 14–7. Dolf Luque, thirty-nine, went 14–8. Jumbo Elliott was 10–7. Ray Moss's record was 9–6. Watty Clark went 13–13. Sloppy Thurston was 6–4. Except for Vance's superlative ERA, however, only Thurston, at 3.40, was likely to surrender fewer runs in an outing than his teammates could score.

Luque had been around since 1914, and in a 20-year career the right-hander from Cuba won 194 games. His lifetime ERA was a solid 3.24. He recorded some seriously memorable moments, winning a major-league–leading 27 games in 1923 for the Cincinnati Reds, as well as a league-best 1.93 ERA. Luque led the NL in ERA one other year, as well (1925, 2.63). He also lost 23 games one season (1922).

A native of Havana, Luque was the first Latino pitcher to make a mark in the majors, and was enshrined in the Cuban, Cincinnati Reds, and Mexican Baseball Halls of Fame. Luque won 106 games in Cuba. He was a major-league coach and a Mexican League manager who was known for a fiery temper, at least once going into the stands to punch a fan harassing him.

Although there were numerous other Latino stars worthy of major-league affiliations, many in the first half of the twentieth century—such as Martin Dihigo, Jose Mendez, and Cristobal Torriente—were considered too dark-skinned for a roster spot. Luque was lighter skinned and had that advantage against prejudice.

Most of Luque's best years were with the Reds, and his 1930 season was his true last hurrah before picking off some final wins with the Giants.

Phelps was a twenty-six-year-old rookie who gave Robinson the best season of his five-year career in 1930. Watty Clark had a workmanlike 12-year career with 111 total victories, and a 1932 season highlighted by 20 triumphs for Brooklyn.

Although he had a career losing record, Elliott led the National League in wins in 1931 with 19 while appearing in a league-high 52 games. He just never approached the mark again.

Righty "Sloppy" Thurston, of the ill-conceived nickname that was not designed to win over girls, actually was teased by teammates with the moniker because he took such good care of himself to look presentable.

Thurston gave Robinson a good half-season, but in 1924, when hurling for the Chicago White Sox, won 20 games and led the American League in complete games with 28. Also, in his debut game, coming in for the St. Louis Browns in relief, he struck out the first three batters he faced on nine pitches. Lifetime, Thurston, born Hollis John, was barely more than a .500 pitcher (89–86), but was helpful to Brooklyn in 1930.

Those were Robinson's arms. It can be argued that, especially during an erratic season when good arms were at a premium, he fulfilled his basic requirement of having enough pitching at his disposal to win a pennant. It was borderline, at least, and the Robins did stay in contention throughout the summer.

When Robinson placed his takeout order for hitters, he may not have expected room service would really take care of him with sufficient batting, yet the Robins as a team batted .304—you can't ask for much more. Brooklyn had a mix of reliable swingers who, much like some strangers that recorded special achievements on other clubs, also pulled close to their finest statistical years out of hats like so many magicians.

Of the eight regulars, five topped .300, two others were in the .290s, and just one player hit as low as .278. There were also bench guys chipping in. The Robins were in the hunt just about all season, and at one point posted an 11-game winning streak, and spent 75 days in first place. Vance's big shoulders were always in the forefront in big games, and the big bats seemingly gave him a chance to win every start. The main problem Brooklyn seemed to have was not scoring runs when Vance pitched.

A rookie at twenty-eight, first baseman Del Bissonette had a schizophrenic career. He was all-world in 1930, batting .336 with 16 home runs and 113 RBIs, but played just five big-league seasons.

He was ruined by back-to-back injuries and illness, forcing him off the field at age thirty-three despite a lifetime .305 average.

Shortstop Glenn Wright eked out 11 seasons with a solid .294 career average, and gave Brooklyn considerable aid at the plate in 1930, hitting .321 with 22 home runs and 126 runs knocked in. It was his best all-around season. When starting out with the Pittsburgh Pirates in the 1920s, Wright impressed more with his fielding, collecting a record 601 assists, a mark that stood for fifty-six years.

Wright played in two World Series with Pittsburgh, but a shoulder injury in 1929 affected his long-term play at short. Still, Wright's fielding exploits included completing one of the rare unassisted triple plays in history. Wright pulled off his gem against the St. Louis Cardinals on May 7, 1925, and the play featured wiping Rogers Hornsby, Jim Bottomley, and Jimmy Cooney off the bases in the ninth inning.

"That was one of the easiest plays I ever made," Wright said of the triple play. "I couldn't help it."[5] By that he meant the ball came right to him and he didn't have far to run to polish off the other runners.

Bottomley was at the plate and hit a liner to Wright at short, who made the catch. Wright slid over to second base to catch Cooney off the bag. And Hornsby was running full blast towards second, so he was an easy out as well.

"We were in the dugout before the fans realized they had seen an unassisted triple play," Wright said.[6]

Those who saw the young Wright believed he was a phenom. He had forced Pittsburgh manager Bill McKechnie to move future Hall of Famer Rabbit Maranville from short to second base. However, Wright incurred so many physical ailments it was remarkable he manufactured his greatest hitting season in 1930.

Outfielder Johnny Frederick, who played 142 games in 1930, was another of those come-out-of-nowhere stars of the moment for Brooklyn that season. He batted .334 with 17 home runs and 76 RBIs as a player who previously had one year of big-league experience.

Of course, after his 1929 season, Brooklyn thought it had a superstar. Frederick broke in batting .328 with 24 home runs and 75 RBIs, to go along with 52 doubles. No wonder Frederick was penciled into the starting lineup the next season.

Frederick never batted as high again as in those first two seasons, but had a knack for shaking up starting pitchers. Ten times, Frederick greeted opposing hurlers with leadoff home runs.

Though he made it through just six seasons, and was done at thirty-two, Frederick's career average was .308. His young departure is a little misleading, though. Frederick was shipped from Brooklyn to Sacramento of the Pacific Coast League, and West Coast living agreed with him. He played six more seasons, five in Portland, Oregon, where he became the manager and put up devastating numbers, hitting between .306 and .363 those years.

Outfielder Rube Bressler batted .299, third baseman Wally Gilbert hit .294, and second baseman Neal Finn hit .278, so Robinson had little reason to hunt for pinch-hitters. If he did he could swivel his head and gaze at Jake Flowers, who hit .320 in 89 games—by far his best year.

For all of that, men on the rise, men who were shooting stars, men who were clutch for a year, Brooklyn's lineup was anchored by two Hall of Famers: catcher Al Lopez and outfielder Babe Herman.

Lopez, who had a long career and a long life, broke into the majors in 1928 at age nineteen, playing in three games for Brooklyn. He stayed with the Robins/Dodgers through 1935, but stayed on the field for 19 seasons, through 1947. Regarded as an astute player, he soon became a successful manager. Although Lopez—like so many others who feasted on weak 1930 pitching—batted a career-high .309.

Alfonso Ramon Lopez was Spanish-American, and because he was the gentlemanly sort, gained the nickname "El Señor" in respect. Known for his defensive abilities, Lopez at one time held the record for most games played at catcher with 1,918.

Lopez won two pennants as a manager, leading the 1954 Cleveland Indians and 1959 Chicago White Sox to success. During that stretch, the Casey Stengel–led New York Yankees won 10 pennants in twelve years, with only Lopez finding ways to beat them in the American League.

Lopez's parents emigrated to the Tampa Bay area of Florida, and he spent much of his life in Ybor City and the nearby Bay area. A baseball stadium in the area was later named for him. Although he only hit over .300 for the Dodgers twice, he was a Brooklyn fixture; a much-admired security blanket behind the plate who earned two All-Star selections.

Lopez said he benefited greatly from playing for Wilbert Robinson, in part because of Robinson's personality, but also because he had been a catcher who could teach him.

"He was a nice man, like a father to me," Lopez said. "He treated me real nice and he wanted me to sit next to him on the bench during games. The only way to learn is through repeated observation."[7]

It took time for Brooklyn to heat up in 1930. By the end of April, the Robins were just 5–7. They first moved over .500, at 8–7, on May 4. Then they began winning more consistently. As the weather warmed, so did Brooklyn, and so did Lopez, who was just twenty-one and technically a rookie. He was applying Robinson's lessons simultaneously.

In one of those 1930-type games, as the Robins began that first move toward .500, they won a 19–15 contest over the Giants. Lopez gathered four hits. Then, all of a sudden, the sportswriters liked how Brooklyn was playing. Robinson felt they were overreacting to a little bit of good fortune for a team that not so long before had dropped to 2–7.

"No, I'm not predicting any pennants for Brooklyn," Robinson said. "But I'm not forecasting any pennants for any other club in the National League either. Don't forget that."[8]

Lopez was young and inexperienced, but was maturing fast and was noticed by observers who thought he was a player on the rise.

"I was a young rookie coming up and I tried to catch the same way I always had," he said after the season.[9]

Under Lopez as manager, the Cleveland Indians won a then-record 111 American League games in 1954 and the White Sox won their first pennant in forty years, or since the Black Sox scandal. Both times, his hometown of Tampa threw a parade to celebrate Lopez's successes. He was elected to the Baseball Hall of Fame in 1977.

The White Sox, meanwhile, did not win a World Series crown between 1917 and 2005. Lopez, ninety-seven at the time, died four days after the team broke its eighty-eight-year drought in '05.

To win as often as Brooklyn did in 1930, the Robins had to have one of their own outliers; one hitter who could trump most of the best sluggers other teams could trot out.

That man was Babe Herman. The outfielder was twenty-seven, and already establishing Hall of Fame hitting credentials. He excelled himself in 1930 with a career-high .393 average, though not by much considering Herman batted .381 a season before and concluded his 13-year career at a lifetime .324. Herman saved his best homer and RBI season for 1930, too, supplementing that average with 35 bombs, 130 RBIs, 241 hits, and 18 stolen bases to go with all that. It was one of nine seasons Herman batted at least .300.

Born in Buffalo, New York, Herman grew up in Glendale, California, where he remained close friends with Casey Stengel. The two of them became rich from smart investments, rather than from baseball salaries. Due to his iffy fielding and often-erratic base-running, Herman was sometimes viewed as a flake, but he was a magnificent hitter, with a lifetime .532 slugging percentage who three times hit for the cycle.

When he was young, Herman thought he was going to be a football player. His goal was to suit up for Cal in Berkeley. He got sidetracked to baseball while playing semipro and was recruited as a fill-in for a better team when a starter was injured in an automobile accident. Then Herman went off to Canada for $175 a month and batted .330 in Edmonton.

Officially Floyd Caves Herman, this Babe—who was not Ruth—set several Robins/Dodgers hitting records. Later in life, he clarified to anyone who asked that he did not get beaned by a fly ball, but did take the one on the shoulder.

"Shoulders don't count," Herman said with a straight face.[10]

He also questioned the 1930s team nickname of "Daffiness Boys." "We weren't really daffy," Herman said. "We weren't nearly as screwy as the Gashouse Gang over in St. Louis. Now they were really daffy."[11]

As the presiding genius of those Robins named after him, Robinson sometimes garnered a reputation as the headmaster of an odd bunch. But Herman emphasized Uncle Robbie knew what he was doing in the dugout.

"Uncle Robbie wasn't a clown," Herman said. "He was a sound baseball man and a good manager, especially when it came to handling pitchers. Of course, he had his idiosyncrasies, but who doesn't?"[12]

Not really one of the early crop of sluggers, Herman subscribed more to the practice of contact hitting. "The bat is like a whip," he said. "The driving power is in the quick lunge just as you meet the ball."[13]

Herman was hitting .468 after the first 16 games in 1930, and even drove in seven runs in a game against the New York Giants, on April 29. He was at .411 by the end of that month. As might be expected in such a hitter's season, the statistical lists were crowded at the top, with Herman, Bill Terry of the Giants, Chuck Klein of the Phillies, and Lefty O'Doul of the Phillies vying to hit .400.

Brooklyn hung close in the pennant race and Herman hung in seeking a .400 mark. Herman was at .387 at the end of August, but finished at .393. He was a handful of hits shy of .400.

As tremendous as Vance was in 1930, with that sterling earned-run average, he could not make up for his lost years and late start, and as such began to fade after that season. He never again approached his 17 wins, topping out at 12, and barely came within a full run of matching that league-best ERA. As the days dwindled on his time in the majors, Vance battled to capture three more victories to reach 200, but ultimately fell short.

When he was at his best, Vance could dazzle. He flummoxed Rogers Hornsby in one 1924 game, the season the Rajah hit .424, by striking him out multiple times. One fan yelled he had paid good money to watch Hornsby hit. Hornsby said, "If I were a Brooklyn fan, I'd pay my good money to watch Vance pitch."[14]

Baseball people felt Vance never lost his cool, despite his long, frustrating apprenticeship in the minors. Once, when Vance and

Babe Ruth were both young and on an exhibition tour, Vance seemed to understand the importance of off-field performance even when his team was regularly getting its ears boxed by the Yankees.

"Every day we knocked their ears off on the ballfield," said Babe Ruth. "Every night they took all our dough playing poker."[15]

Vance was fortunate he had the patience to last, and the help of one doctor from his home area of Nebraska who said his regularly sore right arm eventually would get well.

"When I asked him if it would ever be alright again, he said it would," Vance said. "Then I asked him how long it would take. He said about four years. That staggered me."[16]

It did take years for Vance to fight past his problems and at last get his big-time chance. He lied about his age, he said, telling everyone he was two years younger than thirty-one. Yet even though his career was condensed, Vance became a Hall of Famer.

"Gosh," Vance said when the day came. "Can you imagine me in the Hall of Fame?"[17]

20

THE NEW YORK GIANTS

HE WAS FIERCE, determined, arrogant, imperious, and above all breathed to win. There were reasons John J. McGraw was called "Little Napoleon" during his 30-year tenure as manager of the New York Giants.

Including his shorter stay leading the old Baltimore Orioles, McGraw's career record was 2,783–1,948, winning 58.6 percent of his decisions. His Giants won three World Series crowns and ten National League pennants.

Though small at 5-foot-7 and 155 pounds, he was mighty and possessed a loud roar supported by a temper—first shown when he was an outstanding player for the Orioles in the 1890s, batting .334 with 436 stolen bases. Still held in awe as perhaps the greatest manager in baseball history, McGraw never sugarcoated his attitude.

"I hate to lose and I never feel myself beaten until the last man is out," McGraw said. "I have tried to instill that same fighting spirit in all the teams I have managed."[1]

McGraw was neither patient nor terribly forgiving of players who made mental mistakes from lack of concentration, though he was more philosophical about physical errors because he considered them part of the game.

McGraw was hard-nosed and believed no one was going to give an inch on the field so he and his men should take whatever they could get. He never attended spring training without the belief the coming season was going to be his season, his team's season, and that's how New York felt in 1930, too.

By then, approaching three full decades at the helm of the Giants, McGraw was wearing down. He was closer to retirement than anyone knew, something which came to pass when he stepped away from the Giants during the 1932 season as his health began to fail.

New York finished 17 games over .500 in 1929, good for third place in the National League. As stacked as the Giants were with hitters—a common enough bounty that season, but also seemingly with pitching—there was every reason for McGraw to think the 1930 club could make a run at its first pennant since 1924.

The Giants won their first seven games of the season, but then settled into up and down ball. At different points, New York was 60–46, 66–47, and 74–56, but never better than the 87–67 they finished at.

This despite New York having about the greatest one-season group of hitters McGraw ever managed. As a team, the Giants batted an astonishing .319 with excellent batters littering both the starting lineup and bench. Rather remarkably, despite being grateful for guys recording great seasons, McGraw lamented the passing of the old days when clubs played for one run and the home run was a rarity rather than a regular occurrence. Old- timer McGraw was simpatico with Ty Cobb, who called the station-to-station game "scientific baseball." McGraw's brand of science was the same. It seemed he would rather win 1–0 than 8–4.

That was the real McGraw, commenting on how the game he loved had changed, fidgety if the score got too high when all he wanted to see was a good pitching duel, a game that featured "tight pitching, sensational fielding, team play at the bat, basestealing and scientific methods."[2]

When a manager fielded a lineup as loaded as McGraw's and still complained, it was easy to label him cantankerous. McGraw, however, didn't care how anyone referred to his disposition.

Still, he was riding first baseman Bill Terry that season—the last man to hit .400 in the National League—and a crowd of other Hall of Famers whose bats would have met the approval of lumberjacks. Terry clouted 254 hits in 154 games in his season to remember.

From the onset of the season, McGraw began showing signs of advancing health concerns, finding it difficult at times to sit on the bench for entire games. He so alarmed team owner Charles Stoneham, as the boss said, "I don't give a rap about winning pennants. It's McGraw's health that concerns me."[3] At times Stoneham even tried to persuade McGraw to leave the team for a rest, but the manager would not abandon his troops.

McGraw and Terry had personality differences, dating back to when they first met and, the manager—playing the part of general manager—first tried to sign the player. They were far apart on terms and on other occasions had disputes over money. In 1930, Terry, who had batted as high as .372 before in his career, moved to the otherworldly level.

Terry hit .380 in spring training, showing he was more than ready for the season. In an interview he once again expounded on his personal outlook on the sport. He played because it was the best way for him to make a living and he had three children counting on him.

"It's serious business," Terry said of the sport, as if he would only grudgingly have a good time playing. "Conditions on the Giants are a little different than elsewhere. McGraw generally calls for the ball he wants you to hit. That bothers some fellows who seem to chafe under restrictions, but I'm used to McGraw's system now and I can't say that it hampers me any in my individual work."[4]

By May 17, Terry was batting .433. He then slumped so that, after July 4 play, he was down to .381. By early September, though, his average had climbed back to .402. There were a lot of eyes on Terry's swings.

He was also surrounded by other future Hall of Famers in the regular lineup. Shortstop Travis Jackson hit .339 in 1930, the best single-season mark of his career. Third baseman Freddie Lindstrom hit a boggling .379—also his highest-ever average. The remarkable Mel Ott, who played his first games in the majors for the Giants at age seventeen, batted .349.

Which would have been enough, but McGraw could call on others. Shanty Hogan, a player who was never much in the limelight during his career, appeared in 122 games and hit his career high at .339 (though he did reach .300 five other times). Outfielder Freddy Leach, then thirty-two, mashed the ball at a .327 pace in 126 games. Leach did hit .329 one other season and his lifetime average over 10 seasons was .307 . . . but his name didn't carry the same as Terry or Ott.

The bench guys couldn't get off the bench as often as they would have preferred being behind the likes of the gaggle of Hall of Famers. McGraw was never short of pinch-hitters or reliable fill-ins. Catcher Bob O'Farrell got into 94 games and hit .301; Ethan Allen, a solid outfielder, batted .307 in 76 games; and backup shortstop Doc Marshall hit .309 in 78 games.

They got their shots and produced when McGraw asked. If a team is going to bat .319 as an aggregate, the supporting cast must contribute. That amounted to nine Giants with substantial playing time each hitting above .300. Allen was just twenty-six in 1930, on his way to a 13-year career and a career mark of .300 on the dot. In 1934 with the Phillies, Allen hit .330 with 42 doubles.

Although he was basically just wrapping up the final moments of his career, another Hall of Famer briefly passed through the Giants dugout. Shortstop Dave Bancroft was thirty-nine and appeared in his final 10 games in the majors for New York. He only added one hit to his lifetime total in 19 plate appearances, though Bancroft had already been part of two Giants World Series titlists for McGraw in the early 1920s.

Although his lifetime average was just .279, Bancroft was inducted into the Hall of Fame in 1971, on the strength of his brilliant fielding.

"Bancroft is one of the greatest shortstops in the history of the game," said manager Hughie Jennings. "He can go equally well to his left or right, had a great arm and is a good hitter. The best thing about Bancroft is he can think. He uses his brain."[5]

Bancroft was more coach than player in 1930. Realizing McGraw might be nearing the end of the line, Bancroft hoped he would be a handy successor on the scene when the historic moment came. However, things did not play out that way.

Bancroft was a loyal McGraw man and had been a player-manager for the Boston Braves for four seasons in the 1920s. But the Braves were losers every season with Bancroft in charge, and Giants owner Stoneham was not a Bancroft backer. Bancroft never managed again in the majors. He did handle some minor-league clubs and spent three seasons managing in the All-American Girls Professional Baseball League.

The Lindstrom of 1930 was never better. He grew up a White Sox fan in Chicago, but signed a contract with the Giants when he was just sixteen after a scout saw him have a big day. In 1924, at eighteen, Lindstrom was then the youngest player to appear in a World Series—and he played well for New York that year . . . except for a single moment.

Lindstrom became infamous for allowing a ball to bounce over his head, handing a seventh-game victory to the Washington Senators. The play followed him throughout his career. Lindstrom said he was not uncomfortable when inserted into the championship round and piled up four hits.

"No, I wasn't scared or nervous," Lindstrom said. "But I should have been. I was too dumb then."[6]

He recalled the prevailing mood on the team and during that era, where veterans often formed a protective cocoon to help ward off challenges of up-and-coming players.

"How little those fellows did to help us take their jobs," Lindstrom said later about the lack of advice proffered.[7]

Lindstrom had an extraordinary all-around year in 1930. He banged out 231 hits, cracked 22 home runs, knocked in 106 runs, and stole 15 bases. He was the spirt behind the Giants' success. He also could not have guessed he was experiencing the high point of his 13-season career. Beginning in 1931, although Lindstrom continued to be a top-flight player, his numbers were more down to earth. He went through a series of debilitating injuries and often was utilized in the outfield instead of at third.

During the offseason between 1930 and 1931, McGraw toyed with the notion of Lindstrom spending more time in the wide open spaces than guarding the third-base line. A rookie seemed to be sneaking up on the major-league roster.

"But if he is as good as I have been led to believe," McGraw said of Johnny Vergez, "he should be able to fill Lindstrom's place, and thus make it possible for Lindstrom to play in the outfield, where he wants very much to play, and I believe he will be at his best. It isn't generally known, but as a kid around Chicago he was an outfielder, and I believe, a very good one. He has been at me for a couple of years to give him a break in center field."[8]

That seemed a false cover story. Much later, Lindstrom admitted he was not the same guy during the final few years of his career, especially after breaking his leg sliding in 1931. He also proclaimed he and McGraw feuded about his shift to the outfield.

"Taking me out for a busher," Lindstrom said, "and sticking me in a position I never played before. I don't like it."[9] So much for McGraw's soothing words.

Still, Lindstrom recognized his body was starting to let him down and that injuries hastened his 1936 retirement at thirty after a short stint with the Brooklyn Dodgers.

"But it was my bad back more than the effects of the broken leg," Lindstrom said. "Why, I couldn't play five holes of golf, much less swing properly."[10]

Lindstrom was called "the boy wonder" after his splash in the 1924 World Series, and seven times hit at least .300 on his way to a lifetime average of .311. During one doubleheader in 1928, Lindstrom cranked out nine hits.

The key mistake in that 1924 World Series was not something Lindstrom, even when being inducted into the Hall of Fame, could easily forget.

A ball hit by Earl McNeely of Washington in the 12th inning of the last game struck a rock and instead of making an easy fielding grab, Lindstrom saw the ball bound over his head.

"Muddy Ruel was on second with two outs," Lindstrom recalled, "and Earl McNeely was batting. Earl hit a ground ball that ordinarily would have been a routine out for me. But it hit a pebble right in front of me and bounced over my head into left field, enabling Ruel to score from second with the winning run. Any degree of immorality I might have is tied up with that pebble."[11]

Lindstrom's persistent bad back was later cured, and he was able to contest long days of golf as an older man. Only he wasn't quite as good at that sport.

"It's funny, though," Lindstrom said. "All my years of playing baseball I didn't have any trouble hitting a ball that was thrown every which way at me. Yet the golf ball is just sitting there, waiting to be hit, and I have trouble hitting it."[12]

In some ways, Travis Jackson was a second Lindstrom. He also was eighteen when he first appeared in the New York Giants lineup in 1922. He also had his best hitting year in 1930, reaching .339—one of six seasons he topped .300. And New York's regular shortstop was also selected for the Hall of Fame after a 15-year career that ended for him at thirty-two.

Jackson also was cut down by a series of injuries and illnesses, notably a nagging knee problem, but also mumps, the flu, and appendicitis in various seasons. It was a sign of the times, and Jackson's perennial knee woes were referred to as a "trick knee." That meant it could not be fixed and the problem kept recurring.

Although raw in the beginning, once Jackson gained experience, he became more renowned for fielding than hitting. Many acclaimed Jackson the best fielding shortstop in the game. He could not deny that when he was young, growing up in Arkansas, and playing his first minor-league games, he was far from polished.

"I guess I set a world record for errors," Jackson said of his 1922 season with the Arkansas Travelers when he committed 73 of them. "At least a league record. I had a pretty good arm, see, but I didn't have much control. And even if I booted a ball, I had to throw it. A lot of those were double errors, two on the same play, a boot and then a wild throw. The people in the first base and right-field bleachers knew me. When the ball was hit to me, they scattered: 'Watch out! He's got it again!'"[13]

Jackson was the anointed successor to Dave Bancroft, so there was considerable pressure when he broke in with the Giants.

Even after Jackson stepped away from the majors with a lifetime .291 average, he stayed in baseball as a minor-league manager, though one still often being treated by doctors. His knees held him back from doing much playing as a player-manager, and then he contracted tuberculosis. At different times, however, he returned to the Giants as a coach.

Sportswriters more than once wrote the obituary to his career, only to be surprised when he bounced back.

"It's a great sensation to read your own obituary—and you baseball writers certainly wrote enough of them about me," Jackson said, "and then figuratively to kick off the top of your casket and go out to the wars once more."[14]

Compared to other great hitters of the time, Mel Ott does not always receive much attention. If you look at the early signings—some of it attributable to the astuteness of McGraw's eye for talent—one might think New York was running an American Legion team. But the trio of teenagers—Lindstrom, Jackson, and Ott—all became Hall of Famers.

Ott played 35 games as a seventeen-year-old in 1926, batting .383. He stood just 5-foot-9 and weighed 170 pounds, but displayed as much power as other bigger, stronger looking contemporaries, concluding his 22-year major-league career with 511 home runs. Ott was the first National League player to reach 500.

By 1930, when the Giants were pounding the stitches off the ball, Ott was just twenty-one. That year he batted .349 with 25 home runs and 119 RBIs. His on-base percentage of .458 led the National League. In addition to his prowess with the bat, he also had a keen eye at the plate, and collected 103 walks, partially because of the loaded New York lineup populated by many hitters hurlers wanted to duck.

Ott led the NL in home runs six times, with a high of 42 in 1929. He featured an odd, yet memorable batting stance, swinging from the left side over his 2,730 regular-season games and knocking in 1,860 runs. A 10-time .300 hitter, Ott's lifetime mark was .304 with a .414 on-base percentage. Despite the start of his career predating the creation of the All-Star Game, Ott was still selected 12 times. He led the Giants team in home runs in 18 consecutive seasons.

Ott was from New Orleans and naïve. When he first arrived in New York, he had difficulty negotiating the subway system. But before he could even suit up for the Giants, McGraw raved about him. He wrote a note to owner Charles Stoneham, saying, "Ott is a stand-out with me. Ott is the best-looking young player at the bat in my time with the club."[15]

When he played semipro, Ott impressed observers as a catcher, and that's where he thought his future lay.

Ott said he was sixteen and quite nervous to be discussing his career when McGraw said, "Go to the outfield, young man." He didn't know how he found the words to protest, but said, "But I'm a catcher, Mr. McGraw." McGraw had his own comeback, citing Roger Bresnahan, inventor of the shin guards, "That's all right, Bresnahan always thought he was a pitcher, too."[16]

Ott was so young that season that he was accompanied to spring training by his father. McGraw also took care of him as if he was his own son. He recognized immediately what a valuable commodity Ott would be if nurtured properly. Ott was so young that when he met Lindstrom he teased him about being an old-timer, saying when Lindstrom recorded his marvelous World Series debut as an eighteen-year-old, Ott was still in high school.

"Little did I think that I would grow up to room with the great Lindstrom," Ott joked.[17]

Ott had reached stardom by 1929, at age twenty, when he clouted 42 homers, drove in 151 runs, and batted .328. But he had already hit .322 in 1928, along with showing his first signs of power with 18 homers. "In 1928, I began to get the home-run range and I was feeling pretty proud about that," Ott said.[18]

By most baseball standards, he was still a kid, but one maturing fast. Some sportswriters were calling Ott "the boy bomber of the bayou," because of his Louisiana roots.[19]

Probably the grandest day of 1930 for Ott came on August 31, in the second game of a doubleheader against the Boston Braves. Although the Giants lost, 14–10, Ott slammed three home runs and a double, batted in six runs, and scored three.

However, Ott named August 7, 1940, Mel Ott Night at the Polo Grounds—with 53,000 fans in attendance—as the most memorable of his career.

"All the things that I'd done in baseball for myself just seemed swallowed up in what the fans were doing for me that evening," he said. "I told my wife [Mildred] before going to the park that she'd be lucky if I didn't fall down going after a ball or strike out with the winning run and disgrace her because I was as nervous as a cat."[20]

When Ott retired with 511 homers in 1947, no other National League player was within 200. Ott became a manager, taking over the Giants, but died young, at forty-nine, due to injuries suffered in an automobile accident in 1958.

Unlike the weak links in baseball in 1930, the Giants not only batted that absurd overall .319, but John J. McGraw had some pitching to call on, allowing for a real shot at the pennant.

The Giants even had a Hall of Famer in the pitching rotation at a time when many teams were desperate for hurlers who could just get the ball over the plate. Beyond that, McGraw trotted out seven different hurlers with winning records in 1930. That was being positively greedy.

Southpaw Hub Pruett was presented with a limited number of roses during his seven-season career, but he did end up 5–4 in 1930, his only winning season. Not that his earned-run average of 4.78 was particularly helpful.

Pete Donohue was a solid workman with 134 career wins who twice won at least 20 games (1934 and 1935). The experienced righty led the NL with 20 victories in 1926 for Cincinnati and in 1922 his winning percentage of .667 was best in the league. If Donohue had not been near the end of the line in 1930 when he was 7–6 for the Giants, New York might have won the pennant. But in a bright, shining indicator that he was over the hill at twenty-nine, Donohue's ERA with New York was 6.13.

Joe Heving, who never really broke into any team's rotation as a regular despite compiling a lifetime 76–48 record with a 3.90 ERA, was a twenty-nine-year-old rookie who contributed a 7–5 mark. However, like many others, his ERA was awful, at 5.22. The Giants hitting so well helped him win.

As a group, those three fellows with winning records can only be classified as lucky to complete the season above .500. Less so Clarence Mitchell, who went 10–3 with a 3.98 ERA nearly twenty years after he broke into the big leagues. Then thirty-nine, Mitchell sometimes sprinkled in sparkling years like this one.

Lefty Bill Walker never truly attained prominence, but during his 10 seasons in the majors compiled a 97–77 record, and his earned-run average was a very respectable 3.59. The 17 games he won in 1930 (17–15) was a lifetime high, and he kept his ERA just under 4.00, so in this hate-the-pitcher year, it was respectable.

Wrapped around his 1930 season, Walker led the NL in ERA in both 1929 and 1931, the latter year putting up an outstanding 2.26. He also made one All-Star team and was with the Giants for one World Series crown.

Matching Walker with 17 wins in 1930 was Carl Hubbell, the great screwball artist, who unlike that passel of teen prodigies invited to begin their Giants careers early, was not a rookie in the majors until he was twenty-five. He got a look with the Detroit Tigers, but manager Ty Cobb warned he was just going to ruin his arm with the screwball, and so Hubbell was cut. A New York scout, Dick Kinsella, happened to be a delegate to the Democratic National Convention in 1928 in Houston, and took in a Texas League minor-league ballgame. Impressed by Hubbell, then toiling for Beaumont, he followed him and convinced the Giants to buy him.

In 16 years, culminating when he was forty, Hubbell finished with a 253–154 mark and a glittering 2.98 ERA. He topped 20 triumphs in five consecutive seasons (1933–37), was a nine-time All-Star, and twice was the NL Most Valuable Player. He led the league in wins three times—and all of baseball twice—with a best performance of 26–6 with a 2.31 ERA in 1936.

Hubbell was just approaching his prime years in 1930 and was good, but not yet great. He did feel the wrath of the bats that season, his ERA climbing to 3.87 before he became the best around with three ERA titles and a single-season first-rate mark of 1.66 with 10 shutouts in 1933. Over the 1936 and 1937 seasons, Hubbell won a record 24 consecutive games.

At his finest, Hubbell was viewed as unbeatable. Teammates called him "Meal Ticket" because he always provided. Others in awe of his pitching called him "King Carl." His reputation was burnished in the 1934 All-Star Game. The American League's meat of the lineup, anchored with power hitters, went after Hubbell and he famously struck out Babe Ruth, Lou Gehrig, Jimmie Foxx, Al Simmons, and Joe Cronin in a row—all of them destined for Cooperstown.

The Ks are what everyone remembers about Hubbell's magnificent showing, but the oddity is the American League actually won the game, 9–7, without him figuring into a decision.

Hubbell possessed a mild demeanor, a high kicking delivery, and a longtime loyalty to the Giants, sticking with the club in different capacities after his retirement. He was also remembered for throwing a no-hitter and an 18-inning game, feats that even impressed other topflight pitchers.

"The source of his skill is his matchless control in using his curveball to set up his screwball," said fellow Hall of Famer Waite Hoyt. "Emotions, if he has any, never affect him. His timing, his conservation of energy and influence on the ballclub are other factors in rating him among the great pitchers of all time."[21]

Hubbell got to know McGraw in 1928 and took it well enough when the sometimes acerbic manager greeted him with sarcasm once following an errant pitch.

"I didn't tell you to throw high and outside the park, Hubbell," McGraw said.[22]

The Giants featured one additional character of note in the 1930 rotation. The player who won the most was not Hubbell or

Walker, but Freddie Fitzsimmons, whose 19–7 record produced the best winning percentage in the National League that year at .731. In a 19-year career that some felt might last forever, Fitzsimmons only won more games in a season two years earlier, when he won 20 in 1928. The right-hander finished with 217 victories and a 3.51 ERA. He was known for his durability, as well as longevity.

Although his battles with pounds gained him the insulting nickname "Fat Freddie," Fitzsimmons was actually somewhat light on his feet and was one of the best fielding pitchers around.

Later, Fitzsimmons managed the Philadelphia Phillies and worked as a big-league coach for many years between 1940 and 1966. He may never have stopped pitching if he hadn't incurred a knee injury. It happened in dramatic and unfortunate fashion in Game Three of the 1941 World Series.

Yankee Marius Russo caromed a line drive off Fitzsimmons's knee, and the ball bounced to Dodger shortstop Pee Wee Reese for an out. Variously described as a thrower of the knuckle-curve and the standard knuckleball, Fitzsimmons's arm probably would not have given out for a while.

"Most people think a knuckleball and a slow ball are the same pitch," Fitzsimmons said. "That isn't true at all, for I have a fast knuckler, as well as a slow one, and there is another pitcher in this league who has, too. The pitcher can never tell really where a slow knuckleball will break."[23]

Fitzsimmons was never as flashy or overpowering as Hubbell, but in this season he was the bigger winner.

No one with the Giants, of course, was a bigger winner in 1930 than Bill Terry. The first baseman was not a runaway victor in the batting race, but hit well enough to place himself on one of the most elite lists of all—a player who completed a season with a .400 average.

Terry finished at .401, eight percentage points ahead of Brooklyn's Babe Herman. Nobody realized at the time that when Terry topped the .400 mark, it would be the last time an NL player did so. Only the Red Sox slugger Ted Williams in 1941 would ever again meet the mark or exceed it.

It was much more commonplace to bat .400 between the 1890s and 1920s. Terry knew he was in good company, but would not have realized he represented the end of a line. It had been just five years, 1925, since the most recent .400 hitter. When Rogers Hornsby hit .403 in 1925 with the St. Louis Cardinals, it was the second season in a row he had achieved the feat and the third overall.

When Terry was asked by sportswriters what made him such a tough out, he couldn't explain that well.

"I haven't any secrets of success," Terry said. "Either you do or you don't up there at the rubber." He said it was easier to figure out what he was doing wrong in the batter's box than dissect what he was doing right. "But when you're in a slump you do something you don't ordinarily do—stride too far, don't cut as you should. But I haven't had a long slump for three years now."[24]

How many players could claim that?

21

THE CHICAGO CUBS

THE CHICAGO CUBS recorded the longest World Series championship drought in history between 1908 and 2016, and became the butt of a running joke along the lines of "Anyone can have a bad century." However, in and around 1930, Chicago's National League club was one of the best around, a team that regularly won pennants.

The Cubs were a very respectable National League contender for a lengthy period of time, claiming NL pennants in 1929, 1932, 1935, 1938, and again in 1945. No one made fun of the Cubs. Just because the team did not win a world championship during that time block, it did not mean they were ridiculed. That came later, as the team fell on harder times for a longer period.

When the 1930 season began, the Cubs were the reigning NL champs. They were coming off a 98–54 season under manager Joe McCarthy, though they lost in five games to the Philadelphia Athletics in the World Series. That still made them a favorite to capture another pennant, get back to the Series, and perhaps win it this time around.

The Cubs were tough outs in 1930. Led by the almost unmatchable season of outfielder Hack Wilson, Chicago as a team batted .309 and the Cubs had one of the best pitching staffs in all of baseball. They did not quite achieve the same heights in the standings, though. Under McCarthy, a Hall of Fame leader about to notch more outstanding accomplishments with the New York Yankees, the Cubs were sitting at 86–64 with four games to go in the season.

However, in-house backbiting and lobbying led to an ill-advised change by owner Phil Wrigley, who shoved McCarthy aside in favor of Rogers Hornsby, who thought he could do better. Hornsby's end-of-season tenure consisted of going 4–0, so the Cubs won 90 games again—but did not repeat as pennant winners.

Wrigley Field was often lively while the Cubs pounded the ball sufficiently to chase the pennant till season's end, leading the league in attendance with 1,463,624 tickets sold. The fans swooned as Wilson pieced together one of the greatest individual seasons ever recorded. He created so much excitement it almost didn't matter if any other member of the lineup chimed in. Yet Wilson had plenty of help on this high-scoring team. The Cubs scored just shy of 1,000 runs (998), and 228 more runs than their pitchers allowed.

Thank Wilson, a wrecking machine at the plate. Born in Ellwood, Pennsylvania, in 1900, Lewis Robert Wilson was short at 5-foot-6, but powerful at 190 pounds. Much was made of his small feet (size six) and bulging neck muscles (size 18 collar), plus his arm and shoulder muscles. He did hard labor as a youth in shipyards and steel mills, but made hitting a baseball look easy.

Wilson broke into the majors in 1923, and by 1930 was the cornerstone of the Cubs' offense, with a discerning enough eye to bat. 356 with 105 walks, even as he was so grand a slugger as to set a National League home-run record with 56 dingers and a major-league record with 191 runs batted in. (For many years that mark was thought to be 190, but latter-day researchers scouring box scores changed it.)

That season, Wilson's on-base percentage was .454 and his slugging percentage was .723. He carried a monstrous bat of 40 ounces—like a gunfighter toted a favorite firearm—and he had a name for it, too: "Big Bertha."

In 1930, Wilson was coming off a World Series where he batted .471, but lost a critical fly ball in the sun that was costly to his team. Although he was morose about the mistake, when the Cubs returned home by train five hundred loyal fans applauded Wilson for all he had accomplished that season.

"They give me hell with their razzing when I'm going good," Wilson said of trying to make sense out of fan behavior, "and now when I deserve it, they give me cheers. You can't figure 'em."[1]

At the time, the NL single-season record for homers was 43 by the Phillies' Chuck Klein from the year before. Wilson determined early on he was going to break that mark, and did so before August was up. By then most observers wondered if Wilson could top Babe Ruth's 1927 record of 60. When Wilson ended the season with 56, it was a record that stood in the NL until 1998, when Mark McGwire and Sammy Sosa both busted it.

Wilson realized what he achieved, and reveled in it. He was a party animal, a serious drinker. While alcohol cost him dearly later in life, Wilson said those who formed an impression that he drank all the time and brought his habit onto the field were incorrect.

"I guess a lot of people think I was half stiff all the time I was playing," Wilson said. "That's not true. I played 11 years in the big leagues and I never ever took a drink before a game. Sure, afterwards. And sometimes I'd play with a bad hangover. But I never took a drink before a game."[2]

Wilson was the hero of that summer. His career was good enough to warrant inclusion in the National Baseball Hall of Fame, but he was not as great every year as he was in 1930. Too many things went wrong in 1931 for Wilson to repeat, but encapsulated as a great moment in time, his 1930 season was one long highlight reel.

"I batted .307 for 10 years in the majors," Wilson said. "I could draw 40,000 and more out there. They loved me. Why did it have to end? God, it didn't have to end."[3]

The Cubs crew surrounding Wilson was impressive. Catcher Gabby Hartnett batted .339 with 37 home runs and 122 runs batted in, making him the first catcher to amass more than 120 RBIs in a season. So even if a pitcher safely wiggled his way around Wilson, he might be clobbered by a future Most Valuable Player also having his best season.

Although his career total was 236 homers, Hartnett on only two other occasions topped 20, and in just two seasons did he hit higher than his .339 average.

Hartnett played his entire 19-year career for the Cubs, between 1922 and 1940, and many years later, some thought he was an even more significant player for the team than fellow Hall of Famer Ernie Banks, known as "Mr. Cub."

The saddest part of Banks's career was never playing for a championship Cubs team. Hartnett was on four pennant-winners.

"He was the best player on our club all the time I was there," said Billy Herman, another Hall of Famer. "Sure, we had some pretty good players, but there was no way we could have won without him. Gabby Hartnett is the kind of player you can build a team around."[4]

In his later years with the Cubs, headline writers sometimes goofed around, referring to Hartnett as "The Great Gabby," a play on the title of F. Scott Fitzgerald's novel *The Great Gatsby*. Hartnett batted .297 lifetime.

At one point he held the record for most games caught with 1,727. A minor-league manager, big-league scout, and broadcaster, Hartnett was selected for the Hall of Fame in 1955, when he was operating a bowling alley and not thinking about baseball immortality.

"After I recovered from the shock, I said a prayer thanking the Good Lord for allowing me to live long enough to hear this wonderful news and enjoy a thrill I really never expected," he said."[5]

Overall, McCarthy could call on more big sticks than Boy Scouts trying to build a camp fire.

Riggs Stephenson, who must be one of the most underrated hitters of all time, and Kiki Cuyler, another Hall of Famer, kept Wilson company in the outfield. Stephenson batted .367—the best on the team—and Cuyler was in the neighborhood at .355. The outfield potency alone was ridiculous.

Cuyler drove in 134 runs and added 17 triples to his 13 homers and 50 doubles while totaling 228 hits—20 more than Wilson that season. He led the NL in stolen bases with 37, one of four times he was tops in the circuit. In his 18 seasons, Cuyler batted .321. Briefly a football star at West Point, Cuyler chose baseball as his specialty.

Born Hazen Shirley Cuyler, Kiki passed away at fifty before being elected to the Hall of Fame. He suffered a heart attack while ice fishing in his native Michigan, and then incurred a blood clot.

Switching between left field, second, and third, Stephenson never quite found a permanent fielding home, but was definitely at home in the batter's box. (His lifetime batting average was .336.) After coming out of the University of Alabama (where he lettered in four sports), Stephenson hit .330 in 65 games as a rookie with the Cleveland Indians in 1921.

In a 14-year career, Stephenson hit over .300—sometimes by great margins—a dozen times, but many of his seasons were half-seasons as managers shunted him around. He was weak around the second-base bag making the double-play pivot, and his throwing arm was hampered by an old football injury. He may have been the ideal designated hitter before there was a DH. Even in 1930, when he averaged .367, Stephenson could only get into 109 games.

His nickname was "Old Hoss," because he was reliable and consistent, and Stephenson did make himself into an outfielder after committing too many errors in the infield.

The Cubs also featured a player projected as one of the best young infielders in the National League. Woody English was twenty-four, but had been in the majors since 1927. Over a 12-year career, English hit well (.286 lifetime) and manned both shortstop and third base for the Cubs, though he rarely stroked the long ball . . . except in 1930, which turned into his best season at the plate.

English averaged .335 and hit 17 homers and posted an on-base percentage of .430. He scored 152 runs that season with 17 triples and 214 hits.

The next year English batted .319, but that was his only other season topping .300, never quite fulfilling his early promise.

It was Casey Stengel with the Toledo Mud Hens who devoted extra tutoring time to English, although the atmospheric conditions hitting adjacent to a tobacco factory could have been better.

"The factory over there would about make both of us sick," English said, "but he would work with me and I attributed my jump of 100 points to Casey because he would work with me every morning."[6]

The Cubs stayed in the running for years, periodically picking off a flag, but never won the league crown twice in a row during that era.

"It seems like every three years we won, 1929, 1932, and 1935, but we never won a Series," English said."[7]

English first got to know Hack Wilson when they were teammates in Toledo. He said Wilson was a great guy to be around, but it was simply amazing to watch him hit during his surreal 1930 season. It got so that the other Cubs thought Wilson might smack the ball out of the park every at-bat.

"A jolly, likeable guy, good temperament, and had a lot of fun," English said. "Every time he'd go up to home plate the guys in the dugout would call out, 'You got a home run in you this time?'"[8]

Besides English's phenomenal 1930 season, he made one All-Star team, representing the NL in 1933, and was proud of the cache.

"I'm not famous, but I'm proud to say that I played in the first All-Star Game," said English many years later, not long before he passed away at ninety.[9]

After he retired from playing, English became a manager in the All-American Girls Professional Baseball League, though when first approached for the job he said he didn't know anything about girls baseball. Turned out it was just baseball.

English became captain of the Cubs under manager Charlie Grimm, and said he learned a lot being around the man known as "Jolly Cholly." Grimm was the main first baseman for the 1930

Cubs, though he only batted a solid .289. That season, with a .995 mark, Grimm led the league in fielding at first for a fifth time.

Grimm, born in 1898, was as much a Chicago Cub as Banks became, even if he did break in with the Pittsburgh Pirates, an affiliation mostly forgotten. Grimm was seemingly on lifetime call whenever Cubs ownership needed to fill a spot—whether on the field, in the dugout, in the broadcast booth, or scouting. Grimm was an all-round savvy baseball man.

He first appeared as a player with the Cubs in 1925, and filled in as manager three different times over a three-decade period. In 1960, his last stretch as chief in the dugout, Grimm was traded in-house for Lou Boudreau. Boudreau moved from broadcast commentator to manager, and Grimm moved upstairs. In 1961, when team owner P. K. Wrigley tried out his so-called "College of Coaches," a group rotated being in charge of the team, Grimm stayed a coach that time around. Somehow, he squeezed in five years at the helm of the Braves, too.

Grimm spent so much time running the Cubs, sometimes baseball people forget he was a solid player, with a lifetime .290 average in 2,166 games spread over 20 years.

Grimm hardly ever lived down to his last name. He was seemingly always upbeat, known as a chatterbox, and often entertained by singing songs and playing the banjo.

"I had fun playing baseball," Grimm said. "I tried to make it fun for my players. I was 'Jolly Cholly,' and I always thought a pat on the back, an encouraging word, or a wisecrack, paid off a lot more than a brilliantly executed work of strategy."[10]

Over the long, often dark, history of the Cubs, Grimm stands out as a manager for leading Chicago to three of the organization's pennants, two in the 1930s and one in the 1940s. He also started one season when the Cubs won the flag, but was replaced before the end.

Given Grimm's rookie year was 1916 and he was still employed by the Cubs in the 1960s, it definitely felt as if he had been around forever. Even he felt that way.

"Sometimes I'm amazed that with all the years I've been in baseball, and all the things that happened, I'm still around," Grimm said in 1968. "I came into this great game, thanks to Connie Mack, when I was a teenager. As the years pile up, I sometimes feel as old as Connie, who kept waving that scorecard in the Philadelphia Athletics' dugout until he was almost 90."[11]

Grimm said forty years after he teamed with Hack Wilson in 1930, fans still asked about the man and his fabulous season. Grimm said Wilson was a friendly man who related well to children, liked to have a good time, and enjoyed music. Perhaps that meant he was a fan of Grimm's banjo playing.

"He was a slugger in the Babe Ruth manner," Grimm said. "knock the ball over the left-field wall and just as easily, swinging late, had the power to put it away in right field. I'd say his power was to right-center. He frequently struck out, but he always gave it a good riffle." Grimm said Wilson did not seem to be someone who was a brilliant judge of the strike zone. He based that on something Wilson once told him: "Any ball I can reach, I'm going to swing at."[12]

Although the Cubs could not repeat their 1929 pennant in 1930, Grimm said fans still swooned over the home team. Bill Veeck Sr., father of the Hall of Fame owner of the same name, was a great supporter of Ladies Day discounts. Grimm said women's free admission swelled the crowds well beyond listed capacity at Wrigley Field in 1930. The idea was so popular one joke went that the Cubs were kidnapping women off the streets so they could inflate their already-large attendance figures.

Grimm referred to an elderly woman who, as he put it, seemed somewhat indignant to find herself inside the Friendly Confines. "I was just minding my own business, walking down Addison Street," she reportedly said, "when all of a sudden, I was inside the ballpark. I had no intention of watching a ball game. But I couldn't get out, so I just stayed."[13]

What a remarkable group of everyday players and hitters Chicago sported in 1930. And unlike many NL pretenders, the Cubs owned some pitching. Although even most of the successful starters suffered from the same higher-than-usual ERA infectious disease as the rest of baseball, one regular stood out and apart from everyone else.

Pat Malone, the 6-foot, 200-pound right-hander was twenty-seven and went 20–9, the second time he would win more than 20 games in a campaign during a career that saw him retire after just 10 years in the bigs at thirty-four, with 134 wins.

Malone threw 22 complete games and his earned-run average was 3.94; anything below 4.00 that peculiar year being commendable. But Malone's breakthrough registered in 1929, when he won 22 games and stuck out a league-leading 166 batters. Malone was a member of the small fraternity of pitching survivors in 1930 who could say they helped more than hindered their team.

Perce Leigh Malone grew up in Altoona, Pennsylvania, and his behavior bordered on the juvenile delinquent side—not only in his youth, but after becoming a professional ballplayer. His inclination to play hard gave some of his managers heartburn, but Malone certainly had a good time, with few qualms about skirting disciplinary rules.

Before quitting school at age fourteen, Malone said he was not someone who spent all of his free time in the library studying.

"We used to steal chickens, corn, potatoes, and other fowl and vegetables that could be roasted," he said. "We licked every kid caught off his beat, threw rocks into the windows of residents we didn't like, stole apples, milk bottles, dogs and all kinds of loot. We had a swell kid ball team, and I occupied the limelight as the tough, hard-boiled Irish pitcher. If I couldn't strike a guy out, I'd lick him."[14]

Malone joined the Army in time for World War I, and then was discovered playing semipro ball. He signed with the New York Giants, but feuded with John J. McGraw. It was 1928, and Malone was twenty-five by the time he broke in with the Cubs with an 18-win rookie year.

Malone said Cubs manager Joe McCarthy gave him every chance to succeed, and the pitcher was grateful when he could pay him back with 60 victories in his first three seasons. Malone became pals with Hack Wilson and they were a danger to quiet society, often engaging in practical jokes. Besides setting newspapers on fire while they were being read, catching pigeons on the roofs of team hotels, and setting off smoke bombs in cars belonging to opposing players, the duo did manage to star on the field.

Neither did Malone respond well when taken to task for breaking curfew or failing to follow rules. Except for one season with the New York Yankees, when he went 12–4, Malone did most of his winning in a hurry with the Cubs. When New York released him in 1937, he did not want to leave the majors.

"I'd do anything to stay with this ball club," Malone said, probably indicating he would have been pleased to stay with any team. "Why can't they give me a broom and let me sweep out the dressing room just so I can hang around?"[15]

It may have been preordained that Malone died at just forty given his hard living.

The rest of the 1930 rotation included Charlie Root (16–14), Guy Bush (15–10, but with a 6.20 ERA), and Sheriff Blake (10–14). A surprising success was Bud Teachout, who went 11–4, though his ERA was 4.06.

Only in his last season did Root record a lousier earned run average than he did in 1930. Overall, his mark was a very good 3.59, to accompany 201 victories in 17 years of play. In 1927, when he was just starting out, he led the majors with 26 triumphs.

One incident that kept Root famous was his showdown with Ruth and the Yankees in the 1932 World Series. This was the occasion when Ruth was being razzed by Wrigley fans and, after taking two strikes, blasted a critical home run. It has been said Ruth predicted the long ball and it is described as "Ruth's called shot." Root, a hard-nosed competitor, denied that Ruth did any such thing and resented being termed the punch line of the event.

Often punctuated with a squirt of juice from his chewing tobacco, Root spent the rest of his life, until age seventy-one in 1970, protesting the drama's accuracy.

"No, dammit," the pitcher stated firmly, "the Babe didn't call his shot. He just indicated he had one strike left, which was plenty when you were Babe Ruth. I'm tired of being the goat. Hell, the Babe hit 15 World Series home runs, so I wasn't the only guy he teed off on, but no, he didn't take two strikes on purpose.[16]

Bush played 17 years and won 176 games with a lifetime 3.86 ERA. His ERA of 1930 was the worst of his career, something common for many. In four other seasons, he won at least 18 games.

The veteran right-hander had an intriguing perspective on Ruth. In 1935, as Ruth was poised to retire and Bush was pitching for the Pittsburgh Pirates, he gave up the last two regular-season blasts of the Babe's career, numbers 713 and 714.

Bush planned to throw three fastballs right down the middle because Ruth did not seem as if he still had his old swing and had only blooped his first homer.

"He got ahold of that ball and hit it over the triple-deck clear out of the ballpark in right-center," Bush said. "I'm telling you, it was the longest cock-eyed ball I ever saw in my life. That poor fellow. He'd gotten to where he could hardly hobble along. So when he rounds third base, I just look over there at him and he kind of looked at me. I tipped my cap, just to say, 'I've seen everything now.'"[17]

As a member of the 1930 Cubs, Bush also saw another somewhat unbelievable incident. Pitcher Hal Carlson, whose statistical line at age thirty-eight was 4–2 that season, was the focus of one the strangest episodes in the history of major-league baseball.

Preparing to start the Cubs' May 28 game against the Cincinnati Reds, Carlson, a seasoned right-hander with 114 victories on his resume after 14 years in the big leagues, though with an-appropriate-for-the-year soft ERA of 5.05, underwent an offday massage on his perpetually sore elbow. He lay face down on the rubbing table, as was his habit with trainer Andy Lotshaw, who applied his secret potion (just Coca-Cola, but Lotshaw did not trumpet that.).

Then, back at the Hotel Carlos, soon after and abruptly, Carlson was stricken by stomach pains. It was the middle of the night when Carlson awoke in agony. Apparently, he shouted for help, even announced at high volume that he "was dying."[18] (No teammates initially came to the rescue, perhaps because he was known as a practical joker.) A clubhouse attendant came running, and was shocked when Carlson began spitting up blood.

There was no joke and Carlson really was dying. He passed away in the early morning hours on the day of a scheduled start, his life and career ending simultaneously. The cause of death was a stomach hemorrhage.

The Cubs remained in the pennant race, trying to ignore the in-house political lobbying revolving around Rogers Hornsby. No doubt one of the greatest hitters who ever lived, the second baseman who three times batted .400 and won seven batting titles was in his second season with Chicago. Unlike most of the finest hitters of the era, who batted lefty, Hornsby swung from the right side. In 1929, he won the MVP for the Cubs while batting .380 with 149 RBIs. A year later, then thirty-four, he pretty much decided he should be manager of the Cubs—not Joe McCarthy. Instead of matching his year-old numbers, Hornsby was out much of the year recovering from a persistent heel injury and yakking to owner Phil Wrigley. But the owner finally went along, firing McCarthy and appointing Hornsby manager.

Hornsby never did have much success as a field boss, and only appeared in 42 games in 1930. If Hornsby was healthy and played in his usual fashion beyond hitting .308 in limited play, the Cubs might have gone all the way.

Single-mindedly devoted to squeezing every last hit out of his bat, so focused on preserving his hand-eye coordination, he would not attend movies for fear shows would diminish his eyesight. He also shunned drinking and smoking.

Hornsby seemed to be a humorless man who did not make friends easily, but was such a terrific player he could uplift any batting order. Hornsby was blunt to the point of insulting, but was acknowledged at the plate as "The Rajah." His prime was the 1920s, mostly with the St. Louis Cardinals, but over his 23 seasons made major contributions to the Cubs, Giants, and even Brooklyn briefly.

Hornsby's lifetime average of .358 is second all-time to Ty Cobb's. In addition, he led his league in home runs twice and in RBIs four times. In 1924, Hornsby batted .424. Given the pitching of 1930, and what so many nondescript hitters were accomplishing, a healthy Hornsby might have come close to .450. Wilson may have knocked in 200 runs with Hornsby getting on in front of him.

Jesse Burkett, another great hitter, marveled at Hornsby's skill.

"He stands up there and bats sensibly," Burkett said. "That wonderful batting eye, combined with an ability to place a hit, will make a batting record for all time."[19] Almost did.

Hornsby not only had confidence from a young age, he possessed a naturally smooth batting stance and once when asked how it was that he could hit so well, he said, "I simply can't help it."[20]

When Hornsby managed the Cubs, the players—many of them outstanding—said he set a nearly impossible standard to match. A grumpy Hornsby was constantly let down by his aspirations for them. Only he never let himself down.

"You must believe in yourself," Hornsby said. "I know I can hit the baseball. I didn't care if a pitcher threw the ball with his foot as long as the ball came in the strike zone. The only emotion or thought I ever had for a pitcher was to feel sorry for him."[21]

Yes, Hornsby knew he could hit. Like almost no one else who came before or after.

22

THE ST. LOUIS CARDINALS

SHOWBOAT FISHER. AS much as Hack Wilson epitomized the grandeur of hitting in 1930, and put a stamp on the season for all time's sake, George "Showboat" Fisher did in his own way, too. Wilson set an all-time record for runs batted in, one that is likely to last forever. Fisher set an all-time Fisher record, for one season crazily, wildly, dramatically thrusting his name into the forefront of baseball's best hitters.

Fisher was a rookie in 1923 who had excelled in the minors, but after having not appearing in a professional game in six years, was kept on the roster by the St. Louis Cardinals. For a few months he was one of the hottest hitters on the planet, a batter keeping company with Chuck Klein, Babe Herman, Bill Terry, and Wilson in the National League. The 1930 season was fantasyland for Fisher.

Born in 1899, Fisher had some semi-heroic swings through minor-league organizations, most notably on repeat occasions with the Minneapolis Millers for whom he periodically stopped in to bat over .300. But he also wielded an effective bat in other big towns that, in scope, were just below major league, such as Buffalo, Milwaukee, and Rochester.

Fisher had few chances to rise in the 1920s, though he made cameo appearances with the Washington Senators in 1923 and 1924. In limited shots totaling 28 games, of all things, Fisher couldn't hit, putting up mediocre numbers.

He stood 5-foot-10 and weighed 170 pounds, and never was a truly serious power hitter, yet battered hurlers senseless in the Western League representing the Class A St. Joseph Saints of Missouri. Showboat hit .352 and. 359 in the early 1920s before the Senators beckoned.

The most notable aspect of Fisher's stay with the Senators was being a member of Washington's 1924 World Series team. Although much frustrating time passed in between, when Fisher got another call from the Cardinals for 1930, he also latched on to a pennant winner. Fisher lived to be ninety-five years old, and became the last living member of either Series team.

When asked about that in 1993, Fisher replied, "Seems like a hundred years ago, but I wouldn't trade it for anything."[1]

The ride with the Cardinals in 1930 was special, especially at thirty-one. Fisher fit right in with a team endowed with magnificent hitting. He got into 92 games, with 286 plate appearances, as St. Louis pursued the NL pennant and batted .374 with a .432 on-base percentage. He belted eight home runs and drove in 61 runs, at no time looking out of place in faster company. His showing was greeted with astonishment by the rest of the league.

His stay may not have been long in the limelight, but Fisher loved talking baseball for the rest of his life and was pleased to reminisce. Pretty much a lifetime resident of Minnesota, following a brief stay after birth in Iowa, Fisher was compatible with the signature hobbies of the outdoors in the state, hunting and fishing. Rediscovered late in life by students of the sport, Fisher found himself the object of autograph seekers in his eighties, fans mailing him notes.

One might think the Cardinals would view Fisher more fondly after his marvelous season, but he and the club fought over money and he ended up back in the minors before an 18-game stint with the St. Louis Browns in 1932, when he mustered just a .182 average. The main thing holding Fisher back was his poor fielding; he dropped too many flies in the outfield.

Oh, it wasn't so much Fisher being a showoff that earned him the nickname of "Showboat." musical show *Show Boat* played in St. Louis almost as long as the Cardinals did that summer. Fisher also had his own flashy stance at home plate.

"My style of hitting was quite a bit different than most hitters," Fisher said.[2]

It was an unusual career, but the high point was indisputably 1930. One of the least-known hitters in the sport outperformed so many famous ones.

The Cardinals had a surfeit of .300 hitters crowded into the lineup—all eight regulars, plus another four main backups. As a team, St. Louis hit .314. Sometimes it seemed the Cardinals would never make an out.

Catcher Jimmie Wilson was a lifetime .284 hitter, but batted .318 that season. Hall of Fame first baseman Jim Bottomley was a .310 hitter lifetime, though came in under that at .304. Frank Frisch, another Hall of Famer, manned second and hit .346, on his way to a lifetime .316 mark. Shortstop Charlie Gelbert was not as famous, but hit famously at .304, easily his best single season at the plate. Sparky Adams played third and hit .314.

The main outfielders were Hall of Famer Chick Hafey (.336), Taylor Douthit (.303), and rookie George Watkins—a veritable unknown—who was in Showboat Fisher territory with a .373 average. Coming off the bench for various amounts of time, although receiving substantial looks, were Fisher, Gus Mancuso (.366) , Ray Blades (.396), and Ernie Orsatti (.321).

Manager Gabby Street could close his eyes and point in the darkness and still come up with a worthy pinch hitter. Street probably had as much fun as the hitters that season. He had a track record of having a good time before he became a manager.

Street's most famous escapade was taking on a challenge in 1908, with $500 at stake, that he could catch a ball dropped from the top of the Washington Monument. A couple well-heeled fans dreamed up the stunt. It took more than ten tries for a ball to land close enough for Street to try and spear it. Those tosses drifted sideways and bounced off the monument.

Ultimately, Street got a chance. This type of thing had been tried before with other catchers, but no player made the grab. Street pulled it off on the thirteenth ball thrown over the side.

"I didn't see the ball until it was halfway down," Street said. "It was slanting in the wind and I knew it would be hard to catch."[3]

Street was selected as the new Cardinals manager in the off-season, receiving his hiring call for 1930 when he was home helping his wife wash clothes. The Mrs. was hard to impress. She reacted with: "That was a fine how-do-you-do for Mr. [Sam] Breadon to pick his new manager out of a wash tub."[4]

Street believed he was ready for the job. "Of course I considered myself as a fine prospect," he said, "and I told myself that if Breadon picked anybody else but The Old Sergeant, the National League would lose a damn fine manager. We don't need much help in the way of players and I believe I have a good chance to win the pennant in my first year as a big-league manager."[5]

He was right without even knowing he would have a dozen players hit .300.

Gelbert was a young, promising star in his second season, and 1930 would be his best in a career cut short after nine years. Those were hard-fought years, too, as Gelbert was nearly killed in a hunting accident in November 1932, as he and friends gathered to chase rabbits and birds with shotguns and dogs in the woods of Pennsylvania.

Near the conclusion of the day's hunt, Gelbert made a misstep, catching a foot on a vine, dropped his gun, took a tumble, and had the bad luck to be shot in his left leg. It was a serious wound. "When I think about it now," Gelbert reflected later, "the gun was right up against my leg when it went off. If it had been a few inches away it would have cut my foot off."[6] Gelbert's friends helped him to a nearby farm and then he was in for a rough car ride over a logging road.

Hard times followed. Gelbert did not play from 1932 to 1935, and only once, that latter season, did he ever hit well again, reaching .292. Gelbert battled back to the diamond, but while in the hospital, he pledged to his wife he was finished with hunting. "From now on," Gelbert said while recuperating, "I'll confine myself to golf."[7]

Watkins, a rookie, was as big a surprise to the Cardinals front office in 1930 as Showboat Fisher. Already thirty years of age, Watkins had never played an inning in the majors. He kicked around the minors for five years, mostly in Texas, and regularly produced .300 seasons. Even that was a late start, as he had joined the Navy for World War I in his late teens. The Cardinals gave him a shot and, in 1930, he recorded the highest average ever by a National League rookie. It was a stunning showing for a man who resembled the cowboy image and was considered to be as tough as leather. He made good in the game as essentially a substitute for his older brother, Henry. They were among seven children who barely knew their father, and Henry volunteered to take care of the rest of the family while George sought to make baseball pay off for him.

Watkins's 1930 season was semi-miraculous. Besides that stratospheric .373 average, he hit 17 home runs, knocked in 87 runs, and recorded a .415 on-base percentage. The high times were limited for Watkins, who played seven seasons with a lifetime average of .288. Still, he had a few other major moments, including in World Series play.

"He was as tough as he looked," said one-time Cardinals' teammate Andy High.[8]

On June 24, 1931, in the same game of a doubleheader, Watkins smashed three homers—a performance those who saw raved about. It made an impression on manager Street, for sure.

"One day he hits three out of sight and you think he's Babe Ruth," Street said. "The next day he knows he can't hit [Dazzy] Vance, so he bunts. Then he plays it like Ty Cobb and now I find he's been sick. I'm telling you, a quitter never wins and a winner never quits."[9]

The .300 hitters just kept pouring out of the woodwork for Street. It was insane. Why not Douthit, too? In 11 big-league seasons, he averaged .291. Though he batted .336 the year before, it seems he may have actually slumped in 1930, at only .303. Douthit, a righty hitter who stood 5-11 and weighed 175 pounds, featured other attributes as well. He was a highly complimented fielder roaming center, earning the nickname "Ballhawk." Fly balls went to die in his glove.

In June 1931, Douthit pulled off his greatest feat at the plate. It was a weekend, and Douthit stroked nine straight hits. The only problem was that the Cardinals had decided to trade Douthit on Friday and not announce the deal to the Cincinnati Reds until Monday.

"I got the nine hits in a row, all right," Douthit said, "but I had no idea they were trading me."[10]

Douthit, just thirty-two when he retired in 1933, was suffering the first ill effects of arthritis when St. Louis shipped him off to Cincinnati. Still, he contributed to three Cardinals pennants, including the 1926 team when Rogers Hornsby was manager. Hornsby had no flaws at the plate, but the second baseman had one big problem in the field: he hated to track popups and did not do very well at that task going backward. Sometimes Douthit, the expert fielder, tutored Hornsby, and other times he yelled for his assistance to run in and grab them.

"He'd say to me, 'Taylor, Taylor,'" Douthit said. "One day, backing up, Rog fell over backward, hit his head on a water sprinkler, and was knocked out cold. Frankie Frisch, who took Hornsby's place at second base, would stagger under pop flies, but my, he could go get them."[11]

Even though he did not hit a home run, infielder Adams, a veteran at thirty-five, posted his best season in 1930. A lifetime .286 hitter over 13 years, Adams took pride protecting the bases in the field, even though he stood just 5-foot-4 1/2.

"If somebody kept coming in high, I'd throw the ball right for his head," Adams said. "If he tried to spike me, I'd walk all over his hands, face, anything."[12]

Teams liked that spirit. Catcher Gus Mancuso made a very good early impression with his 76-game, .366 introduction to the Cardinals after playing in just 11 games in 1928. Mancuso was at the beginning of a 17-season career, but never came close to hitting that well again.

And none of those high hitters included the Hall of Famers. Street could switch between guys fans had hardly ever heard of who were batting .373, to old reliables as if he was shuffling cards.

Outfielder Chick Hafey was in the middle of a 13-year big-league career and had been a staple in St. Louis since breaking in during the 1924 season. When Hafey stroked the ball at a .336 clip in 1930, it was one of five times with the Cardinals when he hit at least .329. A year later, Hafey led the NL with a .349 average. Consistent with the live-ball era, Hafey also had good power, smacking 26 homers with 107 RBIs. His statistical line somewhat mirrored the club as a whole, someone who could do it all.

Hafey became the first player to record a hit in All-Star Game history in 1933—when the event was established—although by then he was with the Cincinnati Reds. Hafey was traded because he made a habit of holding out for more money, and in 1931 and 1932 was at odds with Cardinals management.

It was Cardinals executive Branch Rickey whom Hafey later feuded with over money.

Anyone who watched Hafey spray line drives all over the ballpark could see how solid a hitter he was, but he suffered from one handicap during a less enlightened era. In order to pick up the pitched balls flying at him with sufficient precision, he needed to wear glasses. There were many skeptics of that aid in the sport. In Hafey's case, an ongoing sinus problem interfered with his daily duties, too.

Hafey's vision problem was not all natural, either. It had deteriorated somewhat because he had been hit in the head with pitches during his career. He became one of the first major-league players to wear glasses in games, and had an emergency supply of glasses on hand—three pairs, in case of breakage.

During August 1930, Hafey saw the ball just fine. He connected for hits in 10 straight at-bats, which tied the National League record. In 1931, Hafey hit for the cycle and that year, when he claimed the batting crown, edged the Giants' Bill Terry by .002. In the records, they are listed as hitting the same .349.

Hafey was just thirty-two when he retired, blaming the continuing hassles and pain from his sinus woes more than his vision. After playing just 15 games in 1935, Hafey took time off and tried to make a comeback the following spring. Though not making an appearance in 1936, he did play 89 games in 1937, but wasn't his previous self at the plate, batting just .261.

"I don't know what's the matter," Hafey said. "Just when I think everything is all right, I get a dizzy spell. I don't want to try to play again if I'm going to have this trouble. The last season I played I had to have my glasses fitted with new lenses four times. Every time I caught cold, it would impair my vision."[13]

No one could blame Hafey for being somewhat gloomy, but his counterpart at first base, Jim Bottomley, was nicknamed "Sunny." A left-handed hitter and thrower, Bottomley hit .300 nine times, including a limited rookie season in 1922 when he cemented a spot in the lineup by batting .325 in 37 games. By 1930, Bottomley had hit .371 and .367. In his case, swinging for just .304 in 1930 was an "only."

It was not difficult to see how Bottomley received his nickname. He was always in a good mood; always gracious, whether it was inviting a sportswriter to join he and his wife for dinner, to how he approached the game.

A high school dropout from Nokomis, Illinois, Bottomley went to work as a coal miner, railroad clerk, grocery store clerk, and truck driver to help support his family. He was playing semipro ball when scouted, and emerged as a big-league star by twenty-one. That was after family circumstances had been made worse when a younger brother was killed in a mining accident.

Bottomley drove in more than 100 runs in a season six times, and twice led the NL in RBIs. His biggest claim to fame was knocking in a record 12 runs in a single game. On September 16, 1924, Bottomley went wild at bat versus the Brooklyn Robins. In a game won by St. Louis, 17–3, Bottomley went 6-for-6 with three runs scored. His production included two home runs and a double to account for the 12 RBIs. Nearly a century later, the record still stands, though it was tied by Mark Whiten, also of the Cardinals, in 1993.

Due to money haggling with Cincinnati, Bottomley thought his career might end a little earlier than hoped.

"I've played National League ball for 13 years and have $100,000 saved and if I never play ball again it will be all right with me," Bottomley said. "I did not attempt any hold-up on the Reds. If I am sold or traded and the club taking title to my services offers the right kind of a contract I'll gladly get back into uniform. Otherwise, I expect old Sunny Jim is leaving baseball and leaving it as he entered—with a smile."[14]

Bottomley was traded to the St. Louis Browns, a landing spot that pleased him because of his fondness for the city.

"I am glad I have played most of my baseball here. When I'm no longer wanted, I'll slide out gracefully and forget it," Bottomley said of his impending retirement. "Until then, I'll just do the best I can."[15]

Bottomley, who also became a manager, did the best he could until he passed away at fifty-nine.

Second baseman Frankie Frisch was already famous before he became the manager of the Cardinals' Gashouse Gang teams. A fierce and fiery player—first with the New York Giants, where his once-close bond with John J. McGraw frayed sufficiently for him to be traded to St. Louis—Frisch led with his performance and his vocabulary.

"The Fordham Flash" went directly from New York's Fordham University to the Giants in 1919, as a twenty-one-year-old, and was an established star by the time he was traded to St. Louis in 1927. With the Cardinals, Frisch won two of his three National League stolen-base titles, and had a .312 batting average over his 11 seasons in St. Louis. When he retired, Frisch owned a lifetime average of .316, and was an easy choice for the Hall of Fame.

Frisch batted .346 for the 1930 Cardinals—two points shy of his career best—hit 10 home runs, drove in 114 runs, and stole 15 bases. His on-base percentage was .407. Although that was probably his best all-around season, Frisch actually won the NL Most Valuable Player Award the next year (.311 average, 161 hits, 82 RBIs, 28 stolen bases).

The Cardinals were one of the most memorable and colorful outfits of the era (and in baseball history) while Frisch served and led them, routinely capturing pennants and brashly taking on the best in several World Series. St. Louis won pennants in 1926, 1928, 1930, 1931, and 1934, with more stars than seen in the galaxy, from Rogers Hornsby to Dizzy Dean to, of course, Frisch. The Cardinals took home three world championships in that span (1926, 1931, and 1934).

In one of baseball's most controversial and analyzed trades, Frisch and pitcher Jimmy Ring were traded from New York to St. Louis for Hornsby. Although it may have seemed doubtful at the time, the Cardinals appeared to get the better of the deal over the long run. Frisch and Hornsby both believed in imposing discipline, but somehow Hornsby's methods seemed to grate on players while Frisch's appeared to inspire them. It may be that

Frisch built a reputation as a leader who would fight for his players. while Hornsby built a reputation as a leader who would fight with anyone.

St. Louis made a lousy first impression on Frisch as a young ballplayer, who thrilled to the excesses of New York, though he was more mature when he moved there to stay.

"You can have it," Frisch said of St. Louis in 1919, after his first Giants road trip to the city, when asked how the middle of the country compared to New York. "Being with the Giants is swell. But if I was traded to one of those other clubs I would quit."[16] When it happened, Frisch did not quit, he adapted. Frisch spent longer playing in St. Louis than he did in New York and was still with the Cardinals when he played his last game at thirty-nine in 1937.

Frisch said he realized it was time to retire after exhausting himself on the bases. "Somehow I managed to last until I reached the plate and then I almost collapsed," Frisch said. "That's when I realized I was positively through."[17]

The 1930 Cardinals were so flush with hitters, compared to most other seasons, it was embarrassing. Yet other teams that were going nowhere in the standings, the Phillies as Exhibit A, hit just about as well overall. The difference was having some pitching to back up the hitting. Two starters, Jesse Haines and Burleigh Grimes, were future Hall of Famers, and "Wild Bill" Hallahan was a Hall of Fame character. The lesser lights in the mix just about all managed winning records, even if they were not able to brag about their earned run averages.

Syl Johnson lasted 19 years in the bigs and finished 112–117. One of his three best seasons, closely bunched for results, was 1930 when he went 12–10. Jim Lindsey's 7–5 record was his best in parts of seven years. Al Grabowski pitched parts of two seasons, but went 6–4. Hi Bell's 4–3 was up there among his best efforts. Bill Sherdel spent part of 1930 with St. Louis, going 3–2. And Hal Haid also went 3–2. Except for Johnson, the others were all relievers.

One pitcher of consequence too young to make a difference in 1930, injected himself into the season roundup. The blooming right-hander Jerome Hanna "Dizzy" Dean, soon to erupt in baseball consciousness, was twenty years old. He was handed one start, on September 28—the very last day of the season—and pitched a complete-game three-hitter to go 1–0 (the Cardinals beating the Pittsburgh Pirates, 3–1). A few seasons later, Dean won 30 games in one year, one of the last of that breed.

At his best, Flint Rhem had the potential to be an ace. But the righty, who won 20 games for St. Louis in 1926, was erratic on the mound. In addition to his struggles on the field, he did not take care of himself off the field, and put himself at risk through drink. Rhem was once so hungover in the bullpen that he fell asleep and, when he awoke with his eyes taped shut by teammates, he thought he had gone blind. His earned-run average in 26 games in 1930 wasn't much, at 4.45, but he still finished 12–8.

Rhem had an unusual last name, but was also born in Rhems, South Carolina, which was named after his family. Whether he displayed much wisdom is open to discussion, but Rhem was a college man at Clemson, where he also pitched. He won 22 games in the minors in Fort Smith, Arkansas, and threw a no-hitter, too, before the Cardinals looked him over in 1924.

Rhem's breakthrough came in 1926. Recognizing his long-term battle with alcoholism, the Cardinals front office offered him a \$2,500 bonus as part of his contract if he refrained from drinking during the season. But the most notorious story surrounding Rhem occurred late in the 1930 season. In mid-September, he was missing when Street called roll for a game against Brooklyn at Ebbets Field. He did not appear in the manager's sight until the next day.

When Rhem contritely presented himself to Street, he came with an explanation, an explanation everyone across the country recounted, but that no one believed. "Guns, bandits, kidnapping," is how Rhem began his story to Street, summarizing his night by saying two men kidnapped him at gunpoint, transported him to a remote roadhouse in New Jersey, and forced liquor down his throat. "They made me drink the awful stuff." The reasoning behind this escapade was murky, although perhaps the mugs wanted to place bets on the game and thought Rhem might beat them out of their cash.

"And I'm sorry to say that I got drunk," Rhem said of how the imbibing affected him. "Imagine that happening to me! Of all people, me! I was helpless, always in fear of my life."[18]

This was one of the most fantastical stories in baseball history. Major League Baseball wanted to pursue an investigation, following the gambling angle, but the Cardinals urged discretion. St. Louis let the matter go and continued using Rhem on the mound during the pennant race.

"Rhem is a good pitcher," Street said. "I think he can help us win the pennant. I am sorry this happened, but we are going to give the Kid another chance. Whether Rhem's story is true, I do not know. It may be true, but I prefer to let the matter drop."[19]

Rhem completed parts of 12 seasons in the majors, mostly with the Cardinals since the team traded him twice and acquired him three times, including his original signing. In between his adventures, Rhem compiled a 105–97 record with 91 complete games.

It may be that Gabby Street was blessed with so many good hitters he didn't have to strain his brain to put together a solid starting lineup. But it also may be that the pitchers caused enough to worry about on their own.

When the season began, it was no certainty "Wild Bill" Hallahan would produce a 15–9 record. Since 1925, Hallahan had been in and out of Cardinals training camp and had compiled a 6–8 record over three seasons. Finally, 1930 was his year. If Rhem was wild for his own reasons, Wild Bill earned his nickname by frequently missing the plate while trying to throw strikes.

The southpaw from upstate New York provided a sneak preview of 1930 three years earlier, when he was with Syracuse of the International League. That season, Hallahan won 19 games, but also led the league in both strikeouts *and* walks. For the Cardinals, Hallahan won his 15 games, but also led the National League in walks and strikeouts.

Hallahan pitched when it was difficult for left-handers to get respect. They were automatically classified as wild throwers and goofy off the mound, and Hallahan did his worst to enhance both reputations. Once he went to the wrong train station because he thought the traveling secretary, who made the arrangements, had the departure location wrong.

"All left-handers are dumb, all of 'em," said Clarence Lloyd, the Cardinals official in question.[20]

In those days, parents sometimes attempted to train their children out of being left-handed, which Hallahan's parents attempted as well. Tilting him toward the right never took, but Hallahan was able to make a living with his left in baseball. Once, Hallahan's hand was smashed in the door of a crowded taxi and he had to ice it, but pitched the next day because the injured one was his right hand.

Hallahan was even better in 1931, winning an NL-high 19 games, and although his lifetime mark of 102–94 was just OK, he was at his best at World Series time, coming through in the clutch repeatedly for the Cardinals. In seven Series appearances, he went 3–1 with an ERA of 1.36. He was also a card-carrying member of the Gashouse Gang, along with Dean, Frisch, Pepper Martin, and the rest of the bunch that won big and played hard.

Later in life, Hallahan thought players had gone softer; that they wouldn't fight one another. When he played, Hallahan said, he stuck to certain rituals. For him, that meant a change of outlook when the season was about to begin.

"I never chewed off the field, or in winter," Hallahan said of his use of tobacco on the diamond. "But when I reported for spring training, into my jaw it went. It was almost like part of my uniform."[21]

The three aspects of baseball pitcher Burleigh Grimes is most closely identified with are being a member of the National Baseball Hall of Fame, a long association with the Brooklyn Dodgers, and being designated as the last legal spitball thrower after the pitch was banned.

He was not as crucial a member of the 1930 St. Louis Cardinals' pitching staff. Grimes was thirty-six, yet finished 13–6 with one of the best earned-run averages in the game, at 3.01, when others were blowing up. Most of Grimes's best seasons were in his rearview mirror, such as his 25-victory campaign of 1928, but he was an essential part of the Cardinals' success.

Grimes was nearing the end of his career, but went 17–7 in 1929 for the Pittsburgh Pirates. Pittsburgh lost interest, though, and made a careless trade of Grimes to the Boston Braves for Percy Jones, who was nearer the end than Grimes. Grimes made a slow start with Boston, going 3–5, but the Cardinals showed more faith, parting with pitchers Fred Frankhouse and Bill Sherdel for Grimes. Overall that season, Grimes concluded at 16–11, but

13–6 for the Cardinals before doing an even better job in 1931 with a 17–9 mark. So Grimes contributed to two pennant-winners at his advanced age as he moved toward 270 career triumphs.

Grimes and Frisch, now teammates, were snarling enemies when the former was with Brooklyn and the latter batted against him. Although Frisch did not become the dugout boss until after Grimes left the Cardinals, they did take time to make peace.

"He started throwing at my head and then he switched and threw at my knees," Frisch recalled of his early relationship with Grimes. "When he discovered I was a low-ball hitter, he switched back to the head."[22]

Years later, when sitting around Cooperstown at the Hall of Fame talking baseball with Bill Terry, Terry's thoughts gravitated to the same subject.

"Why, Burleigh, did you always throw at my feet?" he asked the then ninety-year-old Grimes. "Because you hit with your feet close together," Grimes responded, "and couldn't move them as fast as you could your head."[23]

The last legal spitballer was throwing the pitch when it was outlawed, so Grimes was grandfathered in under major-league rules. He was a hard-nosed player who always went full speed and was never willing to surrender an inch. The batters were the enemy, and he wanted team managements to pay fair value.

"I'm afraid I was too demanding," said Grimes, who played for seven big-league teams and bargained hard for a good payday. "But I was worth it. Nobody ever gave more, whether pitching, fielding, or hitting."[24]

Grimes and holdover veteran Jesse Haines were good friends, so when Grimes joined the Cardinals he had someone to schmooze with. Haines had also been in the game a long time. He was thirty-six, and threw his first pitch in the majors in 1918.

The 6-foot, 190-pound righty—an early adherent to the knuckleball—Haines was a three-time 20-game winner for the Cardinals, and was enshrined in the Hall of Fame after winning 210 games in a 19-year career. He was not at his baffling best in 1930, but his 13–8 record was certainly helpful. His earned-run average climbed to 4.30, but seemed to pitch around calamity, recalling seasons when he was sub-3.00.

In 1925, Haines, who spent 18 consecutive years with the Cardinals, pitched a no-hitter versus the Boston Braves, and in 1927 won 24 games and notched a 2.72 ERA.

As an older pitcher after becoming a devotee of the knuckleball, Haines once had to leave a game with bleeding knuckles. Another sign of his advancing age was his having to wait five days between starts. That may be regular duty now, but not then.

"Of course, I can't work as often as these young fellows," Haines said, "or as long, either, but I can pitch every once in a while and be the ph of some value."[25]

23

WINNERS AND LOSERS

JESSE HAINES AND Burleigh Grimes, old-timers of the pitching staff, complemented by a dozen .300 hitters, made the St. Louis Cardinals impossible to beat during the 1930 pennant race. Yet, despite finishing 92–62, and with all of those weapons, the Cardinals still had to stage one of the great late-season rallies to wrest the pennant away from the other top teams in the National League.

On August 8, after falling to Brooklyn, 11–5, the Cardinals resided in fourth place, 12 games out of first.

As was obvious, the NL was jam-packed with tremendous hitters—hitters having the year of their lives. When teams are batting well over .300, it is difficult to shut them out or shut them down. The Cardinals may not have seemed quite buried, but they were over the horizon from teams powering the ball about as well as they were.

On the date of the dismal loss to Brooklyn, the Cardinals' record was 53–52. If they were showing a pulse it was only to demonstrate they could still finish over .500.

From then on, however, the Cardinals—with those dozen men stroking the ball, aided by those old-time pitchers—set the league ablaze. St. Louis rushed to the end at 39–10 (including winning streaks of nine, seven, and five (three times) and glided into the World Series, capturing the flag by two games.

The Chicago Cubs came in second with a 90–64 record, while the Giants and Brooklyn fell off. Brooklyn was tied for first as late as September 16, then lost six games in a row. The Giants also went backwards.

In first place as late as September 12, the Cubs were unable to push to the front, even when finishing the season with six straight victories (the last four under new leader Rogers Hornsby).

As the Cardinals slammed the door, Haines, Grimes, and Flint Rehm won two games apiece. "Wild Bill" Hallahan was in the mix, too, obtaining the win when the Cardinals moved into first for good in mid-September.

Hallahan marveled at the talent the Cardinals of that era pulled together, starting with the 1926 pennant and running into the 1930s. They had a special player at just about every position, including the overabundance of swingers in 1930. He credited front office honcho Branch Rickey, who had the foresight to invent the farm system.

"I'll never know where Rickey found all of those wonderful prospects," Hallahan said. "The word 'genius' is terribly overused, but that is what he was when it came to finding and polishing gems."[1]

Haines might never have been admitted to the National Baseball Hall of Fame if he had not joined the exclusive club as a knuckleball thrower when he was losing the steam on his fastball. The new pitch extended his career just enough for Haines to represent the Cardinals in the World Series a couple of extra times. Those games provided opportunity.

There are few born knuckleball throwers. Few come into the game with that dipsy-doodle pitched readymade. More often they turn to it as an emergency backup when their original good stuff starts to fade. That was Haines's tale.

"I worked on a knuckleball quite a while before I started using it consistently," Haines said. "Mine acted like a spitball. I had very good control of it and threw it from different positions. I'd say that some years it added eight to 10 victories to my total."[2]

When the Cardinals pulled the trigger on the trade that brought in Burleigh Grimes, he understood he was going to a better place. The Boston Braves were going nowhere. The two pitchers he was swapped for, Fred Frankhouse and Bill Sherdel, were sad to leave.

Grimes probably forgot the Braves the moment he peeled off the jersey. He was going to St. Louis to win. Grimes revved up just when the team got hot, and padded his win total in August and September.

Owner Sam Breadon seemed to surrender when the Cardinals were 10 games behind. Breadon made a foot-in-the-mouth statement in mid-August while chewing the fat with sportswriters. "It's too bad our club didn't start a little earlier," he said. "I would have had you guys all back here for the World Series. We're playing the best ball in the league right now, but we're too far behind to make up ground we lost earlier in the season."[3]

On September 18, Grimes beat Brooklyn, 4–3, in front of his old fans, who did not view him with nostalgia. The feeling was reciprocated. Grimes took his share of jeering, but didn't mind it one bit.

"Naw, I liked it," Grimes said. "Hey, there's nothing I enjoy more than to have 'em hollering for my head and then be able to strike a slugger out in a pinch. That's sweet music to my ears."[4]

* * *

When the roulette wheel stopped spinning in the American League, the Philadelphia Athletes, in the midst of their own mini-dynasty, strolled away with the pennant. The A's warded off early challenges from the always powerful New York Yankees, the resurgent Washington Senators, and the slightly improving Cleveland Indians.

In the end, the A's flexed their muscles and waved Lefty Grove's arm at pretenders, finishing the season at 102–52. Second place went to Washington, eight games behind at 94–60. The Yankees, for all of the slugging mustered by Babe Ruth, Lou Gehrig, and their cohorts, dropped down to 86–68—16 games behind first place.

The Red Sox came in last and were a full 50 games behind Philadelphia, which meant they had a better shot of winning the International League than the American League.

Philadelphia offered less suspense than the Cardinals. Except for a chunk of May, and a few days in July, Philadelphia was never out of first place again all summer. It was in July when their lead began to bulge.

Philadelphia had a nuclear weapon in Grove that season when the rest of the league was defenseless. He stood alone in 1930.

"His control was his biggest asset," said Bill Veeck, the Hall of Fame owner, sometime later. "When you could throw as hard as he could with his accuracy, you didn't have to do much else. He came to the park to beat you."[5]

Then, of course, the Athletics could supplement Grove with their killers in their lineup. Al Simmons drove in 165 runs, but was aided and abetted by Jimmie Foxx, who drove in 156. Comparatively unheralded was second baseman Max Bishop, who walked

128 times. Bishop was always hanging around on base waiting to be driven in; he scored 117 times. For that matter, five of the starters in the A's lineup compiled on-base percentages of .414 or higher. They were relentless.

Foxx finished with 534 home runs at a time when only Babe Ruth had more. Ted Williams, his teammate with the Boston Red Sox, said the ball made a different sound when it exploded off of Foxx's bat. Longtime Baltimore sportswriter John Steadman said Foxx was "so strong he could take a brand new ball out of the box, squeeze it with his hands and loosen the cover."[6]

During a tribute to Foxx in his hometown of Sudlersville, Maryland, two decades after he died, jokes were made about him clouting about baseballs to far-off lands like Alaska.

In 1930, Foxx launched 37 home runs and his on-base percentage led the quartet of Athletics at .429.

That season, Foxx and Simmons were even more potent poisons together, two fabulous Hall of Famers at their best. Simmons was one home run behind Foxx and .06 behind in on-base percentage while outhitting him at .381. Those who saw Simmons said he swaggered when he came to the plate.

"I wish I had nine players named Al Simmons," said A's manager Connie Mack.[7]

Catcher Cy Perkins froze Simmons in time in his mind as someone who almost could not be topped on the diamond. "I've always classed him next to Ty Cobb as the greatest player I ever saw," Perkins said.[8]

On May 1, the A's beat the Detroit Tigers, 19–2, and during one stretch in July, scored double figures in six out of nine games (the other three scoring nine runs). In the 15–1 win that ended that streak (July 18), Foxx drove in six runs.

St. Louis scored at least 15 runs in a game eight times. Those hitting-deep Cardinals topped 1,004 runs, a National League record. The Yankees managed 1,062, a new big-league record.

As the best hitters of their generation feasted on the shakiest pitching of all time, and as the opportunistic hitters who had suffered and been rebuffed, had their moments in the sun, the World Series lined up the Athletics against the Cardinals.

Given the year just completed, it seemed a sure thing the impressive commanders of the bat of St. Louis and the big sluggers of the Athletics would collide to provide the most explosive World Series of all. A best four-out-of-seven championship loomed and was sure to set records for hits, runs, average, and fireworks. The .314-hitting Cardinals feared no pitcher. The merely .294-hitting Athletics believed they could out-slug any opponent.

In this strangest of all hitting seasons, when nine teams averaged more than .300, some twenty players collected at least 200 hits, one player topped .400, and another set the now-ninety-year-old record for RBIs, it seemed inevitable the world would see a World Series unlike any other.

* * *

The World Series showdown between the 102-victory, defending champion Athletics and the 92-win Cardinals began on October 1 at Shibe Park in Philadelphia.

Manager Connie Mack started Grove for the A's in Game One, as everyone expected. Everyone would have questioned whether Mack suffered a mental lapse if he picked anyone else to throw. It was less obvious when Gabby Street gave the ball to Grimes.

St. Louis actually outhit Philadelphia, 9–5—a pretty good haul off Grove—but they were not big blows. Grimes surrendered just five hits, but they accounted for the same number of runs. When one hour and 48 minutes of entertainment expired for the 32,295 customers, the Athletics had banked a 5–2 victory.

St. Louis led, 2–1, after three innings, but the prosperity didn't last long. The Athletics scored single runs in five innings, with Al Simmons and Mickey Cochrane each ripping solo homers and Jimmie Foxx contributing a triple and a double.

The teams played again the next afternoon, and George Earnshaw handcuffed the Cardinals with efficiency. The A's remembered how to hit, and three times in the first four innings scored two runs. Cochrane homered again. Philadelphia pulled away, winning, 6–1.

During that era teams did not take long breaks between Series games, but they did throw in the occasional travel day. October 3 was an offday, as the clubs rode the train to St. Louis for Game Three at Sportsman's Park. The Cardinals had to pick off a win or they were almost surely done for.

For a moment in the top of the first inning, it appeared Philadelphia might be on its way to a romp. Facing Bill Hallahan, the Athletics loaded the bases. It was a turning point. Hallahan wiggled out of trouble and settled in for the most important victory of his career. He cruised the rest of the way, as St. Louis' bats acted up in the fashion demonstrated all season.

The Cardinals scored here and there all day, with Jim Bottomley and Chick Hafey each crushing run-scoring doubles in a 5–0 win that reinvigorated the hosts. St. Louis rapped out 10 hits in pushing aside Philadelphia's third starter, Rube Walberg. The triumph turned Hallahan into a local hero and burnished his long-term reputation in St. Louis. Hallahan, though, provided little insight to his success.

"After that first inning, I knew I was going to have a good day," Hallahan said. "That first inning was tough, but after that I had as much stuff as I had in Brooklyn [referring to a recent game]. Those fellows are no better hitters than the Robins. Just pitch the same way."[9]

"Wild Bill" provided new life, and Jesse Haines followed suit in Game Four with the same type of critical performance. Haines bested Philadelphia, 3–1, and the Cardinals even made Grove look human . . . but only in the sense that accidents happen. Grove pitched eight innings, allowed five hits and three runs (only one of them earned), taking the defeat.

Haines gave the Sportsman's Park crowd of 39,946 a show, going the distance, quieting the A's to the point where he permitted just four hits and one run. It was one of the major clutch performances of Haines's career and, after Hallahan's effort, the Series was tied at two apiece. As Haines aged past forty, people began calling him "Pop." But he did not pitch like an old man in this game. Sometimes Haines referred back to this victory as his favorite of all time because of the circumstances, spotlight, and besting Grove.

"Beating the great Lefty Grove in the 1930 World Series," Haines said, highlighting the memory. "Not many were beating him in big games in those days."[10]

Haines gave St. Louis hope, but the Athletics eliminated it back at Shibe Park. Earnshaw started for Mack in Game Five and was electric, going seven innings and giving up just two hits and no runs. Of all the bullpen options, it was Grove who came on in relief and picked up the win, pitching two innings of one-hit ball. It was close, but Philadelphia gained its critical third win with a 2–0 victory, St. Louis' passel of .300 hitters were reined in.

It was obvious that, in big games, Mack cared little for starting anyone but Grove or Earnshaw. Earnshaw got the call on one full day's rest and delivered. This time Philadelphia batsmen reacted with fury, crushing Hallahan, 7–1. St. Louis touched Earnshaw for just five hits.

Philadelphia won its second world title in a row, four games to two. Though Earnshaw and Grove won two games apiece, the pitching hero was really Earnshaw, a society man of some wealth who shone brighter than the hard-bitten Grove.

Earnshaw, whose work in the Series was favorably compared to Christy Mathewson's postseason finest, was stingier than the Cards expected and made believers of onlookers not so familiar with the American League. Earnshaw pitched 25 Series innings and gave up two earned runs for an 0.72 ERA.

"Wasn't he the greatest thing you ever looked at?" said Cy Rigler, a former umpire, who called balls and strikes in the decisive game. "I had heard a lot about him. All he needed, all he used today, was that fast one and that curve."[11]

After the explosiveness of the regular season, after the compilation of some of the most amazing batting statistics in the history of baseball, the Philadelphia Athletics won the championship by hitting .197 as a team. Their opponent, the St. Louis Cardinals, flush with a dozen regular-season .300 hitters, lost by batting .200.

Ironically, the Year of the Hitter ended with the Week of the Pitcher.

POSTSCRIPT

FOR SOME OF the big men of the summer, 1930 was the greatest year of their career. For some, the season of the hitter was their defining moment. For some, the high point was prelude to other great moments. For others, the high point only presaged decline or tragedy.

The Philadelphia Athletics' pitcher of the year, Lefty Grove, was even better in 1931, finishing 31–4, and three additional times won at least 20 games on his way into the elite club of 300-game winners. Grove was an easy-choice Hall of Famer, but perhaps is underrated even by those standards.

The standard-bearer of the National League, Dazzy Vance, did not have a special record, but was far ahead of the rest of his opponents in earned-run average. Unlike Grove, who hung in trying until he got it for the 300th win, Vance was stopped three shy of 200.

Any pitcher in that abused class of employment in 1930 who won 20 games deserved, if not a bonus payment in his next contract, at the least the praise of his superiors and compatriots. It was a small group, led by Grove's 28 victories. Wes Ferrell won 25 games, George Earnshaw and Ted Lyons 22 apiece. Lefty Stewart, Ray Kremer, and Pat Malone each 20. To one degree or another, they were all miracle workers on the mound that season.

To make the top ten in average that season, a player had to bat .356. The Chicago Cubs' Hack Wilson held down that position, which comparatively speaking did not come close to matching his production in home runs or runs batted in.

The king of the batsmen that season was the New York Giants' Bill Terry with his .401 mark. Some ninety-plus years later, no other big-league player has topped .400 in the National League, and only Ted Williams did so in the American League, in 1941 (.406).

Others in the National League top ten: 2: Babe Herman, .393; 3: Chuck Klein, .386; 4: Lefty O'Doul, .383; 5: Freddy Lindstrom, .379; 6: George Watkins, .373; 7: Paul Waner, .368; 8: Riggs Stephenson, .367; 9 (tied): Pie Traynor and Hack Wilson, .356.

Terry, Herman, and Klein never hit higher. Neither did Lindstrom, Watkins, Stephenson, Traynor, or Wilson. Waner did—three times—hitting as high as .380. So did O'Doul, reaching .398 in 1929.

As for Showboat Fisher, his show did not last very long, but he was remarkable in 1930 with that .374 average, though he did not make enough plate appearances to qualify for the batting race.

Batting .401 made Bill Terry more than the answer to a trivia question. While his selection surprised many, it was the rangy, sharp-hitting first-baseman who replaced John J. McGraw as manager when after three decades the front man of the New York Giants stepped away from the team he shaped because of ill health.

Terry took command in 1932 and managed the Giants through 1941. His record was a solid 823–661, for a .555 winning percentage. Not in McGraw's class, but a typical fate for a coach or manager who succeeds a legend. He did win a World Series early in his tenure, in 1933, as well as one more pennant, and also served as general manager for several years.

The Giants had a love affair going with Terry for some time. He played his entire career for New York and after he won that 1933 World Series, the team signed him to a new, five-year managerial contract at $40,000 a year. That was real money during the Depression.

Terry was a player-manager through 1938, and concluded his playing days with a .341 average, one of the best totals ever. He was less of a home run and RBI man, but gifted with the glove. His No. 3 uniform jersey was retired by the Giants.

One of the most memorable statements Terry made as manager was a pointed remark aimed at archenemy Brooklyn. When someone asked Terry about the Dodgers' prospects in 1934, he said, "Oh, are they still in the league?"[1]

Terry never backtracked on the remark that inflamed so many Brooklyn fans. He was not a chatterbox with sportswriters, and often criticized their work. Later, he wondered if sour relations with the old-timers kept him out of the Hall of Fame until 1954. When he was inducted, Terry shed a tear and also exclaimed about his selection, "I thank God for it."[2]

The Hack Wilson of 1930 was never to be replicated—not by Hack or anyone else, really. Things began going wrong for him just about right away and his 1931 season seems to have been recorded by a body double rather than the same man, with Wilson stuck on 13 home runs and a .261 average. All his other best seasons came before his absolute best season of 1930.

Wilson's stupendous numbers, especially in the RBI category, are never to be forgotten. The runs batted in total of 191 has never really been approached and the more years pass, the farther over the horizon contenders seem to become marooned.

Only two players ever took a legitimate swing at Wilson's mark. In 1931, the Yankees' Lou Gehrig drove in 185 runs, the second-highest total ever. In 1937, the Tigers' Hank Greenberg knocked in 184 runs. Jimmie Foxx made an aborted run in 1938 with 175 RBIs. Twice before, Gehrig had been within shouting distance of Wilson's record. Stunningly, Gehrig recorded three seasons where he had at least 170 RBIs. Babe Ruth's highest RBI total was 168 in 1921. He also had seasons of 165 and 162.

Wilson's 1931 was a disaster. He couldn't hit any of the pitches he hit routinely the year before. He wondered if he was trying too hard to live up to his fame, and perhaps lived a little too hard in the offseason. After that debacle, Wilson approached his problems with a very modern solution—he installed a home gym in his basement that featured a rowing machine and weights. Plus a punching bag.

"I'm not overweight, understand," Wilson said. "Just softened up." He said he would be ready for spring training by taking advantage of the equipment. "Can't see why I can't come back." A physical gave him a good report. "My eyes were perfect and my eyes, heart, lungs and everything were found to be OK.

"Some people said I was a batting flop because I was carousing around too much," Wilson said. "That was all wrong. I went out occasionally, but not as much as I did the year before."[3]

The Cubs gave up on Wilson remarkably quickly, perhaps not believing in his commitment to physical fitness, and his last few years he played for other National League teams. In 1934, he retired after 12 major-league seasons with a .307 average.

In his prime, Wilson was married with children and owned his home. But he endured a bitter divorce, and bad investments ate up other baseball earnings. Wilson took odd jobs, settling in Baltimore, but in the autumn of 1948 he took a fall at home that led to complications and his death at forty-eight. Wilson was broke at the time, and National League President Ford Frick paid for his funeral. It was also said the hat was passed at one of Wilson's favorite saloons, raising $350 to contribute and buy a tombstone. Later, his Cubs manager, Joe McCarthy, organized a splashier memorial service where baseball people spoke of his great feats with the bat.

That seemed appropriate. Wilson thought McCarthy was the best manager he ever played for, calling him "a nice guy, knew how to handle men and get the best out of 'em." He also singled out Dazzy Vance, the NL menace of 1930, as the one thrower who bothered him. "I could hit 'em high, low, on the inside, or on the outside. Which pitcher gave me the most trouble? Why, Dazzy Vance."[4] He said Vance found his weakness, the fast one down the middle.

The amiable, always friendly, generous, and gregarious Hack Wilson did not say anything at the time about his other weakness, the alcohol.

Wilson's super season lives on in baseball lore, especially the forbidding sounding number of 191. After 1930, the crazy, fluke, stunning hitting season of 1930, was examined and baseball officials fixed things so there would be no repeat, no posse of hitters imitating that season's herd.

Owners and Commissioner Kenesaw Mountain Landis felt the balance between hitting and pitching had been thrown out of balance. Over the winter of 1930–31 changes were made.

The key element came in the manufacture of baseballs, They were doctored at the factory site to ensure they would not travel so far on contact with a bat. By 1930, the baseball featured a corked center, giving the ball quite the lively step when struck. Under the new plan, a so-called cushion cork served as a replacement. The cushion cork was a mixture of cork and rubber and took a bit of the edge off the traveling nature of the ball.

Some other rules were also altered, notably the sacrifice fly where the at-bat was halted for eight years starting in 1931. In 1930, there were 1,317 sacrifices in the National League that did not count as at-bats, but that dropped to 768 in 1931. In the American League the count fell from 1,283 to 650. That, combined with the change in the ball, yanked down batting averages.

Never again would batters be so dominant in a season as they were in 1930. Major League Baseball is still searching for its next .400 hitter and the next Hack Wilson.

Gradually, too, the nation groaned out of the Great Depression, at last reaching full employment when the country shifted to war footing to combat the threats in Europe from Germany and the South Pacific from Japan.

Herbert Hoover's term as president of the United States ended on March 4, 1933, when Franklin D. Roosevelt was inaugurated and took over in the White House. FDR also came on in relief of Hoover as first thrower. The new president threw out the first pitch to open the 1933 baseball season for the Washington Senators on April 12 at Griffith Stadium.

ABOUT THE AUTHOR

Lew Freedman is a veteran sportswriter who has written for several newspapers, including the *Philadelphia Inquirer*, *Chicago Tribune*, *Anchorage Daily News*, and the *Seymour Tribune* in Indiana.

Freedman is the author of more than one hundred books and has received more than three hundred journalism awards. Freedman lives in Indiana with his wife, Debra, and dog, Boston.

SOURCES

PRELUDE

1 Spartano, Phil. "Lindstrom: Ruth Saved Baseball," *Utica Daily Press,* August 16, 1976.

Chapter 2: Hack Wilson—Man of the Hour

1 Parker, Clifton Blue, *Fouled Away: The Baseball Tragedy of Hack Wilson* (Jeffersonville, North Carolina: McFarland Publishing Co. Inc., 2000), P. 10.

2 Ibid., P. 10.

3 Ibid., P.12

4 Ibid., P. 23.

5 Ibid., P. 34.

6 Chastain, Bill, *Hack's 191: Hack Wilson and His Incredible 1930 Season* (Guilford, Connecticut: Lyons Press, 2012), P. 45.

7 Ibid., P. 47.

8 Ibid., P. 50.

9 Ibid.

Chapter 3: Bill Terry Outhitting Them All

1 Williams, Peter, *When the Giants Were Giants: Bill Terry and the Golden Age of Baseball* (Chapel Hill, North Carolina: Algonquin Books, 1994), P.16.

2 Ibid., P. 67.

3 Ibid.

4 Williams, P. 69.

5 Alexander, Charles C., *John McGraw* (New York: Penguin Books, 1989), P. 254.

Chapter 4: Babe Ruth Still in There Slugging

1 Ruth, Babe and Bob Considine, *The Babe Ruth Story* (New York: Penguin Group, 1992), P. 61.

2 Ibid., P. 65.

3 Ibid., P. 66.

4 Montville, Leigh, *The Big Bam: The Life and Times of Babe Ruth* (New York: Doubleday, 2006), P. 107.

5 Ruth and Considine, P. 87.

6 Montville, P. 109.

7 Creamer, Robert C., *Babe: The Legend Comes To Life* (New York: Pocket Books, 1976), P. 226.

8 Ruth and Considine, P. 153.

Chapter 5: The New York Yankees

1 Gomez, Veronica and Lawrence Goldstone, *Lefty: An American Odyssey* (New York: Ballantine Books, 2012), P. 86.

2 (No byline), "Earle Combs," American League Service Bureau, February 3, 1929.

3 Ibid.

4 Daley, Arthur, "Huggins Made Coombs a 'Waiter" for Ruth and Gehrig," *New York Times*, February 3, 1970.

5 Rueling, Mike, "Earle Combs Surprised by Hall of Fame Call," *Louisville Courier-Journal*, February 2, 1970.

6 Votano, Paul, *Tony Lazzeri: A Baseball Biography* (Jeffersonville, North Carolina: McFarland Publishing Company, Inc., 2005), P. 27.

7 Ibid., P. 95.

8 Ibid.
9 Edwards, Henry P. "Red Ruffing," American League Service Bureau, December 8, 1929.
10 Graham, Frank, "Graham's Corner: News of Pennock's Death Calls up Memories," *New York Journal American* (National Baseball Hall of Fame Library Archives, date missing).
11 Lieb, Frederick G., "Friends He Made as Hurler in Majors Aided Pipgras to Return to American League on Strike-Calling Staff," *The Sporting News*, November 7, 1940.

Chapter 6: The Philadelphia Athletics

1 Murphy, Sam (The Old Scout) (missing newspaper), National Baseball Hall of Fame Library Archives, July 7, 1930.
2 Kieran, John, "Sports of the Times: The Jolly Miller," *New York Times*, September 2, 1938.
3 Morrow, Art, "Al Simmons, Two-Time Hit King of the A.L., Dies at 53," *The Sporting News*, June 6, 1956.
4 Macht, Norman L., *Connie Mack: The Turbulent and Triumphant Years, 1915-1931* (Lincoln, Nebraska: University of Nebraska Press, 2012.) P. 575.
5 Ibid., P. 576.
6 Edwards, Henry P., "Walberg Had Early 'Yen' for Sailors' Life," *Brooklyn Daily Eagle*," January 24, 1932.
7 Ibid.
8 Macht, P. 597.
9 Ibid., P. 376.
10 Bevis, Charles, *Mickey Cochrane: The Life of a Baseball Hall of Fame Catcher* (Jeffersonville, North Carolina: McFarland & Company, 1998), P. 46.
11 Ibid., P. 47.

12 Salsinger, H. G., "Cochrane Writes A Song To Toot On His Sax," *Detroit News*, November 30, 1930.
13 Bevis, P. 110.
14 Ibid., P. 111.
15 Rennie, Rud, "Cochrane, Hit By Ball, Suffers Skull Fracture," *New York Herald Tribune*, May 26, 1937.
16 Kase, Max, "Ball That Hit Mickey Did Mile in 25 Seconds," *New York Journal*, May 27, 1937.
17 Mickelson, Paul, "Mickey Cochrane Still Plagued by Dizzy Spells," Associated Press, July 27, 1937.
18 Gorman, Bob, *Double X: Jimmie Foxx, Baseball's Forgotten Slugger* (Camden, New Jersey: Holy Name Society, 1990), P. 47.

Chapter 7: The Washington Senators

1 DeLuca, Joseph C., "The Wild Goose of the Potomac," *South Jersey* magazine, June, 1988.
2 Ritter, Lawrence, interview for *The Glory of Their Times* not used (National Baseball Hall Of Fame Library Archives), January 31, 1964.
3 Thomas, Henry W., *Walter Johnson: Baseball's Big Train* (Washington, D.C.: Phenom Press, 1995), P. 317.
4 Thomas, P. 318.
5 Armour, Mark, *Joe Cronin: A Life In Baseball* (Lincoln, Nebraska, The University of Nebraska, 2010), P. 42.
6 Able, Stephen, "Sam Rice," Society for American Baseball Research.
7 Carroll, Jeff, *Sam Rice: Biography of the Washington Senators Hall of Famer* (Jefferson, North Carolina: McFarland & Company, 2008), P. 163.
8 Ibid.
9 Ibid., P. 170.

10 Ibid. P. 169.
11 Ibid.

Chapter 8: The Cleveland Indians

1 Thomas, Henry, W., *Walter Johnson: Baseball's Big Train* (Washington, D.C.: Phenom Press, 1995), PP. 318-319.
2 Honig, Donald, *Baseball When the Grass Was Green* (New York: Coward, McCann & Geohegan, 1975), P. 9.
3 Thompson, Dick, *The Ferrell Brothers of Baseball* (Jefferson, North Carolina: McFarland & Company, 2005), P. 51.
4 Ibid., P. 58.
5 Ibid.
6 Thompson, P. 83.
7 Pero, Scott, "Charlie Jamieson," Society for American Baseball Research.
8 Ibid.
9 Nowlin, Bill, "Ed Morgan," Society for American Baseball Research.
10 Nowlin, Bill, "Dick Porter," Society for American Baseball Research.
11 Thompson, P. 273.
12 Honig, P. 24.

Chapter 9: The Detroit Tigers

1 Leerhsen, Charles, *Ty Cobb: A Terrible Beauty* (New York: Simon & Schuster, 2015), Frontispiece.
2 Hornbaker, Tim, *War on the Basepaths* (New York: Sports Publishing, 2015), P. 88.
3 Leerhsen, P. 283.
4 Vitty, Cort, "John Stone," Society for American Baseball Research.
5 Ibid.
6 Ibid.

7 Nowlin, Bill, "Dale Alexander," Society for American Baseball Research.
8 Ibid.
9 Ibid.
10 Wolf, Gregory H., "Vic Sorrell," Society for American Baseball Research.
11 Ibid.
12 Cook, William A., *Waite Hoyt: A Biography of the Yankees' Schoolboy Wonder* (Jefferson, North Carolina: McFarland & Company, 2004), P. 9.
13 Skipper, John C., *Charlie Gehringer: A Biography of the Hall of Fame Tigers Second Baseman* (Jefferson, North Carolina: MacFarland & Company, 2008), P. 17.
14 Ibid., P. 21.
15 Ibid., P. 48.

Chapter 10: The St. Louis Browns

1 O'Neil, Tim, "Look Back 250: Great Depression Settles Hard on St. Louis," *St. Louis Post-Dispatch*, October 25, 2014.
2 Steinberg, Steve, "Phil Ball," Society for American Baseball Research.
3 Ibid.
4 Ibid.
5 Rainey, Chris, "Red Kress," Society for American Baseball Research.
6 Thompson, Dick, *The Ferrell Brothers of Baseball* (Jefferson, North Carolina: McFarland & Company, 2005), P. 261.
7 Red Badgro Pro Football Hall of Fame biography, Canton, Ohio.

Chapter 11: The Chicago White Sox

1 Sandoval, Jim, "Eddie Cicotte," Society For American Baseball Research.

2 Ibid.

3 Sagert, Kelly Boyer, *Joe Jackson* (Westport, Connecticut: Greenwood Press, 2004), P. 138.

4 Corbett, Warren, "Ted Lyons," Society for American Baseball Research.

5 Freedman, Lew, *Knuckleball: The History of the Unhittable Pitch* (New York: Sports Publishing, 2015), P. 32.

6 Ibid. P. 33.

7 Cooper, Brian E., *Red Faber: A Biography of the Hall of Fame Spitball Pitcher* (Jefferson, North Carolina: MacFarland & Company, 2006), PP. 24-25.

8 Ibid., P. 82.

9 Nowlin, Bill, "Johnny Watwood," Society for American Baseball Research.

10 Ibid.

11 Nowlin, Bill, "Smead Jolley," Society for American Baseball Research.

12 Ibid.

13 Ibid.

14 Ibid.

15 Nowlin, Bill, "Carl Reynolds," Society for American Baseball Research.

16 Honig, Donald, *Baseball When the Grass Was Green* (New York, Coward, McCann & Geohegan, 1975), P. 96.

Chapter 12: The Boston Red Sox

1 Nowlin, Bill, "Baby Doll Jacobson," Society for American Baseball Research.

2 Liss, Howard *The Boston Red Sox: The Complete History* (New York: Simon & Schuster, 1982), P. 63.

3 Nowlin, Bill, "Danny MacFayden," Society for American Baseball Research.

4 Golenbock, Peter, *Red Sox Nation* (Chicago: Triumph Books, 1992), P. 70.

5 Ibid.

6 Ibid.

Chapter 13: Lefty Grove Untouchable

1 Honig, Donald, *Baseball When the Grass Was Green* (New York: Coward, McCann & Geohegan, 1975), P. 62.

2 Kaplan, Jim, *Lefty Grove: American Original* (Cleveland: Society for American Baseball Research, 2000), P. 17.

3 Ibid., P. 61.

4 Ibid., P. 62-64.

5 Ibid., P. 67.

6 Ibid., P. 69.

7 Lieb, Frederick, G. *Connie Mack: Grand Old Man of Baseball* (Kent, Ohio: Kent State University Press, 1945), P. 221.

8 Honig, P. 63.

9 McLinn, Stoney. "Connie Mark Experiences Mental Sore Arm Watching Grove Pitch His Fastball," *Philadelphia Public-Ledger*, March 28, 1930.

10 Ibid.

11 Ibid.

12 Honig, P. 68.

Chapter 14: Pennant Races

1 Zardetto, Ray, *'30: Major League Baseball's Year of the Batter* (Jefferson, North Carolina: McFarland & Company, 2008), P. 9.

2 Ibid., P. 22.

3 Ibid., P. 26.
4 Gomez, Veronica and Lawrence Goldstone, *Lefty: An American Odyssey* (New York: Ballantine Books, 2012), P. 118.
5 Carroll, Jeff, *Sam Rice: Biography of the Washington Senators Hall of Famer* (Jefferson, North Carolina: McFarland & Company, 2008), P. 164.
6 Ruth, Babe and Bob Considine, *The Babe Ruth Story* (New York: Penguin Books, 1992), P. 78.
7 Ibid., P. 87.
8 Ritter, Lawrence S., *The Glory of Their Times* (New York: Vintage Books, 1985), PP. 279-280.

Chapter 15: The Philadelphia Phillies

1 Westcott, Rich, *Phillies Essential* (Chicago: Triumph Books, 2006), P. 24.
2 Boessenecker, John, *Texas Ranger: The Epic Life of Frank Hamer, the Man Who Killed Bonnie and Clyde* (New York: Thomas Donne Books, 2016), P. 218.
3 (No byline), National League Service Bureau, "Phil Collins, of the Phillies," December 14, 1930.
4 Ibid.
5 Kelley, Brett, *Sports Collectors Digest* January 1, 1993.
6 Ibid.
7 Ibid.
8 Ibid.
9 (No byline), National League Service Bureau, "The Strange Case of Lester Sweetland," January 25, 1931.
10 Kavanaugh, Jack, *Ol' Pete: The Grover Cleveland Alexander Story* (South Bend, Indiana: Diamond Communications, 1996), P. 65.
11 Ibid., P. 137.
12 Ibid.

13 Kavanaugh, P. 154.

14 Kelley, *Sports Collectors Digest*

15 Kiseda, George, "Hurst Was Quiet, Drab .300 Hitter," *Philadelphia Bulletin*, August 13, 1968.

16 Lane, F. C. "The Last of the Hold-Outs," *Baseball Magazine*, July, 1933.

17 Shapiro, Fred, "Who's The Greatest Phillie Ever?" *Philadelphia Magazine*, 1977.

18 Rice, Stephen V., "Pinky Whitney," Society for American Baseball Research.

19 Small, Collie, "Too Good for the Majors," *Saturday Evening Post*, February 23, 1946.

20 Robert, Harry, "Baseball's Only. 400 Hitter," *Baseball Magazine*, January, 1930.

21 Ibid.

22 (No byline) National Baseball Hall of Fame Library Archives (damaged article, no newspaper), "Ruth's Rival in First Full Year in League," 1929.

23 Yeuter, Frank, "Klein Wasn't Park-Made Slugger," *Philadelphia Bulletin*, March 30, 1958.

Chapter 16: The Cincinnati Reds

1 Tribe, Dr. Ivan M., "Brother Eppa Rixey: Hall of Fame Southpaw Pitcher" (KCT, KYCH).

2 Nowlin, Bill and Emmet R. Nowlin, "Eppa Rixey," Society for American Baseball Research.

Chapter 17: The Boston Braves

1 Huhn, Rick, *The Sizzler: George Sisler, Baseball's Forgotten Great* (Columbia, Missouri: The University of Missouri Press, 2004), P. 154.

2 Jones, Harry, "Maranville Pranks Won Affection of Ball Fans," *New York Journal-American*, February 9, 1957.

3 McGowan, J. Lloyd, "Maranville the Manager," National Baseball Hall of Fame Library Archives, publication name missing, November, 1937.

4 Maranville, Rabbit, "Old or New, It's Baseball," *American Legion Monthly*, October, 1935.

5 Maranville, Rabbit, "Hot Stove Stuff," *American Legion Monthly*, January, 1936.

6 Singelais, Neil, "After 57 Years, Berger's Mark about to Fall," *Boston Globe*, August 13, 1987.

7 Ibid.

8 Murray, Jim, "He Got More Hits Than Recognition," *Los Angeles Times*, July 24, 1988.

9 Lane, F. C. "Did The American League Blunder?" *Baseball Magazine*, June, 1929.

10 Lamberty, Bill, "George Sisler," Society for American Baseball Research.

Chapter 18: The Pittsburgh Pirates

1 Lamb, Bill, "Jewel Ens," Society for American Baseball Research.

2 Wolf, Gregory H., "Larry French," Society for American Baseball Research.

3 Ibid.

4 Ibid.

5 Wolf, Gregory H., "Ray Kremer," Society For American Baseball Research.

6 Ibid.

7 Bartell, Dick "Rowdy Richard" with Norman Macht, *Rowdy Richard* (Berkeley, California: North Atlantic Books, 1987), P. 41.

8 Ibid., P. 57.

9 Ibid., P. 76.
10 Rice, Grantland, "The Sport Light," syndicated column (National Baseball Hall of Fame Library Archives), no date, 1939.
11 Grayson, Harry, "Paul Waner Explains Secret—Expects Vaughan Will Become One of the Greatest," Newspaper Enterprise Association/*New York World-Telegraph*, April 26, 1937.
12 Kirksey, George, "Though Credited with League's Keenest Batting Eyes, Big Poison Always Has Been Nearsighted" (National Baseball Hall of Fame Library Archives), newspaper name missing, June 25, 1942.
13 Lieb, Frederick G., "Pirate 'Big Poison' Copped Three N.L. Batting Titles," *The Sporting News*, September 11, 1965.
14 Ibid.
15 Seitz, Nick, "Modesty, Thy Name Is Lloyd Waner," *The Sporting News*, February 18, 1967.
16 Ibid.
17 McHugh, Roy, "Rare Treat: Session with Traynor the Storyteller," *The Sporting News*, December 11, 1971.
18 Keck, Harry, "Stolen Bats Sweetest: Traynor," *Pittsburgh Sun-Telegraph/Baseball Digest* (National Baseball Hall of Fame Library Archives, date missing).
19 Gentille, Sean, "For $2.22 at a Goodwill, an Intern Bought a Hall of Famer's Baseball Bat," *Pittsburgh Post-Gazette*, August 11, 2017.
20 (No byline), "'Switch from Bunt to Power Biggest Change in Game,'—Pie," *The Sporting News*, January 31, 1962.

Chapter 19: The Brooklyn Robins/Dodgers

1 Skipper, John C., *Dazzy Vance: A Biography of the Brooklyn Dodger Hall of Famer* (Jefferson, North Carolina: McFarland & Company, 2007), P. 17.
2 Ibid., P. 23.

3 Ibid., P 32.
4 Ibid., P 52.
5 Corbett, Warren, "Glenn Wright," Society for American Baseball Research.
6 Ibid.
7 Singletary, Wes, *Al Lopez: The Life of Baseball's El Señor* (Jefferson, North Carolina: McFarland & Company, 1999), P. 59.
8 Ibid., P. 64.
9 Ibid., P. 66.
10 (No byline), Associated Press, "Old Dodgers Were Daffy Enough without Hitting 'Babe' on Head," (National Baseball Hall of Fame Library and Archives), newspaper name missing, November 11, 1979.
11 (Associated Press) ibid.
12 Ritter, Lawrence, *The Glory of Their Times* (New York: Random House, 1985), P. 211.
13 Lane, F. C., "How Babe Herman 'Winds Up' for the Pitcher," *Baseball Magazine*, September, 1929.
14 Holmes, Tommy. "Nobody Like Dazzy Vance, a Hornsby Had to Admit," *Brooklyn Eagle*, February 20, 1961.
15 Drebinger, John, "Sports of the Times," *New York Times*, February 20, 1961.
16 Vance, Arthur (Dazzy), "A Master Workman's Story (National Baseball Hall of Fame Research Library, date and publication missing).
17 Daley, Arthur, "Sports of the Times," *New York Times* (National Baseball Hall of Fame Library, date missing).

Chapter 20: The New York Giants

1 Mink, Michael, "John McGraw Played Hardball to Win Pennants and World Series," www.investors.com, April 4, 2016.

2 Alexander, Charles C., *John McGraw* (New York: Penguin Books, 1988), P. 295.

3 Ibid. P. 296.

4 Williams, Peter, *When the Giants Were Giants: Bill Terry and the Golden Age of New York Baseball* (Chapel Hill, North Carolina: Algonquin Books, 1994), P. 99.

5 (No byline), "Bancroft, Frisch and Nehf Star with the Giants," *Southeast Missourian*, July 18, 1922.

6 Broeg, Bob, "Lindy's Shrine Credential More Than Ample," *The Sporting News*, March 17, 1973.

7 Williams, P. 54.

8 Vila, Joe, "'Lindstrom at Best in Center'—McGraw," *New York Sun*, December 25, 1930.

9 Daley, Arthur, "Sports of the Times: About Freddie Lindstrom," *New York Times*, August 26, 1954.

10 Broeg, "Lindy's Shrine."

11 Martz, Ron, "A Pebble Made Him Immortal," *St. Petersburg Times*, February 3, 1976.

12 Bowman, John, "With Memories of the Hitters of Baseball Fam Comes Fred Lindstrom—who Hit with the Best," *The Times* (Holiday, Florida), July 16, 1979.

13 (No byline) Associated Press, "Travis Jackson, 84: Played Baseball for N.Y. Giants," *Boston Globe*, July 29, 1987.

14 Erion, Greg, "Travis Jackson," Society for American Baseball Research.

15 Williams, P. 75.

16 Carmichael, John P., *My Greatest Day in Baseball* (New York: Grosset & Dunlap, 1968 edition), P. 131.

17 Stein, Fred, *Mel Ott: The Little Giant of Baseball* (Jefferson, North Carolina: McFarland & Company, 1999), P. 18.

18 Ibid. P. 32.

19 Ibid., P. 36.
20 Carmichael, P. 132.
21 Stein, Fred, "Carl Hubbell," Society for American Baseball Research.
22 Blaisdell, Lowell L., *Carl Hubbell: A Biography of the Screwball King* (Jefferson, North Carolina: McFarland & Company, 2011), P. 26.
23 De Kever, Peter J., *Freddie Fitzsimmons: A Baseball Life* (Bloomington, Indiana: AuthorHouse, LLC, 2013), P. 92.
24 Burr, Harold C., "Bill Terry Doesn't Know yet Why He Is Such a Great Hitter," *Brooklyn Eagle* (National Baseball Hall of Fame Library Archives), date missing.

Chapter 21: The Chicago Cubs

1 Chastain, Bill, *Hack's 191: Hack Wilson and His Incredible 1930 Season* (Guilford, Connecticut, Lyons Press, 2012), P. 25.
2 Ibid. P. 226.
3 Ibid. P. 231.
4 Holtzman, Jerome, "Hartnett's All-Around Play, Leadership Earn Nod over Banks," *Chicago Tribune*, February 14, 1983.
5 Enright, James, "Gabby Tells Reaction to 'Immortality,'" *Chicago American*, January 27, 1955.
6 Kelley, Brent, "Former Cubs Shortstop Woody English Interviewed," *Sports Collectors Digest*, July 27, 1990.
7 Ibid.
8 Ibid.
9 Carchidi, Sam, "A 1933 All-Star, He's Glowing Still," *Philadelphia Inquirer*, July 1, 1996.
10 Fields, Dan, "Charlie Grimm," Society for American Baseball Research.
11 Grimm, Charlie and Ed Prell, *Jolly Cholly's Story: Baseball I Love You* (Chicago: Henry Regnery Company, 1968), P. 1.
12 Ibid., P. 52.

13 Ibid., P. 77.

14 Hillman, J. R., "Pat Malone: Threw Hard and Played Harder," *Sports Collectors Digest*, February 7, 1997.

15 Burr, Harold C., "Pat Malone Enjoyed Every Minute of Years in Game," *Brooklyn Eagle*, May 16, 1943.

16 Broeg, Bob, "The Homer That Babe Didn't Call: Charley Root Said So," *The Sporting News*, October 21, 1978.

17 (No byline), Associated Press, "Babe's Homers Not Bush," *South Bend Tribune* (Indiana), March 28, 1974.

18 Fuhr, Ernie, "Hal Carlson," Society For American Baseball Research.

19 Alexander, Charles C., *Rogers Hornsby: A Biography* (New York: Henry Holt and Company, 1995), P. 66.

20 Ibid. P. 32.

21 Ibid. P. 94.

Chapter 22: The St. Louis Cardinals

1 Haag, Ken, "'Showboat' Fisher Revisited at near 95!" *Sports Collectors Digest,* October 29, 1993.

2 Thornley, Stew, "Showboat Fisher," Society for American Baseball Research.

3 (No byline), "Baseball Caught by Gabby Street in Monument Drop Rediscovered," (National Baseball Hall of Fame Library, date and publication missing).

4 Stockton, J. Roy, "Street, New Cardinal Pilot, Is a Popular, Plain Man and a Fountain of Wit and Wisdom," *St. Louis Post-Dispatch*, November 1, 1929.

5 Ibid.

6 Stockton, Roy Jr., "The Cardinals' Forgotten Man," *St. Louis Post-Dispatch* magazine, July, 1954.

7 (No bylie), Associated Press, "'I'll Never Hunt Again, Gelbert Promises Wife," *New York American*, November 23, 1932.

8 Broeg, Bob, "Rugged Watty in Cardinal Tradition," *St. Louis Post-Dispatch*, June 10, 1970.

9 Ibid.

10 Broeg, Bob, "Douthit, the Ballhawk, Recalls Nine Hits, His Trade," *St. Louis Post-Dispatch*, August 23, 1976.

11 Ibid.

12 Sarge, Dick, "Earl "Sparky" Adams: Holds Hall of Fame Credentials, *Harrisburg Patriot-News* (National Baseball Hall of Fame Library, date missing).

13 (No byline), United Press International, "Chick Hafey Gives up Idea of Comeback Try," *Tuscaloosa News* (Alabama), April 14, 1936.

14 Swope, Tom, "'My Wife Says We Have Enough Money,' Is Jim's Reply to Larry MacPhail," *Cincinnati Post*, March 30, 1935.

15 McGoogan, W. J., "'Sunny Jim' Bottomley Looks Back over 15 Happy Years of Baseball," *St. Louis Post-Dispatch*, July 1, 1931.

16 Graham, Frank, "Setting the Pace," *New York Sun*, September 13, 1932.

17 Williams, Joe, "Frankie Frisch Hangs up His Spikes; Star since 1919, *New York World-Telegram*, November 16, 1937.

18 Griffith, Nancy Snell, "Flint Rhem," Society for American Baseball Research.

19 (No byline), "The Kidnapping of Flint Rhem," (Things Have Changed) https://havechanged.blogspot.com.

20 Brundidge, Harry T., "Parents And Teachers Couldn't Subdue Hallahan's Lefthanded Throwing; Now Batters Fail to Solve It," *St. Louis Star-Chronicle*, January 1, 1931.

21 Allen, Lee, "Cooperstown Corner: Wild Bill Hallahan, The Lines Are Softened Now," *The Sporting News*, October 12, 1968.

22 Graham, Frank, "Of Grimes And Frisch," *New York Journal-American*, July 29, 1964.
23 Broeg, Bob, "Last of Legal Spitballers Still Going Strong," *St. Louis Post-Dispatch*, August 14, 1983.
24 Ibid.
25 (No byline), "Jesse Haines Sets Record for Unbroken Service in National Baseball League" (National Baseball Hall Of Fame Library, publication missing), May 27, 1937.

Chapter 23: Winners and Losers

1 Allen, Lee, "Cooperstown Corner: Wild Bill Hallahan, the Lines Are Softened Now," *The Sporting News*, October 12, 1968.
2 Russo, Neal, "Batters Knuckled Under to Haines and Schultz," *St. Louis Post-Dispatch*, September 6, 1964.
3 Niese, Joe, *Burleigh Grimes: Baseball's Last Legal Spitballer* (Jefferson, North Carolina: McFarland & Company, 2013), P. 144.
4 Ibid., P. 145.
5 Schulz, John, "Recalling 'Lefty' Grove . . . No Better Left-Hander," *Washington Star*, May 23, 1975.
6 Lieb, Fred, "Foxx, No. 3 on All-Time Homer List, Dead," *The Sporting News*, August 5, 1967.
7 Broeg, Bob, "'Bucketfoot' Never Lost The Swagger," *The Sporting News*, July 11, 1971.
8 Ibid.
9 Brandt, William E., "Hallahan Receives Cheers of Mates," *New York Times*, October 5, 1930.
10 Rumill, Ed, "Jesse Haines: He Challenged the Hitter," *Baseball Digest*, December, 1970.
11 Corum, Bill, "Had to Beg George to Become Ball Player," *New York Evening Journal*, October 9, 1930.

Postscript

1 Parker, Charles E. "Giants Back up Manager's Crack about Dodgers" (National Baseball Hall of Fame Library archives, paper name missing), May 31, 1934.

2 (No byline), Associated Press, "Terry Wipes Away a Tear Going into Hall Of Fame" (National Baseball Hall Of Fame Library And Archives, name of paper missing), August 9, 1954.

3 (No byline), "'I'll Be in Condition,' Says Hack as He Trains in Home Gym He Built," *Brooklyn Eagle*, January 24, 1932.

4 Hughes, Ed, "Hack Talking," *Brooklyn Eagle*, February 10, 1939.